Fall Baking

© 2022 RDA Enthusiast Brands, LLC.
1610 N. 2nd St., Suite 102, Milwaukee, WI 53212-3906
All rights reserved. Taste of Home is a registered trademark
of RDA Enthusiast Brands, LLC.

Visit us at **tasteofhome.com** for other Taste of Home
books and products.

International Standard Book Number:
Retail: 978-1-62145-828-9
DTC: 978-1-62145-834-0

Executive Editor: Mark Hagen
Senior Art Director: Raeann Thompson
Editor: Hazel Wheaton
Art Director: Maggie Conners
Senior Designer: Jazmin Delgado
Deputy Editor, Copy Desk: Dulcie Shoener
Senior Copy Editor: Ann Walter

Cover:
Photographer: Dan Roberts
Set Stylist: Melissa Franco
Food Stylist: Shannon Norris

Pictured on front cover:
Cranberry Apple Sheet Pie, p. 156

Pictured on back cover:
Cherry Danish, p. 231; Coconut Nutella Brownies, p. 122;
Maple Tree Cake, p. 198; Broccoli Beef Braids, p. 299;
Rustic Cranberry Tart, p. 178

INSTANT POT is a trademark of Double Insight Inc.
This publication has not been authorized, sponsored
or otherwise approved by Double Insight Inc.

Printed in USA
10 9 8 7 6 5 4 3 2 1

Table of Contents

MAKE YOUR KITCHEN A PLACE OF HEARTWARMING COMFORT THIS FALL

Celebrate the changing of the season with mouthwatering, satisfying baked goods.

Autumn is the perfect time of year for baking—for very good reason! After standing unused during the hottest days of summer, the oven now has a chance to shine as enthusiastic bakers turn on the heat and create new homemade treats. Just waiting to be used are all the rich tastes of fall—fruits, vegetables, nuts, berries and spices that are ideal for a host of baked delights. Now, **Taste of Home Fall Baking** shows you how to make the most of that cornucopia of flavors.

Whether it's the perfect pumpkin bread, sweet and gooey cinnamon rolls, a fresh-baked loaf of potato bread, indulgent caramel cupcakes, or sweet and tangy cran-apple gingerbread, harvest flavors lend themselves to baked goods like no others. Reward an afternoon of raking leaves with a warm-from-the-oven hazelnut scone and a cup of hot chocolate. Pull out a tray of caramel-apple shortbread to welcome friends who stop by. Tuck a molasses cookie into your child's lunchbox as a back-to-school treat. Bake up some chocolate-chai loaves for your school's fall fundraiser, or some maple-flavored pastries for a church social.

For your convenience, a special added index highlights recipes by flavor—so you can find just what you're looking for. Whether you're craving something made with maple, looking for a new pumpkin recipe or wanting to make the most of the bounty you brought back from a morning spent picking apples at a local orchard, you'll find lots of ideas quickly and easily.

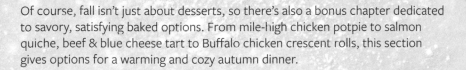

Of course, fall isn't just about desserts, so there's also a bonus chapter dedicated to savory, satisfying baked options. From mile-high chicken potpie to salmon quiche, beef & blue cheese tart to Buffalo chicken crescent rolls, this section gives options for a warming and cozy autumn dinner.

Each and every recipe in this collection has been tested and approved by the experts in the *Taste of Home* Test Kitchen, so they're guaranteed to work— the first time and every time after that. You'll find tips and helpful hints from our home economists scattered throughout the book, full-color photographs on every page, and full nutritional information with each recipe.

With **Taste of Home Fall Baking,** you have a timeless treasury of recipes that you'll pull out each year when the leaves start to turn from green to red and gold. For bakers of all skill levels, whether you're cooking for a crowd or just your family, these are the delicacies that you'll turn to again and again.

Throughout this book, you'll find handy QR codes that provide direct links to extra content, including demonstrations and collections of additional recipes. To use the codes, hover the camera in your smartphone or tablet over the code. When the code comes into focus, the link will appear; then click on the link.

SEE HOW IT'S DONE

For example, use this code to learn how to make the perfect pie crust— with in-depth explanations of not just the *how* but the *why* of each step.

FALL SPICES

Add delicious flavor to your fall baked goods by using spices that taste just right for the season.

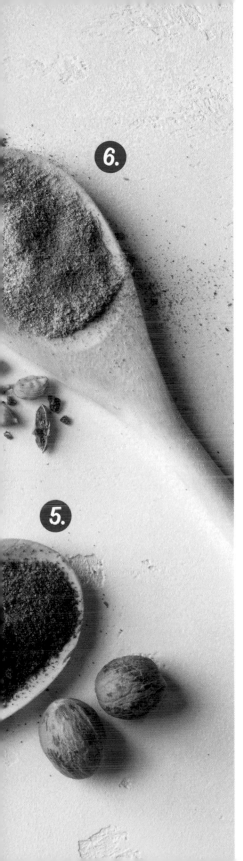

1. Allspice

Available whole or ground, it combines the flavors of cinnamon, nutmeg and cloves. This spice complements stews, carrots, pork, poultry, squash, cakes, cookies and breads.

2. Cinnamon

With its mildly sweet to bittersweet flavor, this is a nice addition to baked goods like coffee cake and crumbles. And it enhances stews, curries, fruit, squash, oatmeal, pork and beef.

3. Anise

These seeds are used ground or whole and give desserts and baked goods like biscotti a licorice flavor. (Don't confuse aniseed with star anise, shown next to the spoon, which is a different spice—it has a similar flavor but is much stronger.)

4. Cloves

Available both whole and ground, they pair well with orange or molasses flavors, and add robust flavor to chocolate and fruit. You'll often find cloves as an added flavor in gingerbread, carrot cake and pumpkin pie.

5. Nutmeg

Warm, sweet and spicy, this adds depth to sweets like pies and custard as well as to savory dishes like white sauces, spinach and squash. You can buy it whole or ground. For the best flavor, grate fresh nutmeg.

6. Cardamom

This warm and aromatic spice is a staple of Indian cuisine and is flavorful in baked goods like shortbread and gingerbread. It pairs well with cinnamon, cloves and chocolate, and is one of the foundation spices in chai.

HOW-TO

**MAKE YOUR OWN
PUMPKIN PIE SPICE**

Mix 4 tsp. ground cinnamon, 2 tsp. ground ginger, 1 tsp. ground cloves and ½ tsp. ground nutmeg. Store in an airtight container in a cool, dry place for up to 6 months.

BUYING
Purchase whole spices whenever possible, and grind them yourself as needed. They'll last longer.

STORING
Store spices in a dark, cool, dry place.

DATING
Spices lose color and flavor as they age, so write the date on jars when you buy them. Toss ground spices after 1 to 3 years and whole spices after 3 to 4 years.

TOASTING
Toasting spices enhances their flavor.

MEASURING
Don't measure spices directly over the bowl. Pour them into your hand first.

WHICH PUMPKIN?

You might think that fresh is always best. But for baking, canned pumpkin is king.

FRESH

CANNED

When it comes to cooking, it's usually a safe assumption that from-scratch just can't be beat, right? However, pumpkin is a major exception. For baking, canned pumpkin (not fresh puree) is best. But why? Our Test Kitchen experts weigh in.

Ease of Use

The idea of going old school sounds like an exciting challenge. But the process of making your own pumpkin puree—scooping seeds and stringy stuff, baking, pureeing and straining—can take up to 2 hours. And then you still have to bake the pie!

Better Taste & Texture

The texture, consistency and flavor of mass-produced canned pumpkin is universal. But fresh pumpkins can vary in the amount of water and sugar content, which can affect flavor and texture.

Year-Round Availability

Although pumpkin is synonymous with autumn and Thanksgiving, serious pumpkin fans want pumpkin more frequently, even when fresh pumpkins aren't available. So for availability and convenience alone, canned pumpkin is the best option. If left unopened, canned pumpkin will last until the expiration date printed on the can. (Once opened, canned pumpkin should be refrigerated and used within 5 days.)

1.

2.

CHOCOLATE

Selecting the right chocolate for your recipe is key to experiencing everything this dreamy indulgence has to offer.

Unsweetened Chocolate

Also known as baking or bitter chocolate, unsweetened chocolate has no sugars or added flavors.

Bittersweet and Semisweet Chocolate

The FDA mandates that bittersweet and semisweet chocolate contain at least 35% pure chocolate (cocoa), but doesn't specify what those percentages should be. Bittersweet is usually 60-72% cocoa; semisweet is generally 35-55% (the higher the percentage of cocoa, the less sweet the chocolate). Both are tasty in baked goods, and they can be used more or less interchangeably; bittersweet chocolate will produce a more dominant chocolate flavor.

Bars vs. Chips

Most solid chocolates are available as bars and chips. Bars usually melt quickly and smoothly; chips have less cocoa butter and contain stabilizers to help them keep their shape. This makes a difference in candies and sauces, but won't cause a significant difference in the texture of a brownie.

Natural Unsweetened Cocoa Powder

Remove most of the cocoa butter from unsweetened chocolate and you get natural unsweetened cocoa powder.

Dutch-Processed Cocoa Powder

Also known as alkalized cocoa powder, this type has been treated to reduce its acidity, giving it a smooth flavor and reddish color. It's best to stick to the cocoa the recipe calls for; the cocoa powders do behave differently. If you want to substitute Dutch cocoa for natural, pay attention to the leavener—if the recipe calls for baking soda, replace it with twice that amount of baking powder.

MELTING CHOCOLATE

There are two rules to melting chocolate, either alone or with other ingredients: Don't get it too hot and don't get it wet. Even small amounts of water will cause the chocolate to seize (become thick and lumpy), making it unusable.

1. Break or chop large pieces of chocolate so it will melt evenly; heat in a double boiler and stir until smooth.

2. To melt chocolate in the microwave, use a microwave-safe bowl and heat at 50% power. Stir frequently until chocolate is melted; do not overheat.

CRUNCH TIME!

Sprinkle in some nuts and your baked goods jump to life with extra flavor and texture. Here are some of the most popular nuts used in fall baking.

1. Almonds

Oval-shaped almonds are sold whole, sliced, slivered and ground. Their mild, rich flavor is perfect for tarts, shortbread, cakes, bars, toffee and biscotti.

2. Cashews

Crescent-shaped cashews are sold shelled—whole, in pieces or ground—and either raw or roasted. They have a rich, buttery flavor that pairs well with chocolate. And they add superb texture, shape and crunch.

3. Pecans

With the highest fat content of any nut, pecans have a rich flavor and brittle texture when they're baked. They're sold whole, in pieces or chopped, and you can buy them toasted, roasted or salted. Sweeter than walnuts, pecans are ideal in desserts like brownies, pies and cakes that have a crunchy streusel topping.

4. Pistachios

Technically a seed, pistachios have a mild, semisweet flavor. They're available all year long shelled, unshelled or ground, raw or roasted, and salted or unsalted. Use whole pistachios in granola. Add ground pistachios to a fruit tart crust or mix them with honey for a sweet pastry filling.

5. Hazelnuts

Also known as filberts, these round nuts are used raw or roasted. (Roast them and remove skins for the best flavor.) The key ingredient in the spread Nutella, sweet-tasting hazelnuts pair beautifully with chocolate and add a pleasing crunch to pastries and desserts.

6. Macadamia Nuts

These large, cream-colored round nuts are high in oil and lend a deliciously rich, buttery flavor to many desserts, including cookies, pies and brittle. They're excellent with tropical flavors like coconut or pineapple as well as with chocolate.

7. Pine Nuts

These tiny beige nuts, almost always used toasted, have a slightly piney flavor. Their soft, chewy texture makes them ideal for baking, so include them in tarts, bars, cakes or cookies.

8. Walnuts

Walnuts are available year-round either shelled or unshelled. High tannins give the light brown kernels a slightly bitter yet mild, dry taste. They are generally used raw in baked items such as cookies, carrot cakes, coffee cakes and more.

KEEP 'EM COOL

Because of their high fat content, nuts can spoil easily. Always store them in airtight containers or resealable plastic freezer bags. Shelled nuts can be stored in a dry, cool location for up to 3 months. Shelled or unshelled nuts can be stored in the fridge for up to 6 months, or in the freezer for up to a year.

TOAST 'EM UP

Toasting nuts brings out their flavor and adds a depth and richness to baked goods. To toast nuts, bake them in a single layer in a shallow pan in a 350° oven for 5-10 minutes, stirring or shaking halfway through. Or cook the nuts in a skillet over low heat until lightly browned, stirring occasionally.

ABOUT EGGS

Eggs really are incredible. They serve many different purposes in baking, whether you're talking just the yolk, just the white, or the entire egg. Here's a quick guide to this essential baking ingredient.

Separating eggs

1. You can separate eggs using the halves of a broken shell, a specially designed egg separator, a slotted spoon, or even your bare hand ! It's easier to separate eggs when they're cold, so it's best to separate them and then let the yolks and whites sit to come to room temperature before using in the recipe.

Beating egg whites

2. Let egg whites stand at room temperature for 30 minutes before beating. For best results, use a clean metal or glass bowl. Any water, egg yolk, or oily residue in the bowl will inhibit the beating of the whites. An acidic ingredient (cream of tartar, lemon juice or vinegar) acts as a stabilizer to keep the egg whites from deflating. Beat on medium speed until soft peaks form, then continue until stiff peaks form.

Testing freshness

3. An easy way to see if your eggs are fresh enough to use is to place them in a bowl of water. If they lie on the bottom, they're fresh. If they tilt upward, they're less fresh, but still perfectly fine. If they float, they're no longer usable and should be discarded.

Egg size equivalents

The recipes in this book were tested with large eggs unless otherwise indicated. Use the following guidelines for substituting other egg sizes for large eggs:

EGG SIZE	SUBSTITUTIONS
1 large egg	1 jumbo, 1 extra-large or 1 medium
2 large eggs	2 jumbo, 2 extra-large, 2 medium or 3 small
3 large eggs	2 jumbo, 3 extra-large, 3 medium or 4 small
4 large eggs	3 jumbo, 4 extra-large, 5 medium or 5 small

TIPS FOR STORING EGGS

- Refrigerate egg whites in an airtight container up to 4 days.
- Refrigerate unbroken egg yolks covered with water in an airtight container up to 2 days.
- Freeze whole eggs by lightly beating them until blended, then pouring them into an airtight, freezer-safe container. Freeze up to 1 year.

SOFT PEAKS

STIFF PEAKS

LOVE ME TENDER

When you want to bake up treats that are a little softer and a smidge tangy, make buttermilk your go-to secret ingredient.

Buttermilk's acidic properties are incredible at breaking down long strands of gluten and other proteins in baked goods, so when you want something to be tender, buttermilk's your answer. (Another bonus: It has more calcium—and other vitamins and minerals—than regular milk.) Best of all, it provides an unexpected "can't-put-my-finger-on-it" flavor to whatever recipes you use it in.

Our Test Kitchen experts tend to use regular (liquid) buttermilk, buying it in amounts as small as 16 ounces. Those 2 cups can take you pretty far. If you have buttermilk left over, experiment with it. You can use it instead of water or regular milk in a recipe, keeping in mind that it adds a yogurty tang to foods. It's also unbeatable for your favorite biscuits, and you can whisk it into a custard for company-worthy French toast.

If you aren't sold on keeping a carton of fresh buttermilk on hand at all times, check out the powdered version. There will be no real difference in the finished product, and the package should last a long time. For most baking, you can use the conversion table on the powder package to determine how much to mix in with the dry ingredients, then use water in lieu of buttermilk with the wet ingredients.

If you're out of both liquid and powdered buttermilk, follow the recipes below to make your own easy substitute.

USING VINEGAR

Combine 1 Tbsp. white vinegar plus enough milk to measure 1 cup. Stir, then let stand for 5 minutes.

USING LEMON JUICE

1 Tbsp. lemon juice plus enough milk to measure 1 cup. Stir, then let stand for 5 minutes.

APPLES TO APPLES

Choosing the perfect fruit can feel like a guessing game, especially in the fall when stores and farmers markets offer so many different varieties of apples. We break down the flavor profiles of the top eight apples sold in the U.S.—and suggest some less well-known options, too!

▼ GOLDEN DELICIOUS

▼ HONEYCRISP

▲ AMBROSIA

► FUJI

GRANNY SMITH

► PINK LADY/ CRIPPS PINK

Ambrosia
Crisp and sweet with a light floral note. Great for eating and baking. *Season: September–October*

Braeburn
Sweet-tart flavor with a hint of spice. Crisp, firm apple. Good for eating, baking and using in salads and sauces. *Season: October–April*

Cortland
Juicy, tender and sweet with a hint of tartness. Resists browning. Good for eating, baking and using in pies, salads and sauces. *Season: September–April*

Empire
Sweet-tart flavor. Juicy, crisp apple. Good for eating, baking and using in pies, salads and sauces. *Season: September–July*

Fuji
Juicy, crisp and very sweet. Good for eating and using in salads and sauces. *Season: October–June*

Golden Delicious
Mild, sweet and juicy. Lighter texture with yellow flesh. Good for eating, baking and using in pies, salads and sauces. *Season: year-round*

Granny Smith
Classic tart flavor with crisp texture. Good for eating, baking and using in pies, salads and sauces. *Season: year-round*

HoneyCrisp
Crisp, sweet and juicy; one of the most popular apple varieties. Great for snacking. Good in a mix with firm, tart apples like Granny Smith or Northern Spy for baking. *Season: year-round*

BRAEBURN

CORTLAND

EMPIRE

JONATHAN

ROME BEAUTY

Jonathan
Tart flavor with a hint of spice. Moderately tender apple. Good for eating, baking and using in pies, salads and sauces. *Season: September–April*

Pink Lady/Cripps Pink
Sweet-tart flavor. Firm, crisp apple. Good for eating, baking and using in salads. *Season: October–June*

Rome Beauty
Mildly tart flavor. Firm apple. Good for baking and using in sauces and pies. *Season: October–May*

HOW TO BUY
Give apples a squeeze; they should be firm with no give. Inspect them for blemishes or dents, as these can accelerate decay. For baking, choose a firm apple that holds up to heat without becoming mushy — and with a tartness to offset sugary baked goods.

HOW TO STORE
Store in a cool place. If storing in the refrigerator, place in a bag with holes in it in the crisper bin. Don't store other fruits or vegetables in the same drawer; apples give off ethylene gas, which causes produce to rot faster. Remove any damaged apples so rot does not spread.

HOW TO PREP
Always wash apples (especially nonorganic ones) before eating or prepping for a recipe. Use 1 tsp. baking soda to 2 cups water as a wash; this has been shown to remove the majority of trace pesticides from apple skin.

ALL-TIME FALL FAVORITES

THESE CLASSIC, TRIED-AND-TRUE FAVORITES

ARE RICH WITH TRADITION AND COMFORT—

THE EPITOME OF FALL BAKING!

GERMAN APPLE CAKE, P. 29

Sweet Potato Dutch Baby with Praline Syrup

PREP: 10 MIN. • **COOK:** 20 MIN.
MAKES: 6 SERVINGS

This recipe reminds me of my favorite Dutch baby breakfast from when I was a child. This is a perfect comfort dish—morning or evening.
—Angela Spengler, Niceville, FL

- 4 **Tbsp. butter, divided**
- 3 **large eggs, room temperature**
- ½ **cup 2% milk**
- ¼ **cup mashed canned sweet potatoes in syrup**
- ½ **cup all-purpose flour**
- ¼ **tsp. salt**
- ½ **cup maple syrup**
- ¼ **cup chopped pecans**

1. Preheat oven to 400°. Place 2 Tbsp. butter in a 10-in. cast-iron or other ovenproof skillet. Place in oven until the butter is melted, 4-5 minutes; carefully swirl butter to coat pan evenly.
2. Meanwhile, in a large bowl, whisk eggs, milk and sweet potatoes until blended. Whisk in flour and salt. Pour into hot skillet. Bake until puffed and edge is golden brown and crisp, 20-25 minutes.
3. In a small saucepan, combine the syrup, pecans and remaining 2 Tbsp. butter. Cook and stir over medium heat until the butter is melted. Remove pancake from the oven; cut into 6 wedges and serve immediately with syrup.
1 SERVING: 261 cal., 14g fat (6g sat. fat), 115mg chol., 210mg sod., 30g carb. (19g sugars, 1g fiber), 5g pro.

Chocolate Eclairs

PREP: 45 MIN. • **BAKE:** 35 MIN. + COOLING
MAKES: 9 SERVINGS

With a creamy filling and thick decadent frosting, these eclairs are extra special. Now you can indulge in classic bakery treats without leaving the house!
—Jessica Campbell, Viola, WI

- 1 **cup water**
- ½ **cup butter, cubed**
- ¼ **tsp. salt**
- 1 **cup all-purpose flour**
- 4 **large eggs, room temperature**

FILLING
- 2½ **cups cold 2% milk**
- 1 **pkg. (5.1 oz.) instant vanilla pudding mix**
- 1 **cup heavy whipping cream**
- ¼ **cup confectioners' sugar**
- 1 **tsp. vanilla extract**

FROSTING
- 2 **oz. semisweet chocolate**
- 2 **Tbsp. butter**
- 1¼ **cups confectioners' sugar**
- 2 **to 3 Tbsp. hot water**

1. Preheat the oven to 400°. In a large saucepan, bring water, butter and salt to a boil. Add flour all at once; stir until a smooth ball forms. Remove from heat; let stand 5 minutes. Add eggs, 1 at a time, beating well after each addition. Continue beating until mixture is smooth and shiny.
2. Using a tablespoon or a pastry tube with a #10 or large round tip, form dough into nine 4x1½-in. strips on a greased baking sheet. Bake for 35-40 minutes or until puffed and golden. Remove to a wire rack. Immediately split eclairs open; remove tops and set aside. Discard the soft dough from inside. Cool eclairs.
3. In a large bowl, beat milk and pudding mix according to package directions. In another bowl, whip the cream until soft peaks form. Beat in sugar and vanilla; fold into pudding. Fill the eclairs (chill any remaining filling for another use). Replace tops.
4. For the frosting, in a microwave, melt the chocolate and butter; stir until smooth. Stir in the sugar and enough hot water to achieve a smooth consistency. Cool slightly. Frost eclairs. Store in refrigerator.
1 ECLAIR: 483 cal., 28g fat (17g sat. fat), 174mg chol., 492mg sod., 52g carb. (37g sugars, 1g fiber), 7g pro.

WHAT IS A DUTCH BABY?

Is it really Dutch? What other flavors can be used? Find out more about this adaptable treat.

White Chocolate Cranberry Blondies

PREP: 35 MIN. • **BAKE:** 20 MIN. + COOLING
MAKES: 3 DOZEN

The family often requests these bars, so they're a regular in our house. For a fancy look on special occasions, I cut them into triangles first and then drizzle the white chocolate over each one individually.
—Erika Busz, Kent, WA

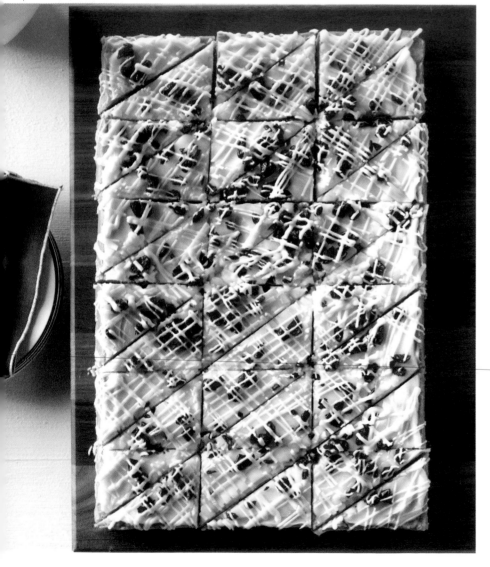

¾ cup butter, cubed
1½ cups packed light brown sugar
2 large eggs, room temperature
¾ tsp. vanilla extract
2¼ cups all-purpose flour
1½ tsp. baking powder
¼ tsp. salt
⅛ tsp. ground cinnamon
½ cup dried cranberries
6 oz. white baking chocolate, coarsely chopped

FROSTING

1 pkg. (8 oz.) cream cheese, softened
1 cup confectioners' sugar
1 Tbsp. grated orange zest, optional
6 oz. white baking chocolate, melted
½ cup dried cranberries, chopped

1. Preheat the oven to 350°. In a large microwave-safe bowl, melt the butter; stir in the brown sugar. Cool slightly.

2. Add eggs, 1 at a time, beating well after each addition. Beat in the vanilla. In another bowl, whisk together flour, baking powder, salt and cinnamon; stir into butter mixture. Stir in cranberries and chopped chocolate (batter will be thick). Spread into a greased 13x9-in. pan.

3. Bake until golden brown and a toothpick inserted in center comes out clean (do not overbake), 18-21 minutes. Cool completely on a wire rack.

4. For the frosting, beat the cream cheese, confectioners' sugar and, if desired, orange zest until smooth. Gradually beat in half the melted white chocolate; spread over blondies. Sprinkle with cranberries; drizzle with the remaining melted chocolate.

5. Cut into triangles. Store in an airtight container in the refrigerator.

1 BLONDIE: 198 cal., 9g fat (6g sat. fat), 27mg chol., 100mg sod., 28g carb. (22g sugars, 0 fiber), 2g pro.

1. In a small bowl, combine the graham cracker crumbs and sugar; stir in the butter. Press into the bottom of a 9-in. springform pan; chill.
2. For filling, in a large bowl, beat cream cheese and sugar until smooth. Add eggs; beat on low speed just until blended. Stir in the pumpkin, spices and salt.
3. Pour into crust. Place pan on a baking sheet. Bake at 350° for 50 minutes.
4. Meanwhile, for topping, combine the sour cream, sugar and vanilla until smooth. Spread over filling; return to the oven for 5 minutes. Cool on rack for 10 minutes. Carefully run a knife around the edge of pan to loosen; cool 1 hour longer.
5. Refrigerate overnight. Remove ring from pan. Top with chopped pecans. Refrigerate leftovers.

1 PIECE: 230 cal., 15g fat (9g sat. fat), 70mg chol., 164mg sod., 20g carb. (15g sugars, 2g fiber), 4g pro.

TEST KITCHEN TIP

A water bath isn't necessary for this cheesecake; the topping will cover any cracks. If you prefer to reduce the chance of cracks, set the springform pan in a larger, deep pan, and add an inch of hot water to the deeper pan before baking.

Pumpkin Cheesecake

PREP: 20 MIN. + CHILLING
BAKE: 55 MIN. + COOLING
MAKES: 16 PIECES

When I was young, we produced several ingredients for this longtime favorite on our farm. We raised pumpkins in the large vegetable garden and made our own butter and sour cream using milk from the dairy herd.
—Evonne Wurmnest, Normal, IL

1 cup graham cracker crumbs
1 Tbsp. sugar
¼ cup butter, melted

FILLING
2 pkg. (8 oz. each) cream cheese, softened
¾ cup sugar
2 large eggs, room temperature, lightly beaten
1 can (15 oz.) pumpkin
1¼ tsp. ground cinnamon
½ tsp. ground ginger
½ tsp. ground nutmeg
¼ tsp. salt

TOPPING
2 cups sour cream
2 Tbsp. sugar
1 tsp. vanilla extract
12 to 16 pecan halves, chopped

Traditional Cheesecake

PREP: 20 MIN. • **BAKE:** 45 MIN. + CHILLING
MAKES: 12 PIECES

Here's a delicious classic cheesecake that tastes great alone or with any number of garnishes. Use this basic recipe as a palette for your creativity!
—Taste of Home *Test Kitchen*

- 1 **cup graham cracker crumbs**
- 1 **Tbsp. sugar**
- 3 **Tbsp. cold butter**

FILLING
- 4 **pkg. (8 oz. each) cream cheese, softened**
- 1¼ **cups sugar**
- 1 **Tbsp. lemon juice**
- 2 **tsp. vanilla extract**
- 3 **large eggs, room temperature, lightly beaten**

1. Preheat oven to 350°. In a small bowl, combine cracker crumbs and sugar; cut in butter until crumbly. Grease the side only of a 9-in. springform pan; press crumb mixture onto bottom of the pan. Place on a baking sheet. Bake for 10 minutes. Cool crust on a wire rack.

2. In a large bowl, beat cream cheese and sugar until smooth. Beat in lemon juice and vanilla. Add the eggs; beat on low speed just until combined. Pour filling onto the crust. Return pan to baking sheet.

3. Bake for 45-55 minutes or until the center is almost set. Cool on a wire rack for 10 minutes. Carefully run a knife around the inside edge of pan to loosen; cool the cheesecake 1 hour longer.

4. Refrigerate overnight before serving. Refrigerate any leftovers.

1 PIECE: 424 cal., 31g fat (19g sat. fat), 144mg chol., 311mg sod., 30g carb. (24g sugars, 0 fiber), 8g pro.

Pumpkin Bread

PREP: 15 MIN. • **BAKE:** 65 MIN. + COOLING
MAKES: 16 PIECES

I keep my freezer stocked with home-baked goodies for our harvest crew—they love this deliciously spicy, easy pumpkin bread.
—Joyce Jackson, Bridgetown, NS

- 1⅔ cups all-purpose flour
- 1½ cups sugar
- 1 tsp. baking soda
- 1 tsp. ground cinnamon
- ¾ tsp. salt
- ½ tsp. baking powder
- ½ tsp. ground nutmeg
- ¼ tsp. ground cloves
- 2 large eggs, room temperature
- 1 cup canned pumpkin
- ½ cup canola oil
- ½ cup water
- ½ cup chopped walnuts
- ½ cup raisins, optional

1. Preheat oven to 350°. Combine the first 8 ingredients. Whisk together eggs, pumpkin, oil and water; stir into the dry ingredients just until moistened. Fold in the walnuts and, if desired, raisins.

2. Pour into a greased 9x5-in. loaf pan. Bake until a toothpick inserted in the center comes out clean, 65-70 minutes. Cool in pan 10 minutes before removing to a wire rack.

1 PIECE: 221 cal., 10g fat (1g sat. fat), 23mg chol., 212mg sod., 31g carb. (20g sugars, 1g fiber), 3g pro.

Cinnamon Swirl Quick Bread

PREP: 15 MIN. • **BAKE:** 45 MIN. + COOLING
MAKES: 16 PIECES

While cinnamon bread is a natural for breakfast, we love it any time of the day. This is a nice twist on traditional cinnamon swirl yeast breads.
—Helen Richardson, Shelbyville, MI

- 2 **cups all-purpose flour**
- 1½ **cups sugar, divided**
- 1 **tsp. baking soda**
- ½ **tsp. salt**
- 1 **cup buttermilk**
- 1 **large egg, room temperature**
- ¼ **cup canola oil**
- 3 **tsp. ground cinnamon**
GLAZE
- ¼ **cup confectioners' sugar**
- 1½ **to 2 tsp. 2% milk**

1. Preheat oven to 350°. In a large bowl, combine flour, 1 cup sugar, baking soda and salt. Combine buttermilk, egg and oil; stir into dry ingredients just until moistened. In a small bowl, combine cinnamon and the remaining ½ cup sugar.
2. Grease the bottom only of a 9x5-in. loaf pan. Pour half the batter into pan; sprinkle with half the cinnamon-sugar. Carefully spread with the remaining batter and sprinkle with the remaining cinnamon-sugar; cut through batter with a knife to create a swirl.
3. Bake 45-50 minutes or until a toothpick inserted in center comes out clean. Cool 10 minutes before removing from pan to a wire rack to cool completely.
4. For the glaze, combine confectioners' sugar and enough milk to reach desired consistency; drizzle over the loaf.
NOTE: To replace a cup of buttermilk, use 1 Tbsp. white vinegar or lemon juice and enough milk to measure 1 cup. Stir, then let stand 5 min. Or, use 1 cup plain yogurt or 1¾ tsp. cream of tartar and 1 cup milk.
1 PIECE: 179 cal., 4g fat (1g sat. fat), 14mg chol., 173mg sod., 34g carb. (21g sugars, 1g fiber), 3g pro.

Old-Fashioned Peanut Butter Cookies

PREP: 15 MIN. • **BAKE:** 10 MIN./BATCH
MAKES: 3 DOZEN

When she got married, my mother insisted my grandmother write down one recipe for her. Grandma was a traditional pioneer-type cook who used a little of this or that until it felt right. This treasured recipe is the only one she ever wrote down!
—Janet Hall, Clinton, WI

- 1 **cup shortening**
- 1 **cup peanut butter**
- 1 **cup sugar**
- 1 **cup packed brown sugar**
- 3 **large eggs, room temperature**
- 3 **cups all-purpose flour**
- 2 **tsp. baking soda**
- ¼ **tsp. salt**

1. Preheat oven to 375°. In a large bowl, cream the shortening, peanut butter and sugars until light and fluffy, 5-7 minutes. Add eggs, 1 at a time, beat well after each addition. Combine flour, baking soda and salt; add to creamed mixture and mix well.
2. Roll the dough into 1½-in. balls. Place balls 3 in. apart on ungreased baking sheets. Flatten with a meat mallet or fork if desired. Bake for 10-15 minutes. Remove to wire racks to cool.
1 COOKIE: 180 cal., 9g fat (2g sat. fat), 18mg chol., 128mg sod., 21g carb. (12g sugars, 1g fiber), 3g pro.

Rustic Nut Bars

PREP: 20 MIN. • **BAKE:** 35 MIN. + COOLING
MAKES: 3 DOZEN

My friends love crunching into the crust—so much like shortbread—and the wildly nutty topping of these chewy, gooey bars.
—Barbara Driscoll, West Allis, WI

- 1 **Tbsp. plus ¾ cup cold butter, divided**
- 2⅓ **cups all-purpose flour**
- ½ **cup sugar**
- ½ **tsp. baking powder**
- ½ **tsp. salt**
- 1 **large egg, room temperature, lightly beaten**

TOPPING
- ⅔ **cup honey**
- ½ **cup packed brown sugar**
- ¼ **tsp. salt**
- 6 **Tbsp. butter, cubed**
- 2 **Tbsp. heavy whipping cream**
- 1 **cup chopped hazelnuts, toasted**
- 1 **cup salted cashews**
- 1 **cup pistachios**
- 1 **cup salted roasted almonds**

1. Preheat oven to 375°. Line a 13x9-in. baking pan with foil, letting the foil ends extend over the sides of the pan by 1 in. Grease foil with 1 Tbsp. butter.

2. In a large bowl, whisk flour, sugar, baking powder and salt. Cut in the remaining ¾ cup butter until the mixture resembles coarse crumbs. Stir in egg until blended (mixture will be dry). Press firmly onto the bottom of the prepared pan.

3. Bake 18-20 minutes or until the edges are golden brown. Cool on a wire rack.

4. In a large heavy saucepan, combine honey, brown sugar and salt; bring to a boil over medium heat, stirring frequently to dissolve sugar. Boil 2 minutes without stirring. Stir in butter and cream; return to a boil. Cook and stir 1 minute or until smooth. Remove from heat; stir in the nuts. Spread over crust.

5. Bake 15-20 minutes or until topping is bubbly. Cool completely in pan on a wire rack. Lifting with foil, remove from pan. Discard foil; cut into bars.

NOTE: To toast nuts, bake in a shallow pan in a 350° oven for 5-10 minutes or cook in a skillet over low heat until lightly browned, stirring occasionally.

1 BAR: 199 cal., 13g fat (4g sat. fat), 21mg chol., 157mg sod., 18g carb. (10g sugars, 1g fiber), 4g pro.

milk, beating well after each addition. Stir in 1⅓ cups toasted pecans.

3. Pour batter into 3 greased and floured 9-in. round baking pans. Bake at 350° for 25-30 minutes or until a toothpick inserted in the center comes out clean. Cool cake for 10 minutes before removing from pans to wire racks to cool completely.

4. For the frosting, cream the butter and confectioners' sugar in a large bowl. Add milk and vanilla; beat until smooth. Stir in remaining toasted pecans. Spread frosting between layers and over the top and side of cake.

1 PIECE: 814 cal., 42g fat (19g sat. fat), 120mg chol., 375mg sod., 107g carb. (86g sugars, 2g fiber), 7g pro.

TEST KITCHEN TIP

If you like, set some of the toasted pecans aside as garnish, as shown in the photo. To take this cake over the top, drizzle each slice with chocolate sauce or hot fudge when serving.

Butter Pecan Layer Cake

PREP: 40 MIN. • **BAKE:** 25 MIN. + COOLING
MAKES: 16 PIECES

Pecans and butter give this cake the same irresistible flavor as the ever-popular ice cream.
—*Becky Miller, Tallahassee, FL*

2⅔ cups chopped pecans
1¼ cups butter, softened, divided
2 cups sugar
4 large eggs, room temperature
2 tsp. vanilla extract
3 cups all-purpose flour
2 tsp. baking powder
¼ tsp. salt
1 cup 2% milk
FROSTING
1 cup butter, softened
8 to 8½ cups confectioners' sugar
1 can (5 oz.) evaporated milk
2 tsp. vanilla extract

1. Place pecans and ¼ cup butter in a baking pan. Bake at 350° for 10-15 minutes or until toasted, stirring frequently; set aside.

2. In a large bowl, cream the sugar and the remaining 1 cup butter until light and fluffy, 5-7 minutes. Add eggs, 1 at a time, beating well after each addition. Stir in the vanilla. Combine the flour, baking powder and salt; add to the creamed mixture alternately with

Two-Layered Apple Crisp

PREP: 30 MIN. • **BAKE:** 45 MIN.
MAKES: 12 SERVINGS

I feel blessed to have had the opportunity to bake this for a local women's homeless shelter. I make it with Honeycrisp or Golden Delicious apples—or a blend of the two.
—Char Morse, Whitehall, MI

- ¾ cup butter, softened
- 1½ cups packed brown sugar
- 2 tsp. ground cinnamon
- ½ tsp. salt
- 2 cups all-purpose flour
- 2 cups old-fashioned oats

FILLING

- 1 cup sugar
- ¾ cup all-purpose flour
- ¼ cup packed brown sugar
- 1 tsp. ground cinnamon
- ⅛ tsp. ground nutmeg
- 3 large Honeycrisp or Golden Delicious apples, peeled and sliced (about 6 cups)
- 3 tsp. vanilla extract
- 1 Tbsp. butter
- Optional: Vanilla ice cream, caramel sundae syrup and salted pecans

1. Beat the butter, brown sugar, cinnamon and salt until crumbly. Add flour and oats; mix well. Press 3 cups oat mixture into the bottom of a greased 13x9-in. baking dish.
2. In another bowl, mix the first 5 filling ingredients. Add apples and vanilla; toss to combine. Spoon over oat layer. Dot with butter; sprinkle with remaining oat mixture.
3. Bake, uncovered, at 350° until crisp is golden brown and the apples are tender, 45-50 minutes. If desired, serve with toppings.

1 SERVING: 478 cal., 14g fat (8g sat. fat), 33mg chol., 207mg sod., 86g carb. (53g sugars, 3g fiber), 5g pro.

German Apple Cake

PREP: 15 MIN. • **BAKE:** 70 MIN. + COOLING
MAKES: 16 SERVINGS

During the long, cold winters we have here, this German apple cake recipe has warmed many a kitchen. It's perfect for breakfast, dessert or an evening snack.
—*Grace Reynolds, Bethlehem, PA*

- 3 **cups all-purpose flour**
- 3 **tsp. baking powder**
- 1 **tsp. salt**
- 4 **large eggs, room temperature**
- 2 **cups sugar**
- 1 **cup canola oil**
- ½ **cup orange juice**
- 2½ **tsp. vanilla extract**
- 4 **cups thinly sliced peeled apples (about 4 to 5 apples)**
- 2 **tsp. ground cinnamon**
- 3 **Tbsp. sugar**
   Confectioners' sugar, optional

1. Preheat oven to 350°. Grease and flour a 10-in. tube pan. Combine flour, baking powder and salt; set aside.

2. In a large bowl, beat eggs and sugar. Combine the oil and orange juice; add alternately with dry ingredients to the egg mixture. Beat until smooth; add the vanilla and beat well.

3. Pour half of the batter into the prepared pan. Arrange half the apples over the batter. Combine cinnamon and sugar and sprinkle half over the apples. Top with the remaining batter, apples and cinnamon mixture.

4. Bake until a toothpick inserted in the center comes out clean, about 70 minutes. Cool for 1 hour before removing from pan. Cool cake, apple side up, on a wire rack. If desired, sprinkle with confectioners' sugar.

1 PIECE: 353 cal., 15g fat (1g sat. fat), 47mg chol., 256mg sod., 50g carb. (31g sugars, 1g fiber), 4g pro.

cider to reach desired consistency; spread or spoon over cake. If desired, sprinkle with freshly grated nutmeg.

1 PIECE: 403 cal., 18g fat (11g sat. fat), 81mg chol., 249mg sod., 56g carb. (38g sugars, 1g fiber), 5g pro.

Snickerdoodles

PREP: 20 MIN. • **BAKE:** 10 MIN./BATCH
MAKES: 2½ DOZEN

The history of these whimsically named treats has been widely disputed, but their popularity is undeniable. Help yourself to one of our soft cinnamon-sugared cookies and see for yourself.
—Taste of Home *Test Kitchen*

- ½ cup butter, softened
- 1 cup plus 2 Tbsp. sugar, divided
- 1 large egg, room temperature
- ½ tsp. vanilla extract
- 1½ cups all-purpose flour
- ¼ tsp. baking soda
- ¼ tsp. cream of tartar
- 1 tsp. ground cinnamon

1. Preheat oven to 375°. Cream butter and 1 cup sugar until light and fluffy; beat in egg and vanilla. In another bowl, whisk together the flour, baking soda and cream of tartar; gradually beat into the creamed mixture.
2. In a small bowl, mix the cinnamon and remaining 2 Tbsp. sugar. Shape dough into 1-in. balls; roll in cinnamon sugar. Place 2 in. apart on ungreased baking sheets.
3. Bake until light brown, 10-12 minutes. Remove from pans to wire racks to cool.
1 COOKIE: 81 cal., 3g fat (2g sat. fat), 15mg chol., 44mg sod., 12g carb. (7g sugars, 0 fiber), 1g pro.

Buttermilk Cake with Cider Icing

PREP: 35 MIN. • **BAKE:** 45 MIN. + COOLING
MAKES: 16 PIECES

One of my favorites, this vintage-style beauty has a rich, buttery flavor. The buttermilk gives the cake an irresistibly tender texture, and watching the rich apple cider icing drizzle down the sides is almost as delicious as taking your first bite. Almost.
—Gina Nistico, Denver, CO

- 1 cup butter, softened
- 2⅓ cups sugar
- 3 large eggs, room temperature
- 1½ tsp. vanilla extract
- 3 cups all-purpose flour
- 1 tsp. baking powder
- ½ tsp. baking soda
- 1 cup buttermilk

ICING
- 1 cup confectioners' sugar
- 4 oz. cream cheese, softened
- ¼ cup butter, softened
- ¼ to ½ cup apple cider or juice
  Freshly grated whole nutmeg, optional

1. Preheat oven to 350°. Grease and flour a 10-in. fluted tube pan.
2. Cream butter and sugar until light and fluffy, 5-7 minutes. Beat in eggs, 1 at a time, beating well after each addition. Beat in the vanilla. In another bowl, whisk flour, baking powder and baking soda; add to creamed mixture alternately with buttermilk (batter will be thick). Transfer to prepared pan.
3. Bake until a toothpick inserted in center comes out clean, 45-50 minutes. Cool in pan 10 minutes before removing to a wire rack to cool completely.
4. For icing, beat confectioners' sugar, cream cheese, butter and enough apple

Caramel Creme Brulee

PREP: 20 MIN. • **BAKE:** 40 MIN. + CHILLING
MAKES: 14 SERVINGS

This recipe comes out perfect every time and it's always a crowd pleaser! A torch works best to get the sugar caramelized while keeping the rest of the custard cool. You may want to use even more sugar to create a thicker, more even crust on top.
—Jenna Fleming, Lowville, NY

- 4½ cups heavy whipping cream
- 1½ cups half-and-half cream
- 15 large egg yolks, room temperature
- 1⅓ cups sugar, divided
- 3 tsp. caramel extract
- ¼ tsp. salt
- ⅓ cup packed brown sugar

1. Preheat oven to 325°. In a large saucepan, heat whipping cream and cream until bubbles form around the side of the pan; remove from the heat. In a bowl, whisk egg yolks, 1 cup sugar, caramel extract and salt until well blended but not foamy. Slowly stir in the hot cream mixture.

2. Place an ungreased broiler-safe 13x9-in. baking dish in a baking pan large enough to hold it without touching the sides. Pour egg mixture into the 13x9-in. dish. Place baking pan on oven rack; carefully add very hot water to the outer pan to within 1 in. of the top of the baking dish. Bake until the center is just set and the top appears dull, 40-50 minutes. Immediately remove dish from water bath to a wire rack; cool 1 hour. Refrigerate until cold.

3. Mix brown sugar and remaining ⅓ cup sugar. Sprinkle custard evenly with sugar mixture. To caramelize the topping with a kitchen torch, hold torch flame about 2 in. above custard surface and rotate it slowly until sugar is evenly caramelized. Serve immediately or refrigerate up to 1 hour.

TO CARAMELIZE TOPPING IN A BROILER: After removing custard from oven, let stand at room temperature for 30 minutes. Preheat broiler. Sprinkle custard evenly with sugar mixture. Broil 3-4 in. from heat until sugar is caramelized, 2-3 minutes. Serve immediately or refrigerate up to 1 hour.

½ CUP: 452 cal., 35g fat (21g sat. fat), 298mg chol., 86mg sod., 28g carb. (27g sugars, 0 fiber), 6g pro.

**Optional: Turbinado or coarse
sugar, ground cinnamon, vanilla
bean ice cream and caramel sauce**

1. Preheat oven to 375°. On a lightly
floured surface, roll half the dough to
a ⅛-in.-thick circle; transfer to a 9-in. pie
plate. In a small bowl, combine sugars, flour
and spices. In a large bowl, toss apples with
lemon juice. Add sugar mixture; toss to
coat. Add filling to crust; dot with butter.
2. Roll the remaining dough to a ⅛-in.-thick
circle. Place over filling. Trim, seal and flute
edge. Cut slits in top. Beat egg white until
foamy; brush over crust. If desired, sprinkle
with turbinado sugar and ground cinnamon.
Cover edge loosely with foil.
3. Bake 25 minutes. Remove foil; bake until
crust is golden brown and filling is bubbly,
20-25 minutes longer. Cool on a wire rack.
If desired, serve with vanilla bean ice cream
and caramel sauce.
1 PIECE: 467 cal., 25g fat (15g sat. fat),
64mg chol., 331mg sod., 58g carb. (26g
sugars, 2g fiber), 5g pro.

TEST KITCHEN TIP

If you want to save a few calories, you
can reduce the sugar by up to half in this
recipe or use a sugar substitute made
for baking.

Apple Pie

PREP: 20 MIN. + CHILLING
BAKE: 45 MIN. + COOLING
MAKES: 8 PIECES

*I remember coming home sullen one
day because we'd lost a softball game.
Grandma, in her wisdom, suggested,
"Maybe a slice of hot apple pie will
make you feel better." She was right.*
—Maggie Greene, Granite Falls, WA

Dough for double-crust pie (p. 154)
⅓ cup sugar
⅓ cup packed brown sugar
¼ cup all-purpose flour
1 tsp. ground cinnamon
¼ tsp. ground ginger
¼ tsp. ground nutmeg
6 to 7 cups thinly sliced
  peeled tart apples
1 Tbsp. lemon juice
1 Tbsp. butter
1 large egg white

Honey Pie

PREP: 20 MIN. + CHILLING
BAKE: 40 MIN. + CHILLING
MAKES: 8 PIECES

A hint of honey flavors this old-fashioned custard pie. Don't be afraid of blind-baking the crust—it's easy to do!
—Taste of Home *Test Kitchen*

    Dough for single-crust pie (p. 154)
  4 **large eggs**
2½ **cups whole milk**
  ½ **cup packed brown sugar**
  ½ **cup honey**
  1 **tsp. ground nutmeg**
  1 **tsp. vanilla extract**
  1 **tsp. almond extract**
  ½ **tsp. salt**
    Optional: Whipped cream, additional honey and flaky sea salt

1. On a lightly floured surface, roll dough to a ⅛-in.-thick circle; transfer to a 9-in. pie plate. Trim to ½ in. beyond rim of plate; flute edge. Refrigerate 30 minutes. Preheat oven to 400°.

2. Line the unpricked crust with a double thickness of foil. Fill with pie weights, dried beans or uncooked rice. Bake on a lower oven rack until the edge is golden brown, 15-20 minutes. Remove foil and weights; bake until the bottom is golden brown, 3-6 minutes longer. Cool on a wire rack.

3. Whisk eggs, then whisk in remaining ingredients until blended. Pour into crust. Cover edge with foil. Bake at 400° until a knife inserted in the center comes out clean, 40-50 minutes. Cool on a wire rack for 1 hour. Refrigerate at least 3 hours before serving. Top each serving with whipped cream, a drizzle of honey or flaky sea salt as desired. Refrigerate leftovers.

1 PIECE: 374 cal., 17g fat (10g sat. fat), 131mg chol., 375mg sod., 50g carb. (35g sugars, 1g fiber), 8g pro.

Pumpkin Bars

PREP: 20 MIN. • **BAKE:** 25 MIN. + COOLING
MAKES: 2 DOZEN

What could be a better fall treat than a big pan of pumpkin-flavored bars? Actually, my family loves these any time of year!
—Brenda Keller, Andalusia, AL

- 4 **large eggs, room temperature**
- 1⅔ **cups sugar**
- 1 **cup canola oil**
- 1 **can (15 oz.) pumpkin**
- 2 **cups all-purpose flour**
- 2 **tsp. ground cinnamon**
- 2 **tsp. baking powder**
- 1 **tsp. baking soda**
- 1 **tsp. salt**

ICING

- 6 **oz. cream cheese, softened**
- 2 **cups confectioners' sugar**
- ¼ **cup butter, softened**
- 1 **tsp. vanilla extract**
- 1 **to 2 Tbsp. 2% milk**

1. Preheat oven to 350°. Beat eggs, sugar, oil and pumpkin until well blended. Combine the flour, cinnamon, baking powder, baking soda and salt; gradually add to pumpkin mixture and mix well. Pour into an ungreased 15x10x1-in. baking pan. Bake 25-30 minutes or until set. Cool completely.
2. For icing, beat cream cheese, confectioners' sugar, butter and vanilla. Add enough milk to achieve spreading consistency. Spread icing over bars. Store in the refrigerator.
1 BAR: 260 cal., 13g fat (3g sat. fat), 45mg chol., 226mg sod., 34g carb. (24g sugars, 1g fiber), 3g pro.

The Best Pecan Pie

PREP: 15 MIN. • **BAKE:** 55 MIN. + COOLING
MAKES: 8 PIECES

Pecan pie is a Thanksgiving tradition in my house, and I was on a quest to create the ultimate version. This might be it!
—James Schend, Pleasant Prairie, WI

Dough for single-crust pie (p. 154)
- ½ cup butter
- 2½ cups coarsely chopped pecans
- ¾ cup packed brown sugar
- ¾ cup maple syrup
- ½ tsp. salt
- 3 large eggs, beaten

- 2 Tbsp. whiskey or bourbon, optional
- 2 tsp. vanilla extract

1. On a lightly floured surface, roll dough to a ⅛-in.-thick circle; transfer to a 9-in. pie plate. Trim to ½ in. beyond rim of plate; flute edge. Refrigerate while preparing filling.
2. In a Dutch oven or large saucepan, melt butter over medium heat. Add pecans; cook, stirring, until very fragrant and pecans start to brown, 4-5 minutes. Remove nuts with a slotted spoon, reserving butter in pan. Stir in the brown sugar, syrup and salt; bring to a boil. Reduce the heat; simmer 2 minutes. Remove from heat. Whisk a small amount of the hot mixture into the eggs; return all to the pan, whisking constantly. Stir whiskey (if desired) and vanilla into the brown sugar mixture; stir in pecans. Pour into crust.
3. Bake at 350° until a knife inserted in center comes out clean, 55-60 minutes. Cover edge with foil during last 30 minutes to prevent overbrowning if necessary. Cool on a wire rack. Refrigerate leftovers.
1 PIECE: 695 cal., 49g fat (17g sat. fat), 130mg chol., 430mg sod., 60g carb. (40g sugars, 4g fiber), 8g pro.

HOW-TO
MAKE THE BEST PECAN PIE

1. Cooking the pecans in butter as a first step makes a much more flavorful pie than does simply adding them raw.

2. Whisking a small amount of the hot sugar mixture into the beaten eggs before adding the eggs to the pan prevents them from cooking—you don't want to end up with scrambled eggs in your pie!

3. The crust for this pie doesn't need to be blind-baked, but refrigerating it before adding the filling and baking it helps keep it crisp and flaky and also prevents it from shrinking in the pan.

4. Test for doneness at the earliest point of the time range; the nuts and high sugar content of this pie make it vulnerable to overbrowning.

Maple Butter Twists

PREP: 35 MIN. + RISING
BAKE: 25 MIN. + COOLING
MAKES: 2 COFFEE CAKES (16 PIECES EACH)

My stepmother gave me the recipe for a delicious yeast coffee cake shaped into pretty rings. When I make it for friends, they always ask for seconds.
—June Gilliland, Hope, IN

3¼ to 3½ cups all-purpose flour
3 Tbsp. sugar
1½ tsp. salt
1 pkg. (¼ oz.) active dry yeast
¾ cup 2% milk
¼ cup butter
2 large eggs, room temperature

FILLING
⅓ cup packed brown sugar
¼ cup sugar
3 Tbsp. butter, softened
3 Tbsp. maple syrup
4½ tsp. all-purpose flour
¾ tsp. ground cinnamon
¾ tsp. maple flavoring
⅓ cup chopped walnuts

GLAZE
½ cup confectioners' sugar
¼ tsp. maple flavoring
2 to 3 tsp. 2% milk

1. Combine 1½ cups flour, sugar, salt and yeast. In a saucepan, heat the milk and butter to 120°-130°. Add to dry ingredients; beat just until moistened. Add eggs; beat on medium for 2 minutes. Stir in enough of the remaining flour to form a firm dough.

2. Turn dough onto a floured surface; knead until smooth and elastic, 5-7 minutes. Place in a greased bowl, turning once to grease top. Cover and let rise in a warm place until doubled, about 70 minutes.

3. Combine first 7 filling ingredients; beat for 2 minutes. Punch the dough down; turn onto a lightly floured surface. Divide in half; roll each into a 16x8-in. rectangle. Spread filling to within ½ in. of edges. Sprinkle with nuts. Roll up jelly-roll style, starting with a long side.

4. With a sharp knife, cut each roll in half lengthwise. Open halves so cut side is up; gently twist the ropes together. Transfer to 2 greased 9-in. round baking pans. Coil into a circle. Tuck the ends under; pinch to seal. Cover and let rise in a warm place until the dough is doubled, about 45 minutes.

5. Bake at 350° for 25-30 minutes or until golden brown. Cool 10 minutes; remove from the pans to wire racks. Combine the confectioners' sugar, maple flavoring and enough milk to reach desired consistency; drizzle over warm cakes.

1 PIECE: 119 cal., 4g fat (2g sat. fat), 21mg chol., 144mg sod., 19g carb. (8g sugars, 0 fiber), 2g pro.

German Chocolate Cake

PREP: 30 MIN. • **BAKE:** 25 MIN. + COOLING
MAKES: 12 PIECES

This cake is my husband's favorite! Each bite has crunch from the pecans, and sweetness from coconut and chocolate.
—Joyce Platfoot, Wapakoneta, OH

- 4 oz. German sweet chocolate, chopped
- ½ cup water
- 1 cup butter, softened
- 2 cups sugar
- 4 large eggs, separated, room temperature
- 1 tsp. vanilla extract
- 2½ cups cake flour
- 1 tsp. baking soda
- ½ tsp. salt
- 1 cup buttermilk

FROSTING

- 1½ cups sugar
- 1½ cups evaporated milk
- ¾ cup butter
- 5 large egg yolks, room temperature, beaten
- 2 cups sweetened shredded coconut
- 1½ cups chopped pecans
- 1½ tsp. vanilla extract

ICING

- 2 oz. semisweet chocolate
- 1 tsp. shortening

1. Line 3 greased 9-in. round baking pans with waxed paper. Grease waxed paper and set aside. In small saucepan, melt chocolate with water over low heat; cool.

2. Preheat oven to 350°. In a large bowl, cream butter and sugar until light and fluffy, 5-7 minutes. Beat in the 4 egg yolks, 1 at a time, beating well after each addition. Blend in melted chocolate and vanilla. Combine flour, baking soda and salt; add to creamed mixture alternately with buttermilk, beating well after each addition.

3. In a small bowl and with clean beaters, beat the 4 egg whites until stiff peaks form. Fold a fourth of the egg whites into the creamed mixture; fold in remaining whites.

4. Pour batter into prepared pans. Bake 24-28 minutes or until a toothpick inserted in center comes out clean. Cool 10 minutes before removing from pans to wire racks to cool completely.

5. For frosting, in a small saucepan, heat sugar, milk, butter and the 5 egg yolks over medium-low heat until mixture is thickened and golden brown, stirring constantly. Remove from the heat. Stir in the coconut, pecans and vanilla. Cool until thick enough to spread. Spread a third of the frosting over each cake layer and stack the layers.

6. For the icing, in a microwave, melt the chocolate and shortening; stir until smooth. Drizzle over the cake.

NOTE: To replace a cup of buttermilk, use 1 Tbsp. white vinegar or lemon juice and enough milk to measure 1 cup. Stir, then let stand 5 min. Or, use 1 cup plain yogurt or 1¾ tsp. cream of tartar and 1 cup milk.

1 PIECE: 910 cal., 53g fat (28g sat. fat), 237mg chol., 511mg sod., 103g carb. (76g sugars, 4g fiber), 11g pro.

Dutch Oven Apple Cobbler

PREP: 20 MIN. • **BAKE:** 45 MIN.
MAKES: 8 SERVINGS

This homey dessert is always a big hit with my family. We like to serve it with ice cream or whipped cream.
—Cindy Jajuga, Weed, CA

- 8 large tart apples, peeled and sliced
- 1 cup sugar, divided
- ¾ tsp. ground cinnamon, divided
- 2 cups all-purpose flour
- ¾ cup packed brown sugar
- 1 tsp. baking powder
- ½ tsp. salt
- 2 large eggs, room temperature, lightly beaten
- ⅔ cup butter, melted
   Vanilla ice cream, optional

1. Preheat oven to 350°. In a 6-qt. Dutch oven, combine apples, ¾ cup sugar and ½ tsp. cinnamon.

2. In a bowl, whisk the flour, brown sugar, remaining ¼ cup sugar, baking powder, salt and remaining ¼ tsp. cinnamon; stir in eggs (mixture will be lumpy). Spoon batter over apples. Drizzle the melted butter over batter (do not stir).

3. Bake, covered, until lightly browned and apples are tender, 45-50 minutes. Serve warm, with ice cream if desired.

1 SERVING: 531 cal., 17g fat (10g sat. fat), 87mg chol., 354mg sod., 93g carb. (64g sugars, 3g fiber), 5g pro.

First-Place Coconut Macaroons

PREP: 10 MIN. • **BAKE:** 20 MIN./BATCH
MAKES: ABOUT 1½ DOZEN

These cookies earned me a first-place ribbon at the county fair. They remain my husband's favorites—whenever I make them to give away, he always asks me where his batch is! I especially like the fact that this recipe makes a small enough batch for the two of us to nibble on.
—Penny Ann Habeck, Shawano, WI

1⅓ **cups sweetened shredded coconut**
⅓ **cup sugar**
2 **Tbsp. all-purpose flour**
⅛ **tsp. salt**
2 **large egg whites, room temperature**
½ **tsp. vanilla extract**

1. Preheat oven to 325°. In a small bowl, combine the coconut, sugar, flour and salt. Add egg whites and vanilla; mix well.

2. Drop by rounded teaspoonfuls onto greased baking sheets. Bake 18-20 minutes or until golden brown. Cool on a wire rack.

1 COOKIE: 54 cal., 2g fat (2g sat. fat), 0 chol., 41mg sod., 8g carb. (7g sugars, 0 fiber), 1g pro.
DIABETIC EXCHANGES: ½ starch, ½ fat.

TEST KITCHEN TIP

You can use unsweetened coconut if you prefer. Your cookies won't be quite as sweet, but they'll be crispier. You can also mix in additions like nuts or mini chocolate chips.

Frosted Maple Cookies

PREP: 20 MIN. + CHILLING
BAKE: 10 MIN./BATCH + COOLING
MAKES: 4 DOZEN

Living in New England, I appreciate the unique qualities of our area. Many here enjoy maple flavor. I love this adaptation of an old favorite.
—Connie Borden, Marblehead, MA

- ½ cup shortening
- 1½ cups packed brown sugar
- 2 large eggs, room temperature
- 1 cup sour cream
- 1 Tbsp. maple flavoring
- 2¾ cups all-purpose flour
- 1 tsp. salt
- ½ tsp. baking soda
- 1 cup chopped nuts

FROSTING
- ½ cup butter
- 2 cups confectioners' sugar
- 2 tsp. maple flavoring
- 2 to 3 Tbsp. hot water

1. In a large bowl, cream shortening and brown sugar until light and fluffy, 5-7 minutes. Add eggs, 1 at a time, beating well after each addition. Stir in sour cream and maple flavoring. Combine the flour, salt and baking soda; add to creamed mixture and mix well. Stir in nuts. Cover dough and refrigerate for 1 hour.

2. Preheat oven to 375°. Drop dough by rounded tablespoonfuls 2 in. apart onto greased baking sheets. Bake 8-10 minutes or until edges are lightly browned. Cool completely on wire racks.

3. For frosting, in a small saucepan, heat butter over low heat until golden brown. Remove from the heat; blend in the confectioners' sugar, maple flavoring and enough water to achieve spreading consistency. Frost cookies.

1 COOKIE: 147 cal., 8g fat (3g sat. fat), 20mg chol., 86mg sod., 18g carb. (12g sugars, 0 fiber), 2g pro.

Old-Fashioned Gingerbread

PREP: 25 MIN. • **BAKE:** 35 MIN. + COOLING
MAKES: 9 PIECES

My dad always told me that his mother made gingerbread with hot water and that hers was dense and rich with molasses. Over the years, I looked for such a recipe—to no avail. Then one day I was given a book compiled by an elderly woman who recalled recipes from her childhood in Virginia, and there it was! I made only one change, using shortening instead of lard.
—cjwkat, tasteofhome.com

- ½ cup butter, cubed
- ¼ cup shortening, cubed
- 1 cup boiling water
- 2 large eggs, room temperature
- 1½ cups molasses
- 2 cups all-purpose flour
- 1 Tbsp. ground ginger
- 2 tsp. baking powder
- 1 tsp. ground cinnamon
- ½ tsp. salt
- ¼ tsp. baking soda
  Confectioners' sugar, optional

1. Preheat oven to 350°. Grease a 9-in. square baking pan; set aside. In a large bowl, mix butter, shortening and boiling water until smooth; cool slightly. Beat in eggs and molasses until well blended. In another bowl, whisk flour, ginger, baking powder, cinnamon, salt and baking soda; gradually beat into molasses mixture. Pour into prepared pan (batter will be thin).

2. Bake until a toothpick inserted in center comes out clean, 35-40 minutes. Cool cake completely on wire rack. If desired, sprinkle with confectioners' sugar before serving.

1 PIECE: 414 cal., 17g fat (8g sat. fat), 68mg chol., 390mg sod., 62g carb. (40g sugars, 1g fiber), 4g pro.

Mom's Chocolate Chip Cookies

PREP: 20 MIN. • **BAKE:** 10 MIN./BATCH
MAKES: 4 DOZEN

My mom brightening my lunch with these yummy cookies has always been one of my fondest memories from childhood.
—Tammy Orr, Wharton, NJ

- 1 **cup butter, softened**
- ¾ **cup packed brown sugar**
- ¼ **cup sugar**
- 1 **pkg. (3.4 oz.) instant vanilla pudding mix**
- 2 **large eggs, room temperature, lightly beaten**
- 1 **tsp. vanilla extract**
- 2¼ **cups all-purpose flour**
- 1 **tsp. baking soda**
- 2 **cups semisweet chocolate chips**

1. Preheat oven to 375°. In a bowl, cream the butter and sugars until light and fluffy, 5-7 minutes. Add the pudding mix, eggs and vanilla. Combine the flour and baking soda; add to creamed mixture and mix well. Fold in chocolate chips.

2. Drop by teaspoonfuls onto ungreased baking sheets. Bake for 10-12 minutes or until lightly browned.

1 COOKIE: 117 cal., 5g fat (3g sat. fat), 8mg chol., 45mg sod., 20g carb. (14g sugars, 1g fiber), 1g pro.

Kathy Harding

Richmond, MO

Branch out from the usual pecan pie with a creamy-crunchy version that comes out of the oven golden brown.

. . . .

Buttermilk Pie with Pecans

PREP: 40 MIN.
BAKE: 50 MIN. + COOLING
MAKES: 8 PIECES

Dough for single-crust pie (p. 154)
½ cup butter, softened
1¾ cups sugar
3 large eggs
3 Tbsp. all-purpose flour
¼ tsp. salt
1 cup buttermilk
2 tsp. vanilla extract
1 cup chopped pecans
Sweetened whipped cream, optional

1. Preheat oven to 425°. On a lightly floured surface, roll the dough to a ⅛-in.-thick circle; transfer to a 9-in. pie plate. Trim to ½ in. beyond rim of plate; flute edge. Line the unpricked crust with a double thickness of foil. Fill with pie weights, dried beans or uncooked rice.

1. Place on a baking sheet; bake until edge is light golden brown, 15 minutes. Remove foil and weights; bake until bottom is golden brown, 5 minutes longer. Cool on a wire rack. Reduce oven setting to 325°.

2. Beat butter and sugar until blended. Add the eggs, 1 at a time, beating well after each addition. Beat in flour and salt. Gradually stir in the buttermilk and vanilla.

3. Sprinkle pecans onto crust; add filling. Bake until center is set, 50-60 minutes. Cover top loosely with foil during the last 15 minutes if necessary to prevent overbrowning.

4. Cool completely on a wire rack. If desired, serve with whipped cream. Serve or refrigerate within 2 hours.

1 PIECE: 591 cal., 35g fat (16g sat. fat), 132mg chol., 405mg sod., 65g carb. (47g sugars, 2g fiber), 7g pro.

Pecan Pie Bars

PREP: 10 MIN. • **BAKE:** 35 MIN. + CHILLING
MAKES: 4 DOZEN

These bars are decadently rich—just like pecan pie! They're sure to disappear from the dessert table at your next gathering, so you might want to save one for later before putting them out.
—Carolyn Custer, Clifton Park, NY

- 2 cups all-purpose flour
- ½ cup confectioners' sugar
- 1 cup butter, softened
- 1 can (14 oz.) sweetened condensed milk
- 1 large egg
- 1 tsp. vanilla extract
  Pinch salt
- 1 pkg. (8 oz.) milk chocolate English toffee bits
- 1 cup chopped pecans

1. Preheat oven to 350°. In a large bowl, combine flour and sugar. Cut in butter until mixture resembles coarse meal. Press firmly onto the bottom of a greased 13x9-in. baking dish. Bake for 15 minutes.

2. Meanwhile, in a large bowl, beat the condensed milk, egg, vanilla and salt until smooth. Stir in the toffee bits and pecans; spread evenly over the baked crust.

3. Bake until lightly browned, 20-25 minutes longer. Cool. Cover and chill; cut into bars. Store in refrigerator.

1 BAR: 127 cal., 8g fat (4g sat. fat), 18mg chol., 100mg sod., 13g carb. (9g sugars, 0 fiber), 2g pro.

SEE HOW IT'S DONE

These sweet bars come together in a few minutes! Hover your camera here to see how.

Giant Molasses Cookies

PREP: 30 MIN. • **BAKE:** 15 MIN./BATCH
MAKES: 2 DOZEN

My family always requests these soft and deliciously chewy cookies. The generous treats are also great for shipping as holiday gifts or to troops overseas.
—Kristine Chayes, Smithtown, NY

- 1½ cups butter, softened
- 2 cups sugar
- 2 large eggs, room temperature
- ½ cup molasses
- 4½ cups all-purpose flour
- 4 tsp. ground ginger
- 2 tsp. baking soda
- 1½ tsp. ground cinnamon
- 1 tsp. ground cloves
- ¼ tsp. salt
- ¼ cup chopped pecans
- ¾ cup coarse sugar

1. Preheat oven to 350°. In a large bowl, cream the butter and sugar until light and fluffy, 5-7 minutes. Beat in the eggs and molasses. Combine the flour, ginger, baking soda, cinnamon, cloves and salt; gradually add to the creamed mixture and mix well. Fold in pecans.

2. Shape dough into 2-in. balls and roll in coarse sugar. Place balls 2½ in. apart on ungreased baking sheets. Bake for 13-15 minutes or until tops are cracked. Remove to wire racks to cool.

1 COOKIE: 310 cal., 13g fat (7g sat. fat), 48mg chol., 219mg sod., 46g carb. (27g sugars, 1g fiber), 3g pro.

CLASSIC YEAST BREADS

AH, THE AROMA OF FRESH-BAKED BREAD!

NOTHING MAKES YOUR KITCHEN COZIER

AND MORE WELCOMING.

CHERRY-TARRAGON DINNER ROLLS, P. 59

Onion Mustard Buns

PREP: 25 MIN. + RISING • **BAKE:** 20 MIN.
MAKES: 2 DOZEN

I'm an avid bread baker and was thrilled to find this recipe. It makes delectably different rolls that are a hit wherever I take them. The onion and mustard flavors go so well with ham or hamburgers, but the buns are special enough to serve alongside an elaborate main dish.
—Melodie Shumaker, Elizabethtown, PA

1 pkg. (¼ oz.) active dry yeast
¼ cup warm water (110° to 115°)
2 cups warm 2% milk (110° to 115°)
3 Tbsp. dried minced onion
3 Tbsp. prepared mustard
2 Tbsp. canola oil
2 Tbsp. sugar
1½ tsp. salt
6 to 6½ cups all-purpose flour
   Optional: Beaten egg, poppy seeds and additional dried minced onion

1. In a large bowl, dissolve yeast in water. Add milk, onion, mustard, oil, sugar, salt and 4 cups flour; beat until smooth. Add enough of the remaining flour to form a soft dough.
2. Turn out dough onto a floured surface; knead until smooth and elastic, 6-8 minutes. Place in a greased bowl, turning once to grease top. Cover and let rise in a warm place until doubled, about 1 hour.
3. Punch dough down; divide into 24 pieces. Flatten each piece into a 3-in. circle. Place circles 1 in. apart on greased baking sheets. Cover and let rise until doubled, about 45 minutes. If desired, brush with beaten egg and sprinkle with poppy seeds or dried minced onion.
4. Bake at 350° until golden brown, 20-25 minutes. Cool on wire racks.
1 BUN: 138 cal., 2g fat, 0 chol., 181mg sod., 26g carb., 4g pro.

Whole Wheat Pita Bread

PREP: 40 MIN. + RISING
BAKE: 10 MIN. • **MAKES:** 1 DOZEN

On a trip to Israel, I fell in love with the rustic pita breads enjoyed with just about every meal. These nutritious whole-wheat pitas are a favorite with young and old alike.
—Ruby Witmer, Goshen, IN

2 pkg. (¼ oz. each) active dry yeast
2 cups warm water (110° to 115°), divided
½ tsp. honey
¼ cup olive oil
1 Tbsp. salt
5 to 6 cups whole wheat flour
   All-purpose flour
   Cornmeal

1. In a large bowl, dissolve yeast in ½ cup warm water. Add the honey; let stand for 5 minutes. Add the oil, salt, 3 cups of whole wheat flour and remaining 1½ cups water. Beat until smooth. Stir in enough whole wheat flour to form a soft dough.
2. Turn the dough onto a surface dusted with all-purpose flour; knead until smooth and elastic, 6-8 minutes. Place in a greased bowl, turning once to grease top. Cover and let rise in a warm place until doubled, about 1½ hours.
3. Punch dough down; let rest 10 minutes. Turn onto a lightly floured surface; divide dough into 12 pieces. Shape each into a ball. Knead each ball for 1 minute. Cover and let rest for 20 minutes.
4. Grease baking sheets and sprinkle with cornmeal. Roll each ball into an 8-in. circle. Place on prepared baking sheets. Cover and let rise in a warm place until doubled, about 30 minutes.
5. Bake at 475° for 8-10 minutes or until browned. Remove from pans to wire racks to cool. To serve, cut in half and split open. Stuff with fillings of your choice.
1 PIECE: 212 cal., 5g fat (1g sat. fat), 0 chol., 593mg sod., 37g carb. (1g sugars, 6g fiber), 7g pro.

Maple & Bacon Swirl Bread

PREP: 50 MIN. + RISING
BAKE: 35 MIN.
MAKES: 2 LOAVES (12 PIECES EACH)

Swirled with maple syrup, raisins, bacon and brown sugar, this craveworthy bread is one they'll remember. Plus, the dough is easy to work with and roll out!
—Alicia Rooker, Milwaukee, WI

2 pkg. (¼ oz. each) active dry yeast
½ cup warm water (110° to 115°)
5 cups all-purpose flour
¾ cup sugar
½ tsp. salt
½ cup cold butter
½ cup sour cream
2 large eggs, lightly beaten, room temperature
2 large egg yolks, lightly beaten, room temperature
1 tsp. vanilla extract

FILLING
2 Tbsp. butter, melted
2 Tbsp. maple syrup
1 tsp. maple flavoring
½ cup packed brown sugar
8 bacon strips, cooked and crumbled
¼ cup raisins

1. In a small bowl, dissolve yeast in warm water. In a large bowl, mix flour, sugar and salt; cut in butter until crumbly. Add sour cream, eggs, egg yolks, vanilla and the yeast mixture; stir to form a soft dough (dough will be sticky).

2. Turn out dough onto a floured surface; knead until smooth and elastic, 6-8 minutes. Do not let rise. Divide in half. Roll out into two 12-in. squares; cover.

3. In a small bowl, combine melted butter, maple syrup and flavoring. Spread over each square to within ½ in. of edges. Sprinkle with brown sugar, bacon and raisins. Roll up each square jelly-roll style; pinch seams to seal.

4. Place rolls on a parchment-lined rimmed baking sheet. Cover and let rise until nearly doubled, about 45 minutes. Bake at 350° until golden brown, 35-40 minutes. Remove from pan to a wire rack to cool.

1 PIECE: 225 cal., 8g fat (4g sat. fat), 48mg chol., 147mg sod., 34g carb. (13g sugars, 1g fiber), 5g pro.

Autumn Sweet Rolls with Cider Glaze

PREP: 30 MIN. + RISING • **BAKE:** 25 MIN.
MAKES: 1 DOZEN

I love cooking with pumpkin because it's versatile, colorful and nutritious. Combining it with chopped apple and cider gives these glazed rolls their autumn appeal.
—Jennifer Coduto, Kent, OH

- 2 tsp. active dry yeast
- ⅓ cup warm water (110° to 115°)
- 1 Tbsp. honey
- ¾ cup canned pumpkin
- 2 large eggs, room temperature
- ¼ cup packed brown sugar
- 2 Tbsp. butter, softened
- 1½ tsp. pumpkin pie spice
- ½ tsp. salt
- 4 to 4½ cups all-purpose flour

FILLING

- ¼ cup sugar
- 1 tsp. ground cinnamon
- 2 Tbsp. butter, melted
- 1 small apple, peeled and finely chopped (about 1 cup)

GLAZE

- 1 cup confectioners' sugar
- 3 Tbsp. apple cider or juice
- ¼ cup finely chopped walnuts, toasted

1. In a small bowl, dissolve yeast in warm water and honey. In a large bowl, combine pumpkin, eggs, brown sugar, butter, pie spice, salt, the yeast mixture and 1½ cups flour; beat on medium speed until smooth. Stir in enough remaining flour to form a soft dough (dough will be sticky).
2. Turn dough onto a floured surface; knead until smooth and elastic, 6-8 minutes. Place in a greased bowl, turning once to grease the top. Cover and let rise in a warm place until doubled, about 1 hour.

3. For filling, mix sugar and cinnamon. Punch down dough. Turn onto a lightly floured surface. Press dough into a 14x12-in. rectangle. Brush with melted butter up to ½ in. from the edges. Sprinkle with cinnamon sugar and chopped apple. Roll up jelly-roll style, starting with a long side; pinch seam to seal. Cut into 12 slices.
4. Place slices in a greased 13x9-in. baking pan, cut side down. Cover with a kitchen towel; let rise in a warm place until doubled, about 30 minutes.
5. Preheat oven to 350°. Bake until golden brown, 25-30 minutes. In a small bowl, mix confectioners' sugar and apple cider; drizzle over warm rolls. Sprinkle with walnuts.
1 ROLL: 306 cal., 7g fat (3g sat. fat), 41mg chol., 145mg sod., 56g carb. (22g sugars, 2g fiber), 6g pro.

Rosemary Walnut Bread

PREP: 25 MIN. + RISING • **BAKE:** 20 MIN.
MAKES: 1 LOAF (9 PIECES)

*I received this recipe from a friend who
made this bread to celebrate moving into
a new apartment.*
—Robin Haas, Cranston, RI

- 1¼ tsp. active dry yeast
- ½ cup warm water (110° to 115°)
- ¼ cup whole wheat flour
- 1½ to 1¾ cups all-purpose flour
- 2 Tbsp. honey
- 1 Tbsp. olive oil
- 1½ tsp. dried rosemary, crushed
- ½ tsp. salt
- ⅓ cup finely chopped walnuts

1. Dissolve yeast in warm water. In a large
bowl, mix whole wheat flour and ¼ cup
all-purpose flour; stir in yeast mixture. Let
stand, covered, for 15 minutes. Add honey,
oil, rosemary, salt and ¾ cup all-purpose
flour; beat on medium speed until smooth.
Stir in walnuts and enough remaining
all-purpose flour to form a soft dough.
2. Turn dough onto a floured surface; knead
until smooth and elastic, 6-8 minutes. Place
in a greased bowl, turning once to grease
the top. Cover and let rise in a warm place
until doubled, about 45 minutes.
3. Punch down dough. Turn onto a lightly
floured surface; divide into thirds. Roll each
into a 12-in. rope. Place on a greased baking
sheet and braid. Pinch ends to seal; tuck
under. Cover with a kitchen towel; let rise in
a warm place until almost doubled, about
30 minutes.
4. Bake at 375° for 20-25 minutes or until
golden brown. Remove from pan to a wire
rack to cool.
1 PIECE: 145 cal., 4g fat (0 sat. fat), 0 chol.,
132mg sod., 23g carb. (4g sugars, 1g fiber),
4g pro.

Christine Wendland

Browns Mills, NJ

Long ago I decided to make my holiday stuffing with real bread, and not store-bought cubes. But I could never find a bread with all the great flavors of fall, so I developed this recipe. It's also nice for post-Thanksgiving turkey sandwiches.

Sage-Apple Cider Bread

PREP: 30 MIN. + RISING
BAKE: 30 MIN.
MAKES: 1 LOAF (16 PIECES)

- 1 pkg. (¼ oz.) active dry yeast
- 1¼ cups warm apple cider or juice (110°–115°)
- 2½ cups bread flour
- ⅓ cup butter, melted
- 2 Tbsp. sugar
- 1 large egg, room temperature
- ¼ cup fresh sage, thinly sliced
- ¾ tsp. salt
- 1½ to 2 cups all-purpose flour
- 2 tsp. 2% milk

1. In a large bowl, dissolve yeast in warm cider. Add bread flour, butter, sugar, egg, sage and salt. Beat on medium speed for 3 minutes. Stir in enough of the all-purpose flour to form a firm dough.

2. Turn dough onto a floured surface; knead until smooth and elastic, 6-8 minutes. Place in a greased bowl, turning once to grease the top. Cover and let rise in a warm place until doubled, about 1 hour.

3. Punch dough down. Turn onto a lightly floured surface. Shape into a loaf. Place in a greased 9x5-in. loaf pan. Cover and let rise until doubled, about 40 minutes. Brush with milk.

4. Preheat oven to 375°. Bake for 30-40 minutes or until golden brown. Remove from pan to a wire rack to cool.

1 PIECE: 176 cal., 5g fat (3g sat. fat), 22mg chol., 149mg sod., 29g carb. (4g sugars, 1g fiber), 4g pro.

Easy Potato Rolls

PREP: 20 MIN. + RISING • **BAKE:** 20 MIN.
MAKES: 45 ROLLS

This recipe is a mainstay for me. I make the dough ahead of time for company, and keep some in the refrigerator to bake for our ranch hands. Any leftover mashed potatoes are sure to go into these rolls.
—Jeanette McKinney, Belleview, MO

- 2 pkg. (¼ oz. each) active dry yeast
- 1⅓ cups warm water (110° to 115°), divided
- 1 cup warm mashed potatoes (without added milk and butter)
- ⅔ cup sugar
- ⅔ cup shortening
- 2 large eggs, room temperature
- 2½ tsp. salt
- 6 to 6½ cups all-purpose flour

1. In a small bowl, dissolve yeast in ⅔ cup warm water. In a large bowl, combine the mashed potatoes, sugar, shortening, eggs, salt, the remaining ⅔ cup water, the yeast mixture and 2 cups flour; beat until smooth. Stir in enough of the remaining flour to form a soft dough.

2. Do not knead. Shape into a ball; place in a greased bowl, turning once to grease the top. Cover and let rise in a warm place until doubled, about 1 hour.

3. Punch down dough; divide into thirds. Divide and shape 1 portion into 15 balls; place in a greased 9-in. round baking pan. Cover with a kitchen towel. Repeat with remaining dough. Let rise in a warm place until doubled, about 30 minutes.

4. Bake rolls at 375° until golden brown, 20-25 minutes. Remove from pans to wire racks. Serve warm.

1 ROLL: 106 cal., 3g fat (1g sat. fat), 8mg chol., 136mg sod., 17g carb. (3g sugars, 1g fiber), 2g pro.

Amish Potato Bread

PREP: 30 MIN. + RISING • **BAKE:** 40 MIN.
MAKES: 1 LOAF (16 PIECES)

A tasty mix of whole wheat and all-purpose flour—plus a small amount of mashed potatoes—combine to give this golden bread its wonderful texture. The loaf is very moist and stays that way for days.
—Sue Violette, Neillsville, WI

- 1 pkg. (¼ oz.) active dry yeast
- ¼ cup warm water (110° to 115°)
- 1¾ cups warm fat-free milk (110° to 115°)
- ⅓ cup butter, softened
- ¼ cup mashed potatoes (without added milk and butter)
- 3 Tbsp. sugar
- 1½ tsp. salt
- 1½ cups whole wheat flour
- 3½ to 4 cups all-purpose flour

1. In a large bowl, dissolve yeast in warm water. Add milk, butter, mashed potatoes, sugar, salt, whole wheat flour and ½ cup all-purpose flour. Beat until smooth. Stir in enough of the remaining all-purpose flour to form a firm dough.

2. Turn dough onto a lightly floured surface; knead until smooth and elastic, 6-8 minutes. Place in a bowl coated with cooking spray, turning once to coat the top. Cover and let rise in a warm place until doubled, about 1 hour.

3. Punch down dough and turn onto a floured surface; shape into a loaf. Place in a 9x5-in. loaf pan coated with cooking spray. Cover and let rise until doubled, about 30 minutes.

4. Bake at 350° for 40-45 minutes or until golden brown. Remove from pan to wire rack to cool.

1 PIECE: 193 cal., 4g fat (2g sat. fat), 11mg chol., 276mg sod., 33g carb. (4g sugars, 2g fiber), 6g pro.

Sourdough Bread

PREP: 20 MIN. + STANDING
BAKE: 45 MIN. • **MAKES:** 2 LOAVES

This no-knead bread is delicious. It has a crisp crust and distinctive sourdough flavor from the starter yeast mixture you stir up in advance. I was surprised at how easy it is!
—Evelyn Gebhardt, Kasilof, AK

1 pkg. (¼ oz.) active dry yeast
3½ cups warm water (110° to 115°), divided
7 to 8 cups bread flour, divided
¼ cup nonfat dry milk powder
2 Tbsp. butter, melted
2 Tbsp. sugar
2 tsp. salt
Cornmeal

1. In a 4-qt. non-metallic bowl, dissolve yeast in 2 cups warm water; let stand for 5 minutes. Stir in 2 cups flour until smooth. Cover loosely with a clean towel. Let stand in a warm place (80° to 90°) to ferment for 48 hours; do not stir. (The mixture will become bubbly and rise, have a yeasty sour aroma and change color from transparent yellow to gray over the course of 48 hours.)

2. Stir in milk powder, butter, sugar, salt, remaining 1½ cups water and enough of the remaining flour to form a soft dough. (Do not knead.) Cover and let rise in a warm place until doubled, about 1½ hours.

3. Heavily grease baking sheets and sprinkle with cornmeal. Gently punch dough down. Turn dough onto a well-floured surface; divide in half.

4. With floured hands, gently move the dough in a circular motion. Use friction from the counter to stretch the surface and create a smooth top and round loaf. Quickly and gently transfer to prepared pans. Cover and let rise until doubled, about 30 minutes. Preheat oven to 375°.

5. With a sharp knife, make 3 diagonal slashes across tops of loaves. Immediately bake 10 minutes. Gently brush or spray loaves with cold water; bake 25-35 minutes longer or until golden brown.

1 PIECE: 120 cal., 1g fat (1g sat. fat), 2mg chol., 157mg sod., 23g carb. (1g sugars, 1g fiber), 4g pro.

TEST KITCHEN TIP
If baking loaves 1 at a time, after you've divided the dough in step 3, cover and refrigerate half the dough. Remove it from the refrigerator and proceed with its shaping and second rise when the oven is ready for the first loaf; that way the second loaf can be baked immediately after its second rise.

Wholesome Wheat Bread

PREP: 30 MIN. + RISING • **BAKE:** 25 MIN.
MAKES: 2 LOAVES (16 PIECES EACH)

My sister and I were in 4-H, and Mom was our breads project leader for years. Because of that early training, homemade bread like this is a staple in my own kitchen.
—Karen Wingate, Coldwater, KS

- 2 pkg. (¼ oz. each) active dry yeast
- 2¼ cups warm water (110° to 115°)
- ⅓ cup butter, softened
- ⅓ cup honey
- 3 Tbsp. sugar
- 1 Tbsp. salt
- ½ cup nonfat dry milk powder
- 4½ cups whole wheat flour
- 2¾ to 3½ cups all-purpose flour

1. In a large bowl, dissolve yeast in warm water. Add butter, honey, sugar, salt, milk powder and 3 cups whole wheat flour; beat on medium speed until smooth. Stir in the remaining 1½ cups whole wheat flour and enough of the all-purpose flour to form a soft dough.

2. Turn dough onto a floured surface; knead until smooth and elastic, about 10 minutes. Place in a greased bowl, turning once to grease the top. Cover and let rise in a warm place until doubled, about 1 hour.

3. Punch down dough. Turn onto a lightly floured surface; divide into 4 portions. Roll each into a 15-in. rope. For each loaf, twist 2 ropes together; pinch ends to seal. Place in greased 9x5-in. loaf pans. Cover; let the dough rise in a warm place until doubled, about 30 minutes. Preheat oven to 375°.

4. Bake until golden brown, 25-30 minutes. Remove from pans to wire racks to cool.

1 PIECE: 134 cal., 2g fat (1g sat. fat), 5mg chol., 243mg sod., 25g carb. (5g sugars, 2g fiber), 4g pro.

Cherry-Tarragon Dinner Rolls

PREP: 30 MIN. + RISING • **BAKE:** 15 MIN.
MAKES: 1 DOZEN

My grandmother made these during any big holiday, and we were all clamoring at the table to get our hands on one. Use any remaining rolls as the bread for a slider sandwich.
—Jeanne Holt, St. Paul, MN

- 1 pkg. (¼ oz.) active dry yeast
- ¾ cup warm 2% milk (110° to 115°)
- 2 large eggs, room temperature, divided use
- 2 Tbsp. butter, melted
- 4½ tsp. sugar
- 1 Tbsp. minced fresh chives
- 2½ tsp. grated orange zest
- 1¼ tsp. salt
- 1¼ tsp. dried tarragon
- 2½ to 3 cups all-purpose flour
- ½ cup chopped dried cherries
- ⅓ cup chopped pistachios

1. In a small bowl, dissolve yeast in warm milk. In a large bowl, combine 1 egg, butter, sugar, chives, orange zest, salt, tarragon, the yeast mixture and 1½ cups flour; beat on medium speed until smooth. Stir in enough of the remaining flour to form a stiff dough (dough will be sticky).

2. Turn onto a floured surface; knead until smooth and elastic, 6-8 minutes. Knead in cherries and pistachios. Place in a greased bowl, turning once to grease the top. Cover and let rise in a warm place until doubled, about 1 hour.

3. Punch down dough. Turn onto a lightly floured surface; divide and shape into 12 balls. Roll each into a 10-in. rope. Fold in half; twist together. Shape into a ring and pinch ends together. Repeat with remaining ropes. Place 2 in. apart on greased baking sheets. Cover with kitchen towels; let rise in a warm place until almost doubled, about 30 minutes.

4. Preheat oven to 375°. In a small bowl, whisk the remaining egg; brush over rolls. Bake until golden brown, 11-13 minutes. Remove from pans to wire racks to cool slightly; serve warm.

1 ROLL: 179 cal., 5g fat (2g sat. fat), 30mg chol., 293mg sod., 29g carb. (7g sugars, 1g fiber), 5g pro.

Best Ever Breadsticks

PREP: 20 MIN. + RISING
BAKE: 10 MIN. • **MAKES:** 2 DOZEN

Present these breadsticks alongside an Italian favorite like lasagna or spaghetti. They're an attractive and edible addition to the table setting!
—Carol Wolfer, Lebanon, OR

- 3 to 3¼ cups all-purpose flour
- 1 pkg. (¼ oz.) quick-rise yeast
- 1 Tbsp. sugar
- 1 tsp. salt
- ¾ cup 2% milk
- ¼ cup plus 1 Tbsp. water, divided
- 1 Tbsp. butter
- 1 large egg white
   Coarse salt

1. Combine 1½ cups flour, yeast, sugar and salt. In a small saucepan, heat milk, ¼ cup water and butter to 120°–130°. Add to the dry ingredients; beat on medium speed just until moistened. Stir in enough of the remaining flour to form a stiff dough.

2. Turn dough onto a lightly floured surface; knead until smooth and elastic, 6-8 minutes. Place in a greased bowl, turning once to grease top. Cover and let rise in a warm place until doubled, about 30 minutes.

3. Punch down dough. Pinch off golf ball-sized pieces. On a lightly floured surface, shape each piece into a 6-in. rope. Place on greased baking sheets 1 in. apart. Cover and let rise for 15 minutes.

4. Preheat oven to 400°. Beat egg white and remaining water; brush over breadsticks. Sprinkle with coarse salt. Bake until golden, about 10 minutes. Remove from pans to wire racks to cool.

1 BREADSTICK: 69 cal., 1g fat (0 sat. fat), 2mg chol., 108mg sod., 13g carb. (1g sugars, 1g fiber), 2g pro. **DIABETIC EXCHANGES:** 1 starch.

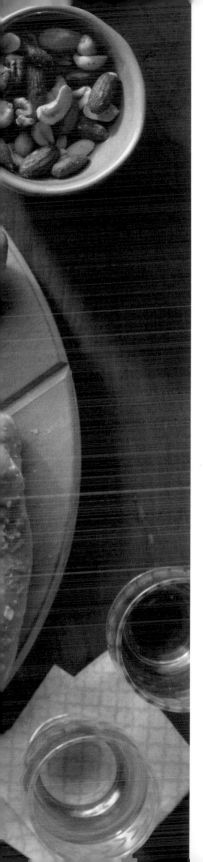

Traditional Pita Bread

PREP: 20 MIN. + RISING • **BAKE:** 5 MIN.
MAKES: 6 PITA BREADS

My husband taught me how to make this pita bread when we were first dating. He always has his eye out for good recipes.
—Lynne Hartke, Chandler, AZ

1	pkg. (¼ oz.) active dry yeast
1¼	cups warm water (110° to 115°)
2	tsp. salt
3	to 3½ cups all-purpose flour

1. In a large bowl, dissolve yeast in warm water. Stir in salt and enough flour to form a soft dough. Turn onto a floured surface; knead until smooth and elastic, 6-8 minutes. Do not let rise.

2. Divide dough into 6 pieces; knead each piece for 1 minute. Roll each into a 5-in. circle. Cover and let rise in a warm place until doubled, about 45 minutes.

3. Preheat oven to 500°. Place circles upside down on greased baking sheets. Bake until puffed and lightly browned, 5–10 minutes. Remove from pans to wire racks to cool.

1 PITA BREAD: 231 cal., 1g fat (0 sat. fat), 0 chol., 789mg sod., 48g carb. (0 sugars, 2g fiber), 7g pro.

Pumpkin Herb Rolls

PREP: 1 HOUR + RISING
BAKE: 15 MIN. + COOLING • **MAKES:** 1 DOZEN

These cute pumpkin rolls are worth the effort. They're a festive fall favorite in my household. If you don't have pumpkin on hand, try using sweet potato.
—Veronica Fay, Knoxville, TN

- 1 **Tbsp. active dry yeast**
- ¾ **cup warm water (110° to 115°)**
- ¾ **cup canned pumpkin**
- 2 **tsp. garlic powder**
- 2 **tsp. onion powder**
- 2 **Tbsp. dried minced onion**
- 1½ **tsp. each minced fresh oregano, sage, rosemary and thyme**
- 1 **tsp. salt**
- ¼ **tsp. cayenne pepper**
- 2¾ **to 3¼ cups bread flour**
- 2 **cups shredded sharp cheddar cheese**
- ¼ **cup butter, melted, optional**
- 6 **honey wheat braided pretzel twists, halved**

1. In a small bowl, dissolve yeast in warm water. In a large bowl, combine pumpkin, garlic powder, onion powder, dried onion, fresh herbs, salt, cayenne, the yeast mixture and 1½ cups flour; beat on medium speed until smooth. Stir in enough remaining flour to form a soft dough (dough will be sticky). Stir in cheese.

2. Turn dough onto a floured surface; knead until smooth and elastic, 6-8 minutes. Place in a greased bowl, turning once to grease the top. Cover and let rise in a warm place until doubled, about 1½ hours.

3. Punch down dough; turn onto a lightly floured surface. Divide and shape into 12 balls; flatten slightly. Wrap each ball in 4 pieces of kitchen string, creating indentions to resemble a pumpkin. Place 2 in. apart on greased baking sheets. Cover with kitchen towels; let rise in a warm place until almost doubled, about 45 minutes.

4. Preheat oven to 375°. Bake until golden brown, 15-20 minutes. If desired, brush with melted butter. Remove from pans to wire racks to cool. Cut and discard string. Before serving, insert a pretzel half in the top of each roll.

1 ROLL: 211 cal., 7g fat (4g sat. fat), 19mg chol., 348mg sod., 28g carb. (1g sugars, 2g fiber), 9g pro.

Angel Biscuits

PREP: 20 MIN. + RISING • **BAKE:** 10 MIN.
MAKES: 2½ DOZEN

I first received these light, wonderful biscuits, along with the recipe, from an elderly gentleman friend. I bake them often as a Saturday-morning treat with butter and honey. They're perfect with sausage gravy and for sandwiches, too!
—Faye Hintz, Springfield, MO

- 2 **pkg. (¼ oz. each) active dry yeast**
- ¼ **cup warm water (110° to 115°)**
- 2 **cups warm buttermilk (110° to 115°)**
- 5 **to 5½ cups all-purpose flour**
- ⅓ **cup sugar**
- 2 **tsp. salt**
- 2 **tsp. baking powder**
- 1 **tsp. baking soda**
- 1 **cup shortening**
  Melted butter

1. Dissolve yeast in warm water. Let stand 5 minutes. Stir in buttermilk; set aside.

2. In a large bowl, combine the flour, sugar, salt, baking powder and baking soda. Cut in shortening with a pastry blender until mixture resembles coarse crumbs. Stir in yeast mixture.

3. Turn onto a lightly floured surface; knead lightly 3-4 times. Roll out to ½-in. thickness; cut with a 2½-in. biscuit cutter. Place 2 in. apart on lightly greased baking sheets. Cover with kitchen towels and let rise in a warm place until almost doubled, about 1 hour.

4. Bake at 450° for 8-10 minutes or until golden brown. Lightly brush tops with melted butter. Serve warm.

1 BISCUIT: 150 cal., 7g fat (2g sat. fat), 1mg chol., 244mg sod., 19g carb. (3g sugars, 1g fiber), 3g pro.

Honey Challah

PREP: 45 MIN. + RISING
BAKE: 30 MIN.
MAKES: 2 LOAVES (24 PIECES EACH)

I use these shiny, beautiful loaves as the centerpiece of my spread. I love the taste of honey, but you can also add chocolate chips, cinnamon, orange zest or almonds. Leftover slices work well in bread pudding or for French toast.
—Jennifer Newfield, Los Angeles, CA

 2 pkg. (¼ oz. each) active dry yeast
 ½ tsp. sugar
1½ cups warm water (110° to 115°), divided
 5 large eggs, room temperature
 ⅔ cup plus 1 tsp. honey, divided
 ½ cup canola oil
 2 tsp. salt
 6 to 7 cups bread flour
 1 cup boiling water
 2 cups golden raisins
 1 Tbsp. water
 1 Tbsp. sesame seeds

1. In a small bowl, dissolve yeast and sugar in 1 cup warm water. Separate 2 eggs; refrigerate the whites. Place egg yolks and remaining 3 eggs in a large bowl. Add ⅔ cup honey, oil, salt, yeast mixture, 3 cups flour and remaining ½ cup warm water; beat on medium speed for 3 minutes. Stir in enough of the remaining flour to form a soft dough (dough will be sticky).

2. Pour boiling water over raisins in a small bowl; let stand 5 minutes. Drain and pat dry. Turn dough onto a floured surface; knead until smooth and elastic, 6-8 minutes. Knead in raisins. Place in a greased bowl, turning once to grease the top. Cover and let rise in a warm place until almost doubled, about 1½ hours.

3. Punch down dough. Turn onto a lightly floured surface. Divide dough in half. Divide 1 portion into 6 pieces. Roll each into a 16-in. rope. Place ropes parallel on a greased baking sheet; pinch ropes together at the top. Braid dough into a 6-strand loaf as shown at right. Repeat process with remaining dough to make a second loaf. Cover with kitchen towels; let rise in a warm place until almost doubled, about 30 minutes.

4. Preheat oven to 350°. In a small bowl, whisk the 2 chilled egg whites and remaining 1 tsp. honey with water; brush over loaves. Sprinkle with sesame seeds. Bake for 30-35 minutes or until bread is golden brown and sounds hollow when tapped. Remove from pans to a wire rack to cool.

1 PIECE: 125 cal., 3g fat (0 sat. fat), 19mg chol., 107mg sod., 21g carb. (8g sugars, 1g fiber), 3g pro.

TEST KITCHEN TIP

It's important for even braiding that the ropes are of equal width and length. Use a kitchen scale to make sure each piece of dough is the same size, and use even pressure when rolling them out so they are the same width from end to end.

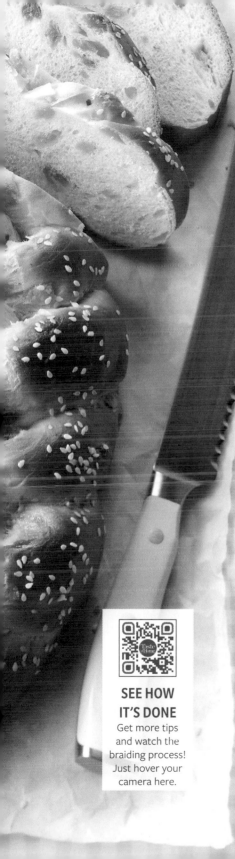

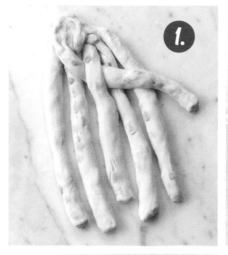

HOW-TO

MAKE A SIX-STRAND BRAID

1. Take the rope on the left and carry it over the 2 ropes beside it, then slip it under the middle rope and carry it over the last 2 ropes. Lay the rope down parallel to the other ropes; it is now on the far right side. Don't leave gaps, but make sure the braid isn't pulled tight—the dough will need space for its second rise.

2. Start again at the new far left rope and weave toward the right in the same pattern— over 2 ropes, under 1 rope, over 2 ropes. (If it's more comfortable for you, feel free to braid from right to left; just be sure you're always starting from the same side of the loaf.)

3. Repeat these steps until you reach the end. Pick up the loaf and recenter it on your work surface as needed.

4. When you've reached the point where the ropes are too short to braid, pinch the ends together. Tuck the pinched ends under to give the loaf a clean look. For a fuller loaf, push the ends of the loaf closer together.

Honey Oatmeal Loaves

PREP: 30 MIN. + RISING
BAKE: 40 MIN. + COOLING
MAKES: 2 LOAVES (16 PIECES EACH)

*A friend gave me her grandmother's
bread recipe as a wedding gift, and
now it's a staple in our house, too.*
—Amy Morrison, Derry, NH

1¾ **cups water**
 1 **cup fat-free milk**
 ½ **cup canola oil**
 ¼ **cup honey**
 ¼ **cup molasses**
1¼ **cups quick-cooking oats**
 4 **to 5 cups bread flour**
 2 **pkg. (¼ oz. each) quick-rise yeast**
 2 **tsp. salt**
 3 **cups whole grain spelt flour**
    or whole wheat flour

1. In a saucepan, heat water, milk, oil,
honey and molasses to a simmer; stir in
oats. Remove from heat; cool to 120°-130°.
In a large bowl, mix 4 cups bread flour, yeast
and salt. Stir in cooled oat mixture. Stir in
spelt flour and enough remaining bread
flour to form a soft, sticky dough.
2. Turn dough onto a floured surface; knead
until smooth and elastic, about 6-8 minutes.
Cover; let rest 10 minutes.
3. Divide dough in half. Roll each into a
12x8-in. rectangle. Roll up jelly-roll style,
starting with a short side; pinch seam and
ends to seal. Place in greased 9x5-in. loaf
pans, seam side down. Cover with kitchen
towels; let rise in a warm place until almost
doubled, about 1 hour.
4. Bake at 350° until golden brown,
40-45 minutes. Remove from pans to
wire racks; cool completely.
1 PIECE: 169 cal., 4g fat (0 sat. fat), 0 chol.,
153mg sod., 27g carb. (5g sugars, 2g fiber),
4g pro.

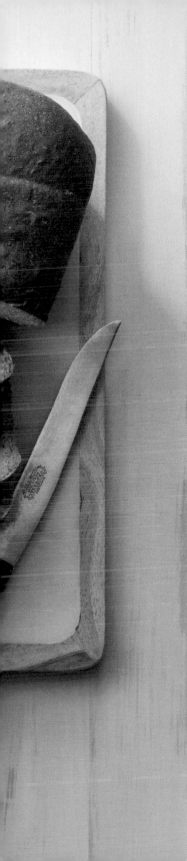

Whole Wheat English Muffins

PREP: 20 MIN. + RISING
BAKE: 20 MIN.
MAKES: 10 SERVINGS

Whole wheat flour gives these muffins a hearty taste, but they still have a light texture. They keep well in the refrigerator or freezer.
—Mildred Decker, Sandy, OR

- 1 pkg. (¼ oz.) active dry yeast
- 3 Tbsp. sugar, divided
- ¼ cup warm water (110° to 115°)
- 1 cup warm 2% milk (110° to 115°)
- 3 Tbsp. butter, softened
- ¾ tsp. salt
- 1 large egg, room temperature
- 1 cup whole wheat flour
- 3 cups all-purpose flour, divided

1. In a large bowl, dissolve yeast and 1 Tbsp. sugar in warm water; let stand for 5 minutes. Add milk, butter, salt, egg, whole wheat flour, 1 cup all-purpose flour and the remaining 2 Tbsp. sugar; beat until smooth. Stir in enough of the remaining all-purpose flour to form a soft dough.

2. Turn dough onto a lightly floured surface; knead until smooth and elastic, 6-8 minutes. Place in a greased bowl, turning once to grease top. Cover and let rise in a warm place until doubled, about 1 hour.

3. Preheat oven to 375°. Punch dough down. Turn onto a lightly floured surface; roll out to ½-in. thickness. Cover and let rest for 5 minutes. Cut into 4-in. circles. Place 2 in. apart on greased baking sheets.

4. Bake until bottoms are browned, 8-10 minutes. Turn muffins over; bake until the second side is browned, about 7 minutes longer. Remove from pan to a wire rack to cool. Store in the refrigerator. To serve, split with a fork and toast.

1 MUFFIN: 246 cal., 5g fat (3g sat. fat), 34mg chol., 232mg sod., 43g carb. (6g sugars, 3g fiber), 7g pro.

Pumpkin Egg Braid

PREP: 30 MIN. + RISING • **BAKE:** 20 MIN.
MAKES: 1 LOAF (12 PIECES)

I developed this bread to celebrate our two favorite holidays, Thanksgiving and Hanukkah. Try it with flavored butters, and use leftovers for French toast or sandwiches.
—Sara Mellas, Hartford, CT

- 1 pkg. (¼ oz.) active dry yeast
- 3 Tbsp. warm water (110° to 115°)
- ½ cup canned pumpkin
- 1 large egg, room temperature
- 2 Tbsp. light brown sugar
- 2 Tbsp. butter, softened
- 1 tsp. pumpkin pie spice
- ½ tsp. salt
- 2 to 2½ cups bread flour

EGG WASH
- 1 large egg
- 1 Tbsp. water

1. In a small bowl, dissolve yeast in warm water. In a large bowl, combine pumpkin, egg, brown sugar, butter, pie spice, salt, the yeast mixture and 1 cup flour; beat on medium speed until smooth. Stir in enough remaining flour to form a soft dough (dough will be sticky).

2. Turn dough onto a floured surface; knead until smooth and elastic, 6-8 minutes. Place in a greased bowl, turning once to grease the top. Cover and let rise in a warm place until doubled, about 1 hour.

3. Punch down dough. Turn onto a lightly floured surface; divide into thirds. Roll each into a 16-in. rope. Place ropes on a greased baking sheet and braid. Pinch ends to seal; tuck under.

4. Cover with a kitchen towel; let rise in a warm place until almost doubled, about 45 minutes. Preheat oven to 350°.

5. For egg wash, in a small bowl, whisk egg and water until blended; brush over loaf. Bake until golden brown, 20-25 minutes. Remove from pan to a wire rack to cool.

1 PIECE: 126 cal., 3g fat (2g sat. fat), 36mg chol., 129mg sod., 20g carb. (3g sugars, 1g fiber), 4g pro. **DIABETIC EXCHANGES:** 1 starch, ½ fat.

Homemade Bagels

PREP: 30 MIN. + RISING
BAKE: 20 MIN. • **MAKES:** 1 DOZEN

Instead of going to a baker, head to the kitchen and surprise your family with homemade bagels. For variation and flavor, sprinkle the tops with cinnamon sugar instead of sesame or poppy seeds.
—Rebecca Phillips, Burlington, CT

- 1 tsp. active dry yeast
- 1¼ cups warm 2% milk (110° to 115°)
- ½ cup butter, softened
- 2 Tbsp. sugar
- 1 tsp. salt
- 1 large egg yolk, room temperature
- 3¾ to 4¼ cups all-purpose flour
  - Optional: Sesame or poppy seeds

1. In a large bowl, dissolve yeast in warm milk. Add the butter, sugar, salt and egg yolk; mix well. Stir in enough flour to form a soft dough.

2. Turn dough onto a floured surface; knead until smooth and elastic, 6-8 minutes. Place in a greased bowl, turning once to grease top. Cover and let rise in a warm place until doubled, about 1 hour.

3. Punch dough down. Shape into 12 balls. Push thumb through centers to form a 1½-in. hole. Stretch and shape dough to form an even ring. Place on a floured surface. Cover and let rest for 10 minutes; flatten bagels slightly.

4. Fill a Dutch oven two-thirds full with water; bring to a boil. Drop bagels, 2 at a time, into the water. Cook 45 seconds; turn and cook 45 seconds longer. Remove with a slotted spoon; drain well on paper towels.

5. Sprinkle with sesame or poppy seeds if desired. Place 2 in. apart on greased baking sheets. Bake at 400° until golden brown, 20-25 minutes. Remove from pans to wire racks to cool.

1 BAGEL: 237 cal., 9g fat (5g sat. fat), 38mg chol., 271mg sod., 33g carb. (3g sugars, 1g fiber), 5g pro.

Dutch-Oven Bread

PREP: 15 MIN. + RISING
BAKE: 45 MIN. + COOLING
MAKES: 1 LOAF (16 PIECES)

Crackling homemade bread makes an average day extraordinary. Enjoy this beautiful crusty bread recipe as is, or stir in a few favorites such as cheese, garlic, herbs and dried fruits.
—Catherine Ward, Mequon, WI

3 to 3½ cups (125 grams per cup) all-purpose flour
1 tsp. active dry yeast
1 tsp. salt
1½ cups water (70° to 75°)

1. In a large bowl, whisk 3 cups flour, yeast and salt. Stir in water and enough of the remaining flour to form a moist, shaggy dough. Do not knead. Cover and let rise in a cool place until doubled, 7-8 hours.

2. Preheat oven to 450°; place a Dutch oven with lid onto the center rack and heat for at least 30 minutes.

3. Once the Dutch oven is hot, turn dough onto a generously floured surface. Using a metal scraper or spatula, quickly shape into a round loaf. Gently place on top of a piece of parchment.

4. Using a sharp knife, make a slash (¼ in. deep) across the top of the loaf. Using the parchment, immediately lower bread into heated Dutch oven. Cover; bake for 30 minutes.

5. Uncover and bake until bread is deep golden brown and sounds hollow when tapped, 15-20 minutes longer, partially covering if browning too much. Remove from pot and cool completely on wire rack.

1 PIECE: 86 cal., 0 fat (0 sat. fat), 0 chol., 148mg sod., 18g carb. (0 sugars, 1g fiber), 3g pro.

TEST KITCHEN TIP

This is a soft, gentle dough that should be baked immediately after shaping. To make a bread that fills your entire Dutch oven, double this recipe: In a large bowl, whisk 6 cups flour, 2 tsp. active dry yeast and 2 tsp. salt. Stir in 3 cups water to form a soft, shaggy dough. Proceed with recipe as directed.

Apple Dumpling Pull-Apart Bread

PREP: 45 MIN. + RISING • **BAKE:** 1¼ HOURS
MAKES: 12 SERVINGS

I converted a basic sweet dough into this incredible apple-filled, pull-apart loaf. The results are anything but basic. It takes time, but I guarantee it's worth it.
—Gina Nistico, Denver, CO

- ¼ cup butter, softened
- 3 lbs. medium Honeycrisp apples, peeled and sliced ¼ in. thick
- ¼ cup sugar
- ¼ cup packed brown sugar
- ½ tsp. salt
- ½ tsp. ground cinnamon
- ¼ tsp. ground allspice
- ¼ cup apple cider
- 1 tsp. vanilla extract

DOUGH

- 1 pkg. (¼ oz.) active dry yeast
- ¾ cup warm water (110° to 115°)
- ¾ cup warm whole milk (110° to 115°)
- ¼ cup sugar
- 3 Tbsp. canola oil
- 2 tsp. salt
- 3¾ to 4¼ cups all-purpose flour

CIDER SAUCE & GLAZE

- 4 cups apple cider, divided
- ½ cup packed brown sugar
- 1 cup confectioners' sugar
- 4 oz. cream cheese, softened
- ½ cup butter, divided
- 1½ tsp. vanilla extract, divided

1. In a Dutch oven over medium heat, melt butter. Add next 6 ingredients; stir to combine. Cook, covered, stirring occasionally, until apples have softened and released their juices, 10-12 minutes. With a slotted spoon, transfer apples to a 15x10x1-in. baking pan; spread in a single layer.

2. Add cider to Dutch oven and bring to a boil; cook, stirring, until the juices thicken and reduce to ½ cup, 10-12 minutes. Remove from heat; add vanilla extract. Pour over apple slices; cool completely. (Filling can be made 24 hours in advance and refrigerated.)

3. For dough, dissolve yeast in warm water. Add milk, sugar, oil, salt and 1¼ cups flour. Beat on medium until smooth, 2-3 minutes. Stir in enough remaining flour to form a soft dough.

4. Turn dough onto a floured surface; knead until smooth and elastic, 6-8 minutes. Place in a greased bowl, turning once to grease top. Cover and let rise in a warm place until doubled, about 1 hour.

5. Punch down dough. Turn onto a lightly floured surface. Roll into an 18x12-in. rectangle; spread apple mixture to within ½ in. of edges. Cut into twenty-four 3x3-in. squares. Make 4 stacks of 6 squares each; place stacks on edges in a greased 9x5-in. loaf pan. Cover and let rise until doubled, about 45 minutes.

6. Preheat oven to 350°. Bake until well browned, 1¼-1½ hours.

7. For sauce, bring 3½ cups cider and brown sugar to a boil. Cook, stirring, until reduced to 1 cup, about 25 minutes. Add ¼ cup butter and ½ tsp. vanilla. Cook and stir until sauce is thickened. Cool slightly.

8. For glaze, beat confectioners' sugar, cream cheese, remaining ¼ cup butter and 1 tsp. vanilla and enough of the remaining apple cider to reach desired consistency. Drizzle sauce and glaze over bread.

1 PIECE: 544 cal., 20g fat (10g sat. fat), 42mg chol., 633mg sod., 88g carb. (54g sugars, 3g fiber), 6g pro.

Dill Bread

PREP: 10 MIN. + RISING • **BAKE:** 35 MIN.
MAKES: 12 SERVINGS

This golden brown loaf is moist and flavorful, with an herbed zest. What's more, no kneading needed!
—Corky Huffsmith, Salem, OR

- 1 **pkg. (¼ oz.) active dry yeast**
- ¼ **cup warm water (110° to 115°)**
- 1 **cup 2% cottage cheese**
- ¼ **cup snipped fresh dill or**
  4 tsp. dill weed
- 1 **Tbsp. butter, melted**
- 1½ **tsp. salt**
- 1 **tsp. sugar**
- 1 **tsp. dill seed**
- 1 **large egg, room temperature,**
  lightly beaten
- 2¼ to 2¾ **cups all-purpose flour**

1. In a large bowl, dissolve yeast in warm water. In a small saucepan, heat cottage cheese to 110°-115°; add to yeast mixture. Add fresh dill, butter, salt, sugar, dill seed, egg and 1 cup flour; beat until smooth. Stir in enough remaining flour to form a soft dough. Do not knead. Cover and let rise in a warm place until doubled, about 1 hour.
2. Punch down dough. Turn onto a lightly floured surface; shape into a 6-in. circle. Place in a greased 9-in. cast-iron skillet or round baking pan. Cover and let rise in a warm place until doubled, about 45 minutes.
3. Preheat oven to 350°. Bake until crust is golden brown and bread sounds hollow when tapped, 35-40 minutes. Remove from pan to a wire rack to cool. Cut into wedges.
1 PIECE: 118 cal., 2g fat (1g sat. fat), 19mg chol., 364mg sod., 19g carb. (1g sugars, 1g fiber), 5g pro. **DIABETIC EXCHANGES:** 1 starch, ½ fat.

SEE HOW IT'S DONE

Watch the simple steps to making this no-knead bread! Just hover your camera here.

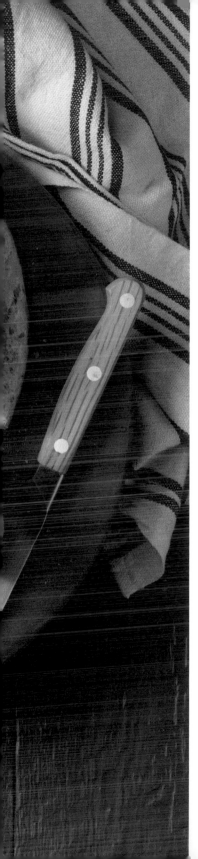

Herbed Accordion Dinner Rolls

PREP: 40 MIN. + RISING • **BAKE:** 20 MIN.
MAKES: 2 DOZEN

To dress up everyday dinner rolls, brush herbed butter over the dough, then form accordion rolls. The aroma from the oven is incredible!
—Taste of Home *Test Kitchen*

- 2 **pkg. (¼ oz. each) active dry yeast**
- ½ **cup warm water (110° to 115°)**
- 1 **tsp. plus ⅓ cup sugar, divided**
- 1¼ **cups warm 2% milk (110° to 115°)**
- ½ **cup butter, melted**
- 2 **large eggs, room temperature**
- 1½ **tsp. salt**
- 6 **to 6½ cups all-purpose flour**
- 3 **Tbsp. butter, softened**
- 1 **tsp. Italian seasoning**
- 1 **large egg white, beaten**

1. In a large bowl, dissolve yeast in warm water with 1 tsp. sugar. Add the milk, melted butter, eggs, salt, 3 cups flour and remaining ⅓ cup sugar; beat until smooth. Stir in enough of the remaining flour to form a soft dough.

2. Turn dough onto a floured surface; knead until smooth and elastic, 6-8 minutes. Place in a greased bowl, turning once to grease the top. Cover and let rise in a warm place until doubled, about 1 hour.

3. Punch dough down; place on a lightly floured surface. Divide into 4 portions. Roll each portion into a 14x6-in. rectangle. Combine softened butter and Italian seasoning; spread over dough.

4. Score each rectangle widthwise at 2-in. intervals. Fold the dough accordion-style back and forth along score lines. Cut folded dough into six 1-in. pieces. Place pieces cut side down in greased muffin cups. Cover and let rise until doubled, about 30 minutes.

5. Preheat oven to 375°. Uncover pans and let dough stand another 10 minutes before baking. Brush with egg white. Bake until golden brown, 18-22 minutes. Remove from pans to wire racks to cool.

1 ROLL: 186 cal., 6g fat (4g sat. fat), 32mg chol., 200mg sod., 28g carb. (4g sugars, 1g fiber), 5g pro.

Honey Beet Bread

PREP: 30 MIN. + RISING • **BAKE:** 30 MIN.
MAKES: 2 LOAVES (16 PIECES EACH)

This bread makes a great accompaniment to a meal when served with honey and butter—but you'll find that any that's left over makes great sandwiches, too!
—Nancy Zimmerman,
Cape May Court House, NJ

- 2 pkg. (¼ oz. each) active dry yeast
- 1½ cups warm water (110° to 115°)
- 2 Tbsp. honey
- 1½ cups grated uncooked fresh beets, squeezed dry
- 1 cup warm 2% milk (110° to 115°)
- 2 Tbsp. butter, softened
- 2½ tsp. salt
- 6¼ to 6¾ cups all-purpose flour
- 1 large egg white, lightly beaten
  Toasted sesame seeds

1. In a large bowl, dissolve yeast in warm water. Add honey; let stand for 5 minutes. Add the beets, milk, butter, salt and 3 cups flour. Beat until smooth. Stir in enough remaining flour to form a soft dough.
2. Turn onto a floured surface; knead until smooth and elastic, 6-8 minutes. Place in a greased bowl, turning once to grease top. Cover and let rise in a warm place until doubled, about 50 minutes.
3. Punch dough down. Turn onto a lightly floured surface; divide dough in half. Shape into 2 loaves. Place in 2 greased 9x5-in. loaf pans. Cover and let rise until doubled, about 40 minutes.
4. Brush with beaten egg white; sprinkle with sesame seeds. Bake at 350° until top begins to brown, 30-35 minutes. Remove from pans to wire racks to cool.
1 PIECE: 108 cal., 1g fat (1g sat. fat), 3mg chol., 203mg sod., 21g carb. (2g sugars, 1g fiber), 3g pro.

Garlic Bubble Loaf

PREP: 35 MIN. + RISING
BAKE: 35 MIN. + COOLING
MAKES: 2 LOAVES (12 PIECES EACH)

Complete your next spaghetti dinner with this eye-catching loaf. Family and friends will have fun pulling off each rich and buttery piece.
—Lynn Nichols, Bartlett, NE

- 2 pkg. (¼ oz. each) active dry yeast
- ¼ cup warm water (110° to 115°)
- 2 cups warm whole milk (110° to 115°)
- 2 Tbsp. sugar
- 1 Tbsp. shortening
- 2 tsp. salt
- 6¼ to 6½ cups all-purpose flour
- ½ cup butter, melted
- 1 Tbsp. dried parsley flakes
- 2 tsp. garlic powder

1. Dissolve yeast in warm water. Add the milk, sugar, shortening, salt and 2 cups flour; beat until smooth. Stir in enough of the remaining flour to form a soft dough.
2. Turn out on a floured surface; knead until smooth and elastic, 6-8 minutes. Place in a greased bowl, turning once to grease top. Cover and let rise in a warm place until doubled, about 1 hour.
3. Punch dough down. Turn onto a lightly floured surface; divide into fourths. Divide each portion into 12 pieces. In a shallow bowl, combine butter, parsley and garlic powder. Shape each piece into a ball; dip in the butter mixture. Place in 2 greased 9x5-in. loaf pans. Pour any remaining butter mixture over dough. Cover and let rise until doubled, about 30 minutes.
4. Bake at 375° for 35-40 minutes or until golden brown. Cool 10 minutes. Remove from pans to wire racks. Serve warm.
2 PIECES : 176 cal., 5g fat (3g sat. fat), 12mg chol., 237mg sod., 27g carb. (2g sugars, 1g fiber), 4g pro.

Gouda & Roasted Potato Bread

PREP: 45 MIN. + RISING • **BAKE:** 40 MIN.
MAKES: 1 LOAF (16 PIECES)

Our family tried roasted potato bread at a bakery on a road trip, and I came up with my own recipe when we realized we lived much too far away to have it regularly. It makes for a really amazing roast beef sandwich and is also great with soups.
—Elisabeth Larsen, Pleasant Grove, UT

½ lb. Yukon Gold potatoes, chopped (about ¾ cup)
1½ tsp. olive oil
1½ tsp. salt, divided
1 pkg. (¼ oz.) active dry yeast
2½ to 3 cups all-purpose flour
1 cup warm water (120° to 130°)
½ cup shredded smoked Gouda cheese

1. Place 1 oven rack at the lowest rack level; place a second rack in the middle of the oven. Preheat oven to 425°. Place potatoes in a greased 15x10x1-in. baking pan. Drizzle with oil; sprinkle with ½ tsp. salt. Toss to coat. Roast until tender, 20-25 minutes, stirring occasionally.

2. In a large bowl, mix yeast, remaining 1 tsp. salt and 2 cups flour. Add warm water; beat on medium speed until smooth. Stir in enough remaining flour to form a soft dough (dough will be sticky).

3. Turn the dough onto a floured surface; knead until smooth and elastic, 6-8 minutes. Gently knead in roasted potatoes and cheese. Place in a greased bowl, turning once to grease the top. Cover and let rise in a warm place until doubled, about 1 hour.

4. Punch down dough. Shape into a 7-in. round loaf. Place on a parchment-lined baking sheet. Cover with a kitchen towel; let rise in a warm place until dough expands to a 9-in. loaf, about 45 minutes.

5. With the oven set at 425°, heat an oven-safe skillet on the bottom oven rack. Meanwhile, in a teakettle, bring 2 cups water to a boil. Using a sharp knife, make a slash (¼ in. deep) across top of loaf. Place bread on top rack. Pull bottom rack out by 6-8 in.; add boiling water to skillet. (Work quickly and carefully, pouring water away from you. Don't worry if some water is left in the kettle.) Carefully slide bottom rack back into place; quickly close door to trap steam in oven. Bake 10 minutes.

6. Reduce oven setting to 375°; remove skillet from oven. Bake bread until deep golden brown, 30-35 minutes longer. Remove loaf to a wire rack to cool.

1 PIECE: 101 cal., 2g fat (1g sat. fat), 4mg chol., 253mg sod., 18g carb. (0 sugars, 1g fiber), 3g pro.

Caramel-Pecan Pumpkin Pull-Aparts

PREP: 40 MIN. + CHILLING • **BAKE:** 25 MIN.
MAKES: 16 SERVINGS

We love sticky buns made with my husband's angel biscuit dough, caramel and pecans. For a twist, try apple butter or applesauce instead of the pumpkin.
—Carolyn Kumpe, El Dorado, CA

- ¼ cup butter, cubed
- 1 cup chopped pecans
- ¾ cup packed brown sugar
- ½ cup heavy whipping cream
- ¼ cup honey

DOUGH

- 1 pkg. (¼ oz.) active dry yeast
- ¼ cup warm water (110° to 115°)
- 2¼ to 2½ cups all-purpose flour
- ¼ cup sugar
- 1 tsp. pumpkin pie spice
- ¾ tsp. salt
- ½ tsp. baking soda
- ½ tsp. baking powder
- ½ tsp. ground cinnamon
- ¼ cup cold butter, cubed
- ½ cup solid-pack pumpkin
- ½ cup buttermilk
- 1 tsp. vanilla extract

1. In a small saucepan, melt butter over medium heat. Add pecans; cook and stir 2-3 minutes or until pecans are fragrant. Stir in brown sugar, cream and honey; cook and stir until sugar is dissolved and mixture begins to darken. Pour into a greased 9-in. square baking pan.

2. In a small bowl, dissolve yeast in the warm water. In a large bowl, whisk 2¼ cups flour, sugar, pie spice, salt, baking soda, baking powder and cinnamon. Cut in the butter until crumbly. Add pumpkin, buttermilk, vanilla and the yeast mixture; mix well.

3. Turn dough onto a floured surface; knead gently 8-10 times, adding additional flour if needed. Roll dough into a 9-in. square. Cut into 16 squares; arrange over the pecan mixture. Cover and refrigerate overnight.

4. Remove pan from the refrigerator 30 minutes before baking. Preheat oven to 400°. Uncover; bake 24-28 minutes or until golden brown. Carefully invert onto a platter; serve warm.

1 PIECE: 266 cal., 14g fat (6g sat. fat), 26mg chol., 219mg sod., 33g carb. (19g sugars, 2g fiber), 3g pro.

TEST KITCHEN TIP

Yeast is very sensitive to high temperatures. Be sure your water is not too hot or you'll risk killing the yeast before it makes the dough light and fluffy.

Milk & Honey White Bread

PREP: 15 MIN. + RISING • **BAKE:** 30 MIN.
MAKES: 2 LOAVES (16 PIECES EACH)

Honey adds special flavor to this traditional white bread. My dad's a wheat farmer—this represents our region and our family well.
—Kathy McCreary, Goddard, KS

- 2 pkg. (¼ oz. each) active dry yeast
- 2½ cups warm whole milk (110° to 115°)
- ⅓ cup honey
- ¼ cup butter, melted
- 2 tsp. salt
- 8 to 8½ cups all-purpose flour

1. In a large bowl, dissolve yeast in warm milk. Add honey, butter, salt and 5 cups flour; beat until smooth. Add enough remaining flour to form a soft dough.

2. Turn onto a floured board; knead until smooth and elastic, 6-8 minutes. Place in a greased bowl, turning once to grease top. Cover and let rise in a warm place until doubled, about 1 hour.

3. Punch dough down and shape into 2 loaves. Place in greased 9x5-in. loaf pans. Cover and let rise until doubled, about 30 minutes.

4. Bake at 375° until golden brown, 30-35 minutes. Cover loosely with foil if tops brown too quickly. Remove from pans and cool on wire racks.

1 PIECE: 149 cal., 2g fat (1g sat. fat), 6mg chol., 172mg sod., 28g carb. (4g sugars, 1g fiber), 4g pro..

TEST KITCHEN TIP

To best test for doneness, use a quick-read thermometer; the internal temperature of yeast bread should be 160-185°. You can also test a loaf by tapping the bottom— it should sound hollow.

Caraway Rye Dinner Rolls

PREP: 35 MIN. + RISING • **BAKE:** 15 MIN.
MAKES: 1½ DOZEN

Caraway seeds give these rye dinner rolls a delicate nutty flavor. Dense and rich, these onion-infused buns are ideal for dipping in hearty stews.
—Deborah Maki, Kamloops, BC

- 1¼ cups rye flour
- ½ cup wheat germ
- 2 Tbsp. caraway seeds
- 1 pkg. (¼ oz.) active dry yeast
- 1 tsp. salt
- 3 cups all-purpose flour
- 1 cup 2% milk
- ½ cup water
- 3 Tbsp. butter
- 2 Tbsp. honey
- ½ cup finely chopped onion

EGG WASH
- 1 large egg
- 2 tsp. water

1. In a large bowl, mix the first 5 ingredients and 1 cup all-purpose flour. In a small saucepan, heat the milk, water, butter and honey to 120°-130°. Add to the dry ingredients; beat on medium speed for 3 minutes. Stir in onion and enough of the remaining all-purpose flour to form a soft dough (dough will be sticky).

2. Turn dough onto a floured surface; knead until smooth and elastic, 6-8 minutes. Place in a greased bowl, turning once to grease the top. Cover; let rise in a warm place until doubled, about 1 hour.

3. Punch down dough. Turn onto a lightly floured surface; divide and shape into 18 balls. Place 2 in. apart on greased baking sheets. Cover with a kitchen towel; let rise in a warm place until almost doubled, about 45 minutes.

4. For egg wash, In a small bowl, whisk egg and water; brush over rolls. Bake at 400° until lightly browned, 11-14 minutes. Remove to wire racks to cool.

1 ROLL: 152 cal., 3g fat (2g sat. fat), 17mg chol., 158mg sod., 26g carb. (3g sugars, 2g fiber), 5g pro.

rise until doubled, about 30 minutes. Preheat oven to 350°.

4. In a small bowl, combine egg and milk; brush over top. Sprinkle with poppy seeds. Bake until golden brown, 40-45 minutes. Cool 20 minutes before slicing. Serve warm.

1 PIECE: 361 cal., 16g fat (10g sat. fat), 62mg chol., 505mg sod., 40g carb. (3g sugars, 2g fiber), 13g pro.

90-Minute Dinner Rolls

PREP: 35 MIN. + RISING • **BAKE:** 20 MIN.
MAKES: 1 DOZEN

Now that our children are grown, I'm cooking for two most of the time. With this recipe, we enjoy fresh rolls for several days.
—Reba Erickson, Edwardsville, KS

- 2 to 2½ cups all-purpose flour
- 2 Tbsp. sugar
- 1 pkg. (¼ oz.) quick-rise yeast
- ½ tsp. salt
- ½ cup 2% milk
- ¼ cup water
- 2 Tbsp. butter

1. In a large bowl, combine ¾ cup flour, the sugar, yeast and salt. In a small saucepan, heat milk, water and butter to 120°-130°. Add to the dry ingredients; beat just until moistened. Stir in enough remaining flour to form a soft dough.

2. Turn onto a floured surface; knead until smooth and elastic, 6-8 minutes. Cover and let rest 10 minutes.

3. Divide dough into 12 pieces; shape each into a roll. Arrange in a greased 9-in. round baking pan. Cover and let rise until doubled, about 35 minutes. Preheat oven to 375°.

4. Bake until golden brown, 20-25 minutes. Remove from pan to a wire rack to cool.

1 ROLL: 109 cal., 2g fat (1g sat. fat), 6mg chol., 123mg sod., 19g carb. (3g sugars, 1g fiber), 3g pro.

Herbed Mozzarella Round

PREP: 20 MIN. + RISING
BAKE: 45 MIN. + COOLING
MAKES: 1 LOAF (12 PIECES)

Served warm with soup or salad, this pretty bread is hearty enough to round out a quick meal on busy evenings.
— June Brown, Veneta, OR

- 4 to 4½ cups all-purpose flour
- 2 pkg. (¼ oz. each) active dry yeast
- 1 Tbsp. sugar
- 1 tsp. salt
- 1 cup warm mashed potatoes (prepared with milk and butter)
- ½ cup butter, softened
- 1 cup warm 2% milk (110° to 115°)
- 3 cups shredded mozzarella cheese
- 1 to 3 tsp. minced fresh thyme
- 1 tsp. minced fresh rosemary

TOPPING
- 1 large egg
- 1 Tbsp. 2% milk
- 1 tsp. poppy seeds

1. In a large bowl, combine 3 cups flour, the yeast, sugar and salt. Add the potatoes and butter. Beat in warm milk until smooth. Stir in enough remaining flour to form a firm dough. Beat for 2 minutes.

2. Turn onto a lightly floured surface; knead until smooth and elastic, 5-7 minutes. Place in a greased bowl, turning once to grease top. Cover and let rise in a warm place until doubled, about 45 minutes.

3. Punch dough down; turn onto a lightly floured surface. Roll into an 18-in. circle. Transfer to a lightly greased 14-in. pizza pan. Sprinkle cheese over center of dough to within 5 in. of edge. Sprinkle with thyme and rosemary. Bring edges of dough to center; twist to form a knot. Cover and let

QUICK BREADS

LOAVES, MUFFINS, SCONES, CORNBREAD AND MORE...

THESE DELICIOUS RECIPES COME TOGETHER

IN A FLASH WHENEVER YOU NEED THEM.

PECAN COFFEE
CAKE MUFFINS, P. 89

One-Bowl Chocolate Chip Bread

PREP: 20 MIN. • **BAKE:** 65 MINUTES
MAKES: 1 LOAF (16 PIECES)

My family of chocoholics hops out of bed on Valentine's Day because they know I'm baking this indulgent quick bread for breakfast. But don't wait for a special occasion to enjoy it—it hits the spot any time of year.
—Angela Lively, Conroe, TX

    3   large eggs, room temperature
    1   cup sugar
    2   cups sour cream
    3   cups self-rising flour
    2   cups semisweet chocolate chips

1. Preheat oven to 350°. Beat the eggs, sugar and sour cream until well blended. Gradually stir in flour. Fold in chocolate chips. Transfer to a greased 9x5-in. loaf pan.
2. Bake until a toothpick comes out clean, 65-75 minutes. Cool in pan for 5 minutes before removing to a wire rack.
1 PIECE: 306 cal., 13g fat (8g sat. fat), 42mg chol., 305mg sod., 44g carb. (25g sugars, 2g fiber), 5g pro.

TEST KITCHEN TIP

As a substitute for the 3 cups self-rising flour in this recipe, place 4½ tsp. baking powder and 1½ tsp. salt in a 1-cup measuring cup. Add all-purpose flour to measure 1 cup; combine with an additional 2 cups all-purpose flour.

Cranberry Muffins

PREP: 15 MIN. • **BAKE:** 20 MIN. + COOLING
MAKES: 18 SERVINGS

There's an abundance of cranberries in our area during the fall, and this recipe is one of my favorite ways to use them. I've often given these fresh-baked muffins as a small gift to friends, and they're always well received.
—Ronni Dufour, Lebanon, CT

    2   cups all-purpose flour
    1   cup sugar
    1½ tsp. baking powder
    1   tsp. ground nutmeg
    1   tsp. ground cinnamon
    ½   tsp. baking soda
    ½   tsp. ground ginger
    ½   tsp. salt
    2   tsp. grated orange zest
    ½   cup shortening
    ¾   cup orange juice
    2   large eggs, room temperature, lightly beaten
    1   Tbsp. vanilla extract
    1½ cups coarsely chopped cranberries
    1½ cups chopped pecans

1. Preheat oven to 375°. In a large bowl, combine the flour, sugar, baking powder, nutmeg, cinnamon, baking soda, ginger, salt and orange zest. Cut in shortening until crumbly. In a small bowl, combine the orange juice, eggs and vanilla. Stir into the dry ingredients just until moistened. Fold in cranberries and nuts.
2. Fill 18 greased or paper-lined muffin cups two-thirds full. Bake until a toothpick inserted in the middle comes out clean, 18-20 minutes. Cool in pans for 10 minutes before removing to wire rack. Serve warm.
1 MUFFIN: 231 cal., 13g fat (2g sat. fat), 24mg chol., 141mg sod., 26g carb. (13g sugars, 2g fiber), 3g pro.

Golden Sweet Onion Cornbread with Cranberry Butter

PREP: 35 MIN. • **BAKE:** 20 MIN. + STANDING
MAKES: 8 SERVINGS

Put your cast-iron skillet to a new use when you bake up this hearty cornbread in it.
—Taste of Home *Test Kitchen*

2 Tbsp. butter
1 large sweet onion, halved and thinly sliced
4 tsp. chopped seeded jalapeno pepper
½ tsp. chili powder, divided
2 Tbsp. brown sugar, divided
1½ cups all-purpose flour
1 cup yellow cornmeal
3 Tbsp. sugar
2 tsp. baking powder
½ tsp. kosher salt
½ tsp. baking soda
1¼ cups buttermilk
2 large eggs, room temperature, lightly beaten
¼ cup butter, melted
¾ cup shredded cheddar cheese
1 can (4 oz.) chopped green chiles

CRANBERRY BUTTER
½ cup whole-berry cranberry sauce
½ tsp. grated lime zest
½ cup butter, softened

1. Preheat oven to 425°. In a 10-in. cast-iron skillet, melt 2 Tbsp. butter; tilt to coat bottom and sides of pan. Add the onion, jalapeno and ¼ tsp. chili powder; cook over medium-low heat until onion is lightly browned and tender. Stir in 1 Tbsp. brown sugar until dissolved; set aside.

2. In a large bowl, combine flour, cornmeal, sugar, baking powder, salt, baking soda and the remaining ¼ tsp. chili powder and 1 Tbsp. brown sugar. In a small bowl, whisk the buttermilk, eggs and melted butter. Stir into dry ingredients just until moistened. Fold in cheese and chiles.

3. Pour over onion mixture in skillet. Bake 20-25 minutes or until golden brown. Meanwhile, in a small saucepan, cook cranberry sauce and lime zest over low heat until heated through. Cool completely.

4. Let cornbread stand for 10 minutes. Invert onto a serving platter; cut into wedges. Pour cranberry mixture over softened butter; serve with cornbread.

NOTE: Wear disposable gloves when cutting hot peppers; the oils can burn skin. Avoid touching your face.

1 PIECE WITH 1 TBSP. CRANBERRY BUTTER: 468 cal., 25g fat (16g sat. fat), 118mg chol., 626mg sod., 52g carb. (17g sugars, 3g fiber), 10g pro.

Chocolate Chai Mini Loaves

PREP: 25 MIN. • **BAKE:** 35 MIN. + COOLING
MAKES: 3 MINI LOAVES (6 PIECES EACH)

This bread is irresistible! A friend gets mad when I make it because I give her a loaf and she can't help but eat the whole thing!
—Lisa Christensen, Poplar Grove, IL

- 2 oz. semisweet chocolate, chopped
- ½ cup water
- ½ cup butter, softened
- 1 cup packed brown sugar
- 2 large eggs, room temperature
- 1 tsp. vanilla extract
- 1½ cups all-purpose flour
- 3 Tbsp. chai tea latte mix
- 1 tsp. baking soda
- ½ tsp. salt
- ½ cup sour cream

FROSTING

- 1 cup confectioners' sugar
- 1 Tbsp. butter, softened
- 1 Tbsp. chai tea latte mix
- ½ tsp. vanilla extract
- 4 to 5 tsp. whole milk

1. Preheat oven to 350°. In a microwave, melt the chocolate with the water; stir until smooth. Cool slightly.

2. In a large bowl, cream butter and brown sugar until light and fluffy, 5-7 minutes. Add 1 egg at a time, beating well after each addition. Beat in the vanilla, then the chocolate mixture.

3. Combine the flour, latte mix, baking soda and salt; add to the creamed mixture alternately with sour cream.

4. Transfer to 3 greased 5¾x3x2-in. loaf pans. Bake for 35-40 minutes or until a toothpick inserted in the center comes out clean. Cool for 10 minutes before removing from pans to a wire rack to cool completely.

5. For frosting, combine the confectioners' sugar, butter, latte mix, vanilla and enough milk to achieve desired consistency. Frost tops of loaves.

1 PIECE: 208 cal., 9g fat (5g sat. fat), 43mg chol., 206mg sod., 30g carb. (21g sugars, 1g fiber), 3g pro.

TEST KITCHEN TIP

Skip the frosting and dust the top of these loaves with confectioners' sugar to cut calories by almost 20 percent.

Apple & Cheddar Mini Scones

PREP: 25 MIN. • **BAKE:** 10 MIN.
MAKES: 32 SCONES

Cheese and sage go well with apples, so why not put them all together in scones? These mini ones make a fall brunch, tailgate or party even more fun.
—Sue Gronholz, Beaver Dam, WI

- 3 **cups all-purpose flour**
- 3 **tsp. baking powder**
- ½ **tsp. salt**
- ½ **tsp. baking soda**
- 1 **cup cold butter, cubed**
- 1 **large egg, room temperature**
- ¾ **cup vanilla yogurt**
- 3 **Tbsp. 2% milk, divided**
- ⅓ **cup shredded peeled apple**
- ⅓ **cup shredded sharp cheddar cheese**
- 1 **Tbsp. minced fresh sage**
- 1 **Tbsp. sugar**

1. Preheat oven to 425°. In a large bowl, whisk flour, baking powder, salt and baking soda. Cut in butter until mixture resembles coarse crumbs. In another bowl, whisk egg, yogurt and 2 Tbsp. milk; stir into crumb mixture until just moistened. Stir in apple, cheese and sage.

2. Turn dough onto a lightly floured surface; knead gently 10 times. Divide dough in half; pat each portion into a 6-in. circle. Cut each circle into 8 wedges; cut each wedge in half.

3. Transfer to parchment-lined baking sheets. Brush tops with the remaining 1 Tbsp. milk; sprinkle with sugar. Bake for 10-12 minutes or until golden brown. Serve warm.

1 MINI SCONE: 109 cal., 7g fat (4g sat. fat), 23mg chol., 159mg sod., 10g carb. (2g sugars, 0 fiber), 2g pro.

Pecan Coffee Cake Muffins

PREP: 25 MIN. • **BAKE:** 20 MIN.
MAKES: 15 MUFFINS

These moist, cakelike muffins with crumb topping are wonderful for entertaining, brunch or any time you want a treat.
—*Shannon Saltsman, Olmsted Falls, OH*

- ½ **cup butter, softened**
- 1 **cup packed brown sugar**
- 1 **cup all-purpose flour**
- 1 **tsp. ground cinnamon**
- ½ **cup chopped pecans**

BATTER

- 1 **cup butter, softened**
- ¾ **cup packed brown sugar**
- ½ **cup sugar**
- 2 **large eggs, room temperature**
- ⅓ **cup half-and-half cream**
- 1½ **tsp. vanilla extract**
- 2 **cups all-purpose flour**
- 2 **tsp. baking powder**
- ½ **tsp. salt**
  Confectioners' sugar, optional

1. Preheat oven to 350°. For streusel, in a small bowl, combine butter, brown sugar, flour and cinnamon until crumbly. Stir in pecans; set aside.
2. In a large bowl, cream butter and sugars until light and fluffy, 5-7 minutes. Add eggs, 1 at a time, beating well after each addition. Beat in cream and vanilla. Combine flour, baking powder and salt; add to creamed mixture just until moistened.
3. Fill greased or paper-lined muffin cups one-fourth full. Drop 1 Tbsp. streusel into the center of each muffin cup; cover with batter. Sprinkle tops with the remaining streusel.
4. Bake until a toothpick inserted in muffin comes out clean, 20-22 minutes. Cool in pan 5 minutes before removing to a wire rack. If desired, dust with confectioners' sugar. Serve warm.
1 MUFFIN: 420 cal., 22g fat (12g sat. fat), 79mg chol., 284mg sod., 52g carb. (32g sugars, 1g fiber), 4g pro.

Homemade Irish Soda Bread

PREP: 20 MIN. • **BAKE:** 1 HOUR
MAKES: 1 LOAF

Some people consider bread to be the most important part of a meal...and this Irish bread satisfies such folks! It is by far the best soda bread I've ever tried. With added raisins, it is moist and delicious.
—Evelyn Kenney, Trenton, NJ

- 4 cups all-purpose flour
- ¼ cup sugar
- 1 tsp. salt
- 1 tsp. baking powder
- 1 tsp. baking soda
- ¼ cup cold butter, cubed
- 1⅓ cups buttermilk
- 1 large egg, room temperature
- 2 cups raisins
- 3 to 4 Tbsp. caraway seeds
- 2 Tbsp. 2% milk

1. Preheat oven to 375°. In a large bowl, combine flour, sugar, salt, baking powder and baking soda. Cut in butter until the mixture resembles coarse crumbs. Whisk buttermilk and egg; stir into the dry ingredients just until moistened. Stir in raisins and caraway seeds.
2. Turn out onto a floured surface. Knead gently 8-10 times. Shape into a ball and place on a greased baking pan. Pat into a 7-in. round loaf. Cut a 4-in. cross about ¼ in. deep on top to allow for expansion. Brush top with milk.
3. Bake until golden brown, about 1 hour. Remove from pan to wire rack.
1 PIECE: 223 cal., 4g fat (2g sat. fat), 20mg chol., 326mg sod., 43g carb. (15g sugars, 2g fiber), 5g pro.

Cinnamon-Sugar Mini Muffins

PREP: 20 MIN. • **BAKE:** 15 MIN.
MAKES: 2 DOZEN

These delightful little muffins are rich and buttery. You can also make them in regular-sized muffin tins—just bake a little longer.
—Jan Lundberg, Nashville, IN

- 5 Tbsp. butter, softened
- ½ cup sugar
- 1 large egg, room temperature
- ½ cup 2% milk
- 1½ cups all-purpose flour
- 2¼ tsp. baking powder
- ¼ tsp. salt
- ¼ tsp. ground nutmeg

COATING

- ⅓ cup butter, melted
- ⅔ cup cinnamon sugar

1. Preheat oven to 350°. In a large bowl, cream butter and sugar until light and fluffy, 5-7 minutes. Beat in egg. Beat in milk. Combine flour, baking powder, salt and nutmeg; add to the creamed mixture just until moistened.
2. Fill greased miniature muffin cups two-thirds full. Bake 14-16 minutes or until a toothpick inserted in a muffin comes out clean. Cool for 5 minutes in pans before removing to wire racks.
3. Dip muffins in melted butter, then roll in cinnamon sugar. Serve warm.
1 MUFFIN: 116 cal., 5g fat (3g sat. fat), 21mg chol., 114mg sod., 16g carb. (10g sugars, 0 fiber), 1g pro.

Apple Cider Biscuits

TAKES: 30 MIN. • **MAKES:** ABOUT 1 DOZEN

My family enjoys these tender, flaky biscuits warm from the oven. We have a lot of apple trees, so we're always looking for apple recipes. This is a tasty way to use some of our cider.
—Harriet Stichter, Milford, IN

2 cups all-purpose flour
1 Tbsp. baking powder
2 tsp. sugar
½ tsp. salt
⅓ cup cold butter
¾ cup apple cider
⅛ tsp. ground cinnamon
Honey, optional

1. Preheat oven to 425°. In a large bowl, combine the flour, baking powder, sugar and salt. Cut in butter until mixture resembles coarse crumbs. Stir in cider just until moistened.
2. Turn onto a lightly floured surface and knead 8-10 times. Roll out to ½-in. thickness; cut with a 2½-in. biscuit cutter. Place on ungreased baking sheets. Sprinkle with cinnamon; pierce tops of biscuits with a fork.
3. Bake until golden brown, 12-14 minutes . If desired, serve with honey.
1 BISCUIT: 131 cal., 5g fat (3g sat. fat), 14mg chol., 252mg sod., 18g carb. (3g sugars, 1g fiber), 2g pro.

Lorraine Caland

Shuniah, ON

This wonderful muffin recipe has been in my files for years. The chunks of fresh pear make each bite moist and delicious.

Ginger Pear Muffins

PREP: 25 MIN. • **BAKE:** 20 MIN.
MAKES: 1½ DOZEN

- ¾ cup packed brown sugar
- ⅓ cup canola oil
- 1 large egg, room temperature
- 1 cup buttermilk
- 2½ cups all-purpose flour
- 1 tsp. baking soda
- 1 tsp. ground ginger
- ½ tsp. salt
- ½ tsp. ground cinnamon
- 2 cups chopped peeled fresh pears

TOPPING
- ⅓ cup packed brown sugar
- ¼ tsp. ground ginger
- 2 tsp. butter, melted

1. Preheat oven to 350°. Beat brown sugar, oil and egg until well blended. Beat in buttermilk. Combine flour, baking soda, ginger, salt and cinnamon; gradually beat into buttermilk mixture until blended. Stir in pears. Fill 18 paper-lined muffin cups two-thirds full.

2. For topping, combine brown sugar and ginger. Stir in butter until crumbly. Sprinkle over the batter.

3. Bake 18-22 minutes or until a toothpick inserted in a muffin comes out clean. Cool for 5 minutes in pans before removing to wire racks. Serve warm.

1 MUFFIN: 174 cal., 5g fat (1g sat. fat), 13mg chol., 162mg sod., 30g carb. (16g sugars, 1g fiber), 3g pro. **DIABETIC EXCHANGES:** 2 starch, 1 fat.

Buttery Cornbread

PREP: 15 MIN. • **BAKE:** 25 MIN.
MAKES: 15 SERVINGS

A friend gave me this recipe several years ago, and it's my favorite. I love to serve the melt-in-your-mouth cornbread hot from the oven with butter and syrup. It gets rave reviews on holidays and at potluck dinners.
—Nicole Callen, Auburn, CA

- ⅔ cup butter, softened
- 1 cup sugar
- 3 large eggs, room temperature
- 1⅔ cups 2% milk
- 2⅓ cups all-purpose flour
- 1 cup cornmeal
- 4½ tsp. baking powder
- 1 tsp. salt

1. Preheat oven to 400°. In a large bowl, cream butter and sugar until light and fluffy, 5-7 minutes. Combine eggs and milk. Combine flour, cornmeal, baking powder and salt; add to the creamed mixture alternately with the egg mixture.

2. Pour into a greased 13x9-in. baking pan. Bake 22-27 minutes or until a toothpick inserted in center comes out clean. Cut into squares; serve warm.

1 PIECE: 259 cal., 10g fat (6g sat. fat), 68mg chol., 386mg sod., 37g carb. (15g sugars, 1g fiber), 5g pro.

Double Corn Cornbread: Stir in 1½ cups thawed frozen corn

Mexican Cheese Cornbread: Stir in 1 cup shredded Mexican cheese blend.

Jalapeno Cheese Cornbread: Stir in 1 cup shredded cheddar cheese and 3 finely chopped seeded jalapeno peppers.

TEST KITCHEN TIP
If you have leftover cornbread, crumble it up to use as bread crumbs or cube it and keep it in the freezer to make stuffing.

GET MORE RECIPES
If you adore cornbread served all different ways, just hover your camera here for more recipes.

Maple-Chai Pumpkin Muffins

PREP: 25 MIN. • **BAKE:** 20 MIN.
MAKES: 1 DOZEN

Why use ordinary pumpkin pie spice when you can up the ante with homemade chai spice? The maple syrup pairs so well with the pumpkin and this warming spice blend. If you prefer, substitute old-fashioned rolled oats, pecans, walnuts or even white chocolate chips for the pepitas topping.
—*Debra Keil, Owasso, OK*

- 1 cup all-purpose flour
- ¾ cup whole wheat flour
- 1 tsp. baking soda
- 1 tsp. ground cardamom
- ½ tsp. salt
- ½ tsp. ground cinnamon
  Dash ground nutmeg
  Dash ground cloves
- 2 large eggs, room temperature
- 1 cup canned pumpkin
- ½ cup maple syrup
- ⅓ cup melted coconut oil
- ¼ cup 2% milk
- 1 tsp. vanilla extract
- ⅓ cup plus 1 Tbsp. pepitas, divided

1. Preheat oven to 325°. In a large bowl, whisk the first 8 ingredients. In another bowl, whisk eggs, pumpkin, syrup, coconut oil, milk and vanilla until blended. Add to the flour mixture; stir just until moistened. Fold in ⅓ cup pepitas.

2. Fill greased or foil-lined muffin cups three-fourths full. Sprinkle with the remaining 1 Tbsp. pepitas. Bake until a toothpick inserted in the center comes out clean, 20-25 minutes. Cool 5 minutes before removing from pan to a wire rack. Serve warm.

1 MUFFIN: 197 cal., 9g fat (6g sat. fat), 31mg chol., 230mg sod., 25g carb. (9g sugars, 2g fiber), 5g pro.

Banana Oat Muffins
TAKES: 30 MIN. • **MAKES:** 1 DOZEN

Chopped pecans add pleasant crunch to these hearty muffins with rich banana flavor. These muffins are low in cholesterol, but you'd never know it. My husband and I love them.
—Marjorie Mott, Galatia, IL

- ¾ cup all-purpose flour
- ¾ cup quick-cooking oats
- 1 tsp. baking powder
- 1 tsp. ground cinnamon
- ½ tsp. baking soda
- ¼ tsp. ground nutmeg
- 2 large egg whites, room temperature
- 1 cup mashed ripe bananas (about 2 medium)
- ½ cup packed brown sugar
- ¼ cup fat-free milk
- ¼ cup canola oil
- ½ cup chopped pecans

1. Preheat oven to 400°. In a large bowl, combine the first 6 ingredients. In a small bowl, beat the egg whites, bananas, brown sugar, milk and oil. Stir into dry ingredients just until moistened. Stir in pecans.
2. Coat muffin cups with cooking spray; fill two-thirds full with batter. Bake for 15-20 minutes or until a toothpick comes out clean. Cool for 5 minutes before removing from pan to a wire rack.
1 MUFFIN: 180 cal., 9g fat (1g sat. fat), 0 chol., 102mg sod., 24g carb. (13g sugars, 2g fiber), 3g pro.

Almond Flour Bread
PREP: 10 MIN. • **BAKE:** 25 MIN. + COOLING
MAKES: 10 SERVINGS

My almond flour bread recipe is keto-friendly. It's low in carbs with a fluffy, crumbly texture like a traditional loaf of bread.
—Caroline Baines, Spokane, WA

- 2 cups almond flour
- ¼ cup chia seeds
- 2 tsp. baking powder
- ½ tsp. salt
- 4 large eggs, room temperature
- ¼ cup unsweetened almond milk or water
- ¼ cup butter, melted or coconut oil, melted

1. Preheat oven to 350°. In a large bowl, whisk almond flour, chia seeds, baking powder and salt. In another bowl, whisk the eggs, almond milk and melted butter; stir into the dry ingredients just until moistened. Pour into a parchment-lined 8x4-in. loaf pan.
2. Bake until a toothpick inserted in center comes out clean and top is golden brown, 25-30 minutes. Let cool for 10 minutes before removing from pan to a wire rack to cool completely.
1 PIECE: 219 cal., 19g fat (4g sat. fat), 87mg chol., 292mg sod., 7g carb. (1g sugars, 4g fiber), 8g pro.

Kelsey's Favorite Cranberry Bread

PREP: 25 MIN. • **BAKE:** 55 MIN. + COOLING
MAKES: 1 LOAF (12 PIECES)

My granddaughter Kelsey and I adapted an old recipe when we first baked this new favorite. She and her sister, Aidan, don't like nuts, so we used golden raisins instead.
—Annette Grahl, Midway, KY

2 cups all-purpose flour
¾ cup sugar
1½ tsp. baking powder
1 tsp. salt
½ tsp. baking soda
¼ cup cold butter, cubed
1 large egg, room temperature
¾ cup orange juice
2 tsp. grated orange zest
1 cup chopped fresh or frozen cranberries
½ cup golden raisins

STREUSEL

⅓ cup packed brown sugar
3 Tbsp. all-purpose flour
2 Tbsp. cold butter

GLAZE

½ cup confectioners' sugar
2 tsp. orange juice

1. Preheat oven to 350°. In a large bowl, combine the first 5 ingredients; cut in butter until crumbly. In a small bowl, whisk the egg, orange juice and zest. Stir into the dry ingredients just until moistened. Fold in cranberries and raisins. Transfer to a greased 8x4-in. loaf pan.

2. For the streusel, combine brown sugar and flour; cut in the 2 Tbsp. butter until crumbly. Sprinkle over batter. Bake until a toothpick inserted in the center comes out clean, 55-65 minutes. Cool for 10 minutes before removing from pan to a wire rack to cool completely.

3. For glaze, combine the confectioners' sugar and orange juice until smooth. Drizzle over bread.

1 PIECE: 260 cal., 6g fat (4g sat. fat), 33mg chol., 349mg sod., 49g carb. (29g sugars, 1g fiber), 3g pro.

Anise Pumpkin Bread

PREP: 15 MIN. • **BAKE:** 45 MIN. + COOLING
MAKES: 1 LOAF (12 PIECES)

We live in a rural area of Long Island where there's plenty of fresh air and friendly country folks. This recipe has traveled from one end of the island to the other.
—P. Marchesi, Rocky Point, NY

- 2 large eggs, room temperature
- 1 cup packed brown sugar
- 1 cup canned pumpkin
- ⅓ cup vegetable oil
- 1 tsp. vanilla extract
- 1¼ cups all-purpose flour
- ¼ cup quick-cooking oats
- 2 tsp. baking powder
- 1 tsp. aniseed
- ½ tsp. salt

GLAZE
- ½ cup confectioners' sugar
- 2 to 3 tsp. 2% milk
- ¼ tsp. anise extract
- ¼ tsp. butter flavoring, optional

1. Preheat oven to 350°. In a bowl, combine the eggs, brown sugar, pumpkin, oil and vanilla. In another bowl, combine the flour, oats, baking powder, aniseed and salt; add to pumpkin mixture and stir until well blended. Pour into a greased and floured 8x4-in. loaf pan.

2. Bake until a toothpick inserted in the center comes out clean, 45-50 minutes. Cool 10 minutes before removing from pan to a wire rack to cool completely.

3. For glaze, combine confectioners' sugar, milk, anise extract and, if desired, butter flavoring. Drizzle over bread.

1 PIECE: 219 cal., 7g fat (1g sat. fat), 31mg chol., 197mg sod., 36g carb. (24g sugars, 1g fiber), 3g pro.

TEST KITCHEN TIP

You can make your glaze thinner or thicker by adjusting the amount of milk and sugar. For a pourable glaze, add more milk. If you want a more distinct design, make a thicker glaze and use a squeeze bottle to drizzle it onto the loaf.

Greek Breadsticks

PREP: 20 MIN. • **BAKE:** 15 MIN.
MAKES: 32 BREADSTICKS

Get ready for rave reviews with these crispy Greek-inspired appetizers. They're best served hot and fresh from the oven with your favorite tzatziki sauce.
—Jane Whittaker, Pensacola, FL

- ¼ cup marinated quartered artichoke hearts, drained
- 2 Tbsp. pitted Greek olives
- 1 pkg. (17.3 oz.) frozen puff pastry, thawed
- 1 carton (6½ oz.) spreadable spinach and artichoke cream cheese, divided
- 2 Tbsp. grated Parmesan cheese, divided
- 1 large egg
- 1 Tbsp. water
- 2 tsp. sesame seeds
   Refrigerated tzatziki sauce, optional

1. Preheat oven to 400°. In a food processor, pulse artichokes and olives until finely chopped. Unfold 1 pastry sheet on a lightly floured surface; spread half of the cream cheese over half of pastry. Top with half the artichoke mixture. Sprinkle with half the Parmesan cheese. Fold plain half over filling; press gently to seal.

2. Repeat with remaining pastry, cream cheese, artichoke mixture and Parmesan cheese. Whisk egg and water; brush over tops. Sprinkle with sesame seeds. Cut each rectangle into sixteen ¾-in.-wide strips. Twist strips several times; place 2 in. apart on greased baking sheets.

3. Bake for 12-14 minutes or until golden brown. Serve warm, with tzatziki sauce if desired.

1 BREADSTICK: 101 cal., 6g fat (2g sat. fat), 11mg chol., 104mg sod., 9g carb. (0 sugars, 1g fiber), 2g pro.

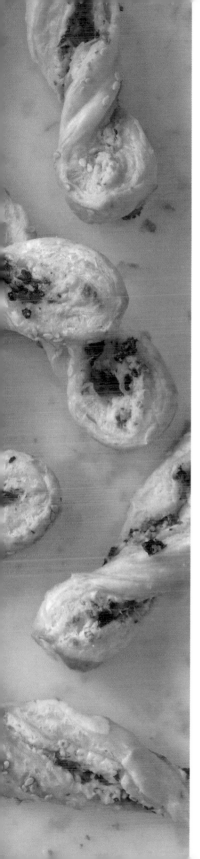

Caraway Scones

TAKES: 30 MIN. • **MAKES:** 8 SERVINGS

These savory scones are perfect next to a soup and salad at a luncheon.
—Brooke Staley, Mary Esther, FL

2	**cups all-purpose flour**
4½	**tsp. sugar**
2	**tsp. baking powder**
2	**tsp. caraway seeds**
½	**tsp. salt**
¼	**cup cold butter**
1	**large egg, room temperature**
⅔	**cup 2% milk**

1. Preheat oven to 400°. In a large bowl, combine the flour, sugar, baking powder, caraway seeds and salt. Cut in butter until mixture resembles coarse crumbs. In another bowl, whisk egg and milk; stir into the dry ingredients just until moistened.

2. Turn onto a floured surface; gently knead 6-8 times. Transfer to a greased baking sheet; pat into an 8-in. circle. Cut into 8 wedges, but do not separate. Bake until golden brown, 17-22 minutes. Remove from pan to a wire rack. Serve warm.

1 SCONE: 197 cal., 7g fat (4g sat. fat), 44mg chol., 284mg sod., 28g carb., 1g fiber), 5g pro.

Sweet Potato Spice Bread

PREP: 15 MIN. • **BAKE:** 25 MIN. + COOLING
MAKES: 2 MINI LOAVES (6 PIECES EACH)

It's a good thing this recipe makes two mini loaves because they'll go fast! For a small household, eat one loaf now and freeze the other for later.
—Ronnie Littles, VA Beach, VA

- 1 cup all-purpose flour
- 1½ tsp. baking powder
- ¼ tsp. each ground cinnamon, nutmeg and allspice
- ⅛ tsp. salt
- 1 large egg, room temperature
- ⅓ cup mashed sweet potato
- ⅓ cup honey
- 3 Tbsp. canola oil
- 2 Tbsp. molasses
- ⅓ cup chopped walnuts

1. Preheat oven to 325°. In a small bowl, combine the flour, baking powder, spices and salt. In another small bowl, whisk egg, sweet potato, honey, oil and molasses. Stir into dry ingredients just until moistened. Fold in walnuts.

2. Transfer to 2 greased 5¾x3x2-in. loaf pans. Bake for 25-30 minutes or until a toothpick inserted in the center comes out clean. Cool for 10 minutes before removing from pans to wire racks.

1 PIECE: 142 cal., 6g fat (1g sat. fat), 18mg chol., 85mg sod., 20g carb. (10g sugars, 1g fiber), 3g pro.

Pumpkin Patch Biscuits

PREP: 20 MIN. • **BAKE:** 20 MIN.
MAKES: 6 BISCUITS

I got smart and started making double batches of these moist, fluffy biscuits to meet the demand. My dad loves their pumpkiny goodness and requests them for Christmas, Father's Day and his birthday!
—Liza Taylor, Seattle, WA

- 1¾ cups all-purpose flour
- ¼ cup packed brown sugar
- 2½ tsp. baking powder
- ½ tsp. salt
- ¼ tsp. baking soda
- ½ cup plus 1½ tsp. cold butter, divided
- ¾ cup canned pumpkin
- ⅓ cup buttermilk

1. Preheat oven to 425°. In a large bowl, combine the flour, brown sugar, baking powder, salt and baking soda. Cut in ½ cup butter until mixture resembles coarse crumbs. Combine the pumpkin and buttermilk; stir into the crumb mixture just until moistened.

2. Turn out dough onto a lightly floured surface; knead 8-10 times. Pat or roll out to 1-in. thickness; cut with a floured 2½-in. biscuit cutter. Place 1 in. apart on a greased baking sheet.

3. Bake 18-22 minutes or until golden brown. Melt the remaining 1½ tsp. butter; brush over biscuits. Serve warm.

1 BISCUIT: 328 cal., 17g fat (11g sat. fat), 44mg chol., 609mg sod., 40g carb. (11g sugars, 2g fiber), 5g pro.

Cast-Iron Chocolate Chip Banana Bread

PREP: 20 MIN. • **BAKE:** 25 MIN.
MAKES: 10 SERVINGS

I love this cast-iron banana bread because it cooks evenly every time. The end result is so moist and delicious!
—Ashley Hudd, Holton, MI

- ¼ cup butter, softened
- 1 cup sugar
- 1 large egg, room temperature
- 3 medium ripe bananas, mashed (about 1¼ cups)
- 1 tsp. vanilla extract
- 2 cups all-purpose flour
- 1 tsp. baking soda
- ½ tsp. salt
- 1 cup semisweet chocolate chips, divided
  Dried banana chips, optional

1. Preheat oven to 350°. In a large bowl, beat butter and sugar until crumbly. Beat in egg, bananas and vanilla. In another bowl, whisk flour, baking soda and salt; gradually beat into banana mixture. Stir in ½ cup chocolate chips.

2. Transfer to a greased 10-in. cast-iron or other ovenproof skillet; sprinkle with remaining ½ cup chocolate chips. If desired, top with dried banana chips. Bake until a toothpick inserted in center comes out clean, 25-30 minutes. Cool in pan on a wire rack.

1 PIECE: 330 cal., 10g fat (6g sat. fat), 31mg chol., 290mg sod., 58g carb. (34g sugars, 3g fiber), 4g pro.

HOW-TO
MAKE BANANA BREAD

1. The best bananas for banana bread are those that are just past their prime. Bananas that have some brown speckles on the skin are perfect; they should mash easily and be full of flavor. If your bananas are underripe, store them in a brown paper bag at room temperature for a day or two, or warm them in a 250° oven (peels and all) for 15-20 minutes.

2. Softened butter should still be a bit cool—around 65°. Butter that is too soft will create a more liquid, slightly greasy mixture when beaten. For this banana bread, your butter and sugar mix should be crumbly, not the "light and fluffy" texture you'll often see called for with cakes and cookies.

3. Whisking the dry ingredients before adding them to the wet ingredients ensures the leavener is evenly distributed. To keep your quick bread tender, mix the dry and wet ingredients together just until combined—you may even want to do it by hand.

Parmesan Zucchini Bread

PREP: 10 MIN. • **BAKE:** 1 HOUR + COOLING
MAKES: 1 LOAF (16 PIECES)

This loaf has a rugged, textured look that adds to its old-fashioned appeal. The mild Parmesan flavor nicely complements the zucchini, which adds bits of green color to every tender slice.
—Chris Wilson, Sellersville, PA

- 3 **cups all-purpose flour**
- 3 **Tbsp. grated Parmesan cheese**
- 1 **tsp. salt**
- ½ **tsp. baking powder**
- ½ **tsp. baking soda**
- 2 **large eggs, room temperature**
- 1 **cup buttermilk**
- ⅓ **cup sugar**
- ⅓ **cup butter, melted**
- 1 **cup shredded peeled zucchini**
- 1 **Tbsp. grated onion**

1. Preheat oven to 350°. In a large bowl, combine flour, cheese, salt, baking powder and baking soda. In another bowl, whisk the eggs, buttermilk, sugar and butter. Stir into the dry ingredients just until moistened. Fold in zucchini and onion.

2. Pour into a greased and floured 9x5-in. loaf pan. Bake until a toothpick inserted in the center comes out clean, about 1 hour. Cool for 10 minutes before removing from pan to a wire rack.

1 PIECE: 156 cal., 5g fat (3g sat. fat), 35mg chol., 288mg sod., 23g carb. (5g sugars, 1g fiber), 4g pro.

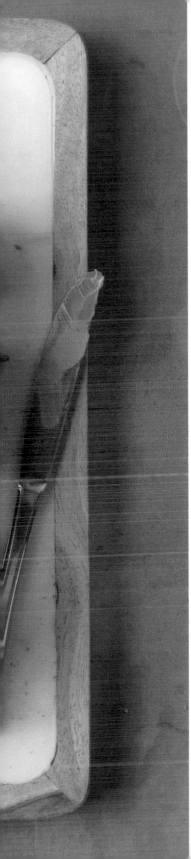

Swiss Beer Bread

PREP: 15 MIN. • **BAKE:** 50 MIN. + COOLING
MAKES: 1 LOAF (12 PIECES)

This recipe is a family favorite in our house because it isn't greasy like many cheese breads. It will not last long in your house, either!
—Debi Wallace, Chestertown, NY

- 4 **oz. Jarlsberg or Swiss cheese**
- 3 **cups all-purpose flour**
- 3 **Tbsp. sugar**
- 3 **tsp. baking powder**
- 1½ **tsp. salt**
- ½ **tsp. pepper**
- 1 **bottle (12 oz.) beer or nonalcoholic beer**
- 2 **Tbsp. butter, melted**

1. Preheat oven to 375°. Divide cheese in half. Cut half into ¼-in. cubes; shred the remaining half. In a large bowl, combine the flour, sugar, baking powder, salt and pepper. Stir beer into dry ingredients just until moistened. Fold in cubed and shredded cheese.
2. Transfer to a greased 8x4-in. loaf pan. Drizzle with butter. Bake until a toothpick inserted in center comes out clean, 50-60 minutes. Cool for 10 minutes before removing from pan to a wire rack.
1 PIECE: 182 cal., 5g fat (3g sat. fat), 11mg chol., 453mg sod., 28g carb. (4g sugars, 1g fiber), 6g pro.

Easy Peasy Biscuits

PREP: 25 MIN. • **BAKE:** 10 MIN.
MAKES: 2 DOZEN

I love that I can make these biscuits and have enough left over to freeze for another meal. They are wonderful with homemade peach preserves.
—Amanda West, Shelbyville, TN

- 4 cups all-purpose flour
- 4 Tbsp. baking powder
- 1 Tbsp. sugar
- 1 Tbsp. ground flaxseed
- 1 tsp. sea salt
- 1 cup solid coconut oil
- 1½ cups 2% milk

1. Preheat oven to 450°. In a large bowl, whisk flour, baking powder, sugar, flaxseed and salt. Add coconut oil and cut in with a pastry blender until mixture resembles coarse crumbs. Add milk; stir just until moistened.

2. Turn onto a lightly floured surface; knead gently 8-10 times. Pat or roll dough into a rectangle ½ in. thick; fold dough into thirds (as you would a letter). Pat or roll dough again into a rectangle ½ in. thick; cut with a pizza cutter or knife into 24 biscuits, each about 2½ in. square. Place 1½ in. apart on ungreased baking sheets. Bake until light brown, 8-10 minutes. Serve warm.

FREEZE OPTION: Freeze cut biscuit dough on waxed paper-lined baking sheets until firm. Transfer to airtight containers; return to freezer. To use, bake biscuits in a preheated 350° oven until light brown, 15-20 minutes. Or, freeze cooled baked biscuits in airtight containers. To use, heat in a preheated 350° oven until warmed, 5-10 minutes.

1 BISCUIT: 167 cal., 10g fat (8g sat. fat), 1mg chol., 328mg sod., 17g carb. (1g sugars, 1g fiber), 3g pro.

Glazed Cranberry Biscuits

PREP: 30 MIN. • **BAKE:** 15 MIN.
MAKES: ABOUT 1 DOZEN

My family likes biscuits for breakfast. One Sunday, I decided to make those golden goodies extra special by adding white chips, dried cranberries and a simple orange glaze.
—Lori Daniels, Beverly, WV

- 2 cups all-purpose flour
- 2 tsp. baking powder
- ½ tsp. salt
- ½ tsp. grated orange zest
- ½ tsp. ground cinnamon
- ¼ cup shortening
- ¼ cup cold butter
- ¾ cup 2% milk
- ¼ cup orange juice
- 1 cup dried cranberries
- ½ cup white baking chips

DRIZZLE
- 1½ cups confectioners' sugar
- 2 Tbsp. orange juice
- ¼ tsp. orange extract

1. Preheat oven to 400°. In a large bowl, combine the first 5 ingredients. Cut in shortening and butter until mixture resembles coarse crumbs. Stir in milk and orange juice just until moistened. Stir in the cranberries and baking chips.

2. Turn dough onto a lightly floured surface; knead gently 8-10 times. Pat or roll out to ¾-in. thickness; cut with a floured 2½-in. biscuit cutter.

3. Place 2 in. apart on a greased baking sheet. Bake for 12-16 minutes or until lightly browned. In a small bowl, combine the confectioners' sugar, orange juice and extract; drizzle over biscuits. Serve warm.

1 BISCUIT: 285 cal., 11g fat (5g sat. fat), 12mg chol., 206mg sod., 45g carb. (26g sugars, 1g fiber), 3g pro.

Lemon-Thyme Tea Bread

PREP: 20 MIN. • **BAKE:** 40 MIN. + COOLING
MAKES: 1 LOAF (16 PIECES)

I received this recipe as part of a gift, along with a lemon thyme plant and a fresh loaf of this pound cake-like bread. Everyone who tries it asks for the recipe.
—Jeannette Mango, Parkesburg, PA

- ¾ cup whole milk
- 1 Tbsp. minced fresh thyme or 1 tsp. dried thyme
- ½ cup butter, softened
- 1 cup sugar
- 2 large eggs, room temperature
- 2 cups all-purpose flour
- 1½ tsp. baking powder
- ¼ tsp. salt
- 1 Tbsp. lemon juice
- 1 Tbsp. grated lemon zest

GLAZE

- ½ cup confectioners' sugar
- 1 Tbsp. lemon juice

1. In a microwave-safe bowl, combine milk and thyme. Microwave, uncovered, on high 1-2 minutes or until bubbly; cover and let stand until cooled to room temperature.

2. Preheat oven to 350°. In a large bowl, cream butter and sugar until light and fluffy, 5-7 minutes. Add eggs, 1 at a time, beating well after each addition. Combine flour, baking powder and salt; add to the creamed mixture alternately with reserved milk mixture. Stir in lemon juice and zest.

3. Pour into a greased 9x5-in. loaf pan. Bake 40-45 minutes or until a toothpick inserted in center comes out clean. Cool 10 minutes before removing from pan to a wire rack.

4. For glaze, in a small bowl, combine confectioners' sugar and lemon juice until smooth; drizzle over bread.

1 PIECE: 187 cal., 7g fat (4g sat. fat), 43mg chol., 92mg sod., 29g carb. (17g sugars, 0 fiber), 3g pro.

Lemon Bread: Omit thyme and step 1.

Lemon-Blueberry Bread: Omit thyme and step 1. Fold in 1 cup fresh or frozen blueberries.

Lemon Poppy Seed Bread: Omit thyme and step 1. Add 2 tsp. poppy seeds to the flour mixture.

Praline-Topped Apple Bread

PREP: 30 MIN. • **BAKE:** 50 MIN. + COOLING
MAKES: 1 LOAF (16 PIECES)

*Apples and candied pecans make this bread
so much better than the usual coffee cakes
you see at brunches.*
—Sonja Blow, Nixa, MO

- 2 **cups all-purpose flour**
- 2 **tsp. baking powder**
- ½ **tsp. baking soda**
- ½ **tsp. salt**
- 1 **cup sugar**
- 1 **cup sour cream**
- 2 **large eggs, room temperature**
- 3 **tsp. vanilla extract**
- 1½ **cups chopped peeled**
  Granny Smith apples
- 1¼ **cups chopped pecans, toasted,**
  divided
- ½ **cup butter, cubed**
- ½ **cup packed brown sugar**

1. Preheat oven to 350°. In a large bowl, mix
flour, baking powder, baking soda and salt.
In another bowl, beat sugar, sour cream,
eggs and vanilla until well blended. Stir into
the flour mixture just until moistened. Fold
in apples and 1 cup pecans.

2. Transfer to a greased 9x5-in. loaf pan.
Bake until a toothpick inserted in center
comes out clean, 50-55 minutes. Cool in
pan 10 minutes before removing to a wire
rack to cool completely.

3. In a small saucepan, combine the butter
and brown sugar. Bring to a boil, stirring
constantly to dissolve sugar; boil 1 minute.
Working quickly, pour over cooled bread.
Sprinkle with remaining ¼ cup pecans;
let stand until set.

NOTE: To toast nuts, bake in a shallow pan in
a 350° oven for 5-10 minutes or cook in a
skillet over low heat until lightly browned,
stirring occasionally.

1 PIECE: 288 cal., 16g fat (6g sat. fat), 42mg
chol., 235mg sod., 34g carb. (21g sugars, 1g
fiber), 4g pro.

Chocolate Chip Pumpkin Bread

PREP: 15 MIN. • **BAKE:** 45 MIN.
MAKES: 4 MINI LOAVES (6 PIECES EACH)

I love making this bread in the fall. The aroma is mouthwatering, and the chocolate chips add so much to an all-time favorite.
—*Vicki Raboine, Kansasville, WI*

- 1 **cup packed brown sugar**
- 1 **cup sugar**
- ⅔ **cup butter, softened**
- 3 **large eggs, room temperature**
- 2⅓ **cups all-purpose flour**
- 1½ **cups canned pumpkin**
- ½ **cup water**
- 2 **tsp. baking soda**
- 1 **tsp. ground cinnamon**
- 1 **tsp. salt**
- ½ **tsp. ground cloves**
- 2 **cups semisweet chocolate chips**

1. Preheat oven to 350°. In a bowl, cream the sugars, butter and eggs. Add flour, pumpkin, water, baking soda, cinnamon, salt and cloves. Mix thoroughly. Fold in chocolate chips.

2. Pour into 4 greased and floured 5¾x3x2-in. loaf pans. Bake 45 minutes or until a toothpick inserted in center comes out clean..

1 PIECE: 239 cal., 10g fat (6g sat. fat), 37mg chol., 258mg sod., 37g carb. (26g sugars, 2g fiber), 3g pro.

Sweet Potato Biscuits with Honey Butter

TAKES: 30 MIN. • **MAKES:** 15 BISCUITS (ABOUT ½ CUP HONEY BUTTER)

Why not give sweet potatoes a starring role at your table? Served with cinnamon-honey butter, these biscuits are downright delicious.
—Cathy Bell, Joplin, MO

- 2 **cups all-purpose flour**
- 4 **tsp. sugar**
- 3 **tsp. baking powder**
- 1 **tsp. salt**
- 1 **tsp. ground cinnamon**
- ½ **tsp. ground nutmeg**
- ¼ **cup shortening**
- 1 **cup mashed sweet potatoes**
- ½ **cup half-and-half cream**

HONEY BUTTER
- ½ **cup butter, softened**
- 2 **Tbsp. honey**
- 1 **tsp. ground cinnamon**

1. Preheat oven to 400°. Combine the first 6 ingredients. Cut in shortening until the mixture resembles coarse crumbs. Combine sweet potatoes and cream; stir into crumb mixture just until moistened. Turn onto a lightly floured surface; gently knead 8-10 times.
2. Pat or roll out to ½-in. thickness; cut with a floured 2½-in. biscuit cutter. Reroll and repeat once. Place 1 in. apart on a greased baking sheet.
3. Bake 9–11 minutes or until golden brown. Meanwhile, in a small bowl, beat the butter, honey and cinnamon until blended. Serve with warm biscuits.

1 BISCUIT WITH 1½ TSP. BUTTER: 186 cal., 10g fat (5g sat. fat), 20mg chol., 312mg sod., 21g carb. (5g sugars, 1g fiber), 2g pro.

2. Bake 40-45 minutes or until a toothpick inserted in center comes out clean. Cool in pans for 10 minutes before transferring to wire racks.

FREEZE OPTION: Securely wrap and freeze individual cooled loaves. To use, thaw at room temperature.

1 PIECE: 189 cal., 9g fat (4g sat. fat), 36mg chol., 223mg sod., 23g carb. (11g sugars, 1g fiber), 5g pro.

Cheese & Garlic Biscuits

TAKES: 20 MIN. • **MAKES:** 2½ DOZEN

My biscuits won the prize for best quick bread at my county fair. One of the judges liked them so much, she asked for the recipe! These buttery, savory biscuits go with just about anything.
—Gloria Jarrett, Loveland, OH

- 2½ **cups biscuit/baking mix**
- ¾ **cup shredded sharp cheddar cheese**
- 1 **tsp. garlic powder**
- 1 **tsp. ranch salad dressing mix**
- 1 **cup buttermilk**

TOPPING
- ½ **cup butter, melted**
- 1 **Tbsp. minced chives**
- ½ **tsp. garlic powder**
- ½ **tsp. ranch salad dressing mix**
- ¼ **tsp. pepper**

1. Preheat oven to 450°. In a large bowl, combine the baking mix, cheese, garlic powder and salad dressing mix. Stir in buttermilk just until moistened. Drop by tablespoonfuls onto greased baking sheets.

2. Bake until golden brown, 6-8 minutes. Meanwhile, combine topping ingredients. Brush over biscuits. Serve warm.

1 BISCUIT: 81 cal., 5g fat (3g sat. fat), 11mg chol., 176mg sod., 7g carb. (1g sugars, 0 fiber), 2g pro.

Yummy Apricot Pecan Bread

PREP: 20 MIN. • **BAKE:** 40 MIN. + COOLING
MAKES: 2 LOAVES (12 PIECES EACH)

Every time I prepare this yummy bread, I receive raves. It's perfect with coffee or as a gift, plus it's really quick and easy to prepare.
—Joan Hallford, North Richland Hills, TX

- 2½ **cups all-purpose flour**
- ¾ **cup sugar**
- 2 **tsp. baking soda**
- 1 **tsp. ground cinnamon**
- ¼ **tsp. salt**
- ¼ **tsp. ground nutmeg**
- 1 **cup 2% milk**
- 2 **large eggs, room temperature**
- ⅓ **cup butter, melted**
- 2 **cups shredded cheddar cheese**
- 1 **cup finely chopped dried apricots**
- ¾ **cup finely chopped pecans**

TOPPING
- 3 **Tbsp. packed brown sugar**
- 1 **Tbsp. butter**
- ½ **tsp. ground cinnamon**

1. Preheat oven to 350°. In a large bowl, combine the first 6 ingredients. In a small bowl, beat the milk, eggs and butter; stir into dry ingredients just until moistened. Fold in the cheese, apricots and pecans. Spoon into 2 greased 8x4-in. loaf pans. Combine the topping ingredients; sprinkle over batter.

SEE HOW IT'S DONE
Watch how quickly these bite-sized biscuits come together! Just hover your camera here.

COOKIES, BROWNIES & BARS

AFTER RAKING LEAVES OR DOING FALL CHORES,

CUDDLE UP WITH A CUP OF COFFEE AND A

SWEET HOMEMADE TREAT AS YOUR REWARD!

BIG SOFT GINGER
COOKIES, P. 138

2. Drop by tablespoonfuls 1 in. apart onto ungreased baking sheets. Bake until edges begin to brown, 10-12 minutes. Cool for 1 minute before removing to wire racks. Store in an airtight container.

1 COOKIE: 81 cal., 5g fat (2g sat. fat), 12mg chol., 61mg sod., 10g carb. (5g sugars, 1g fiber), 1g pro.

Chocolate Mincemeat Bars

PREP: 15 MIN. • **BAKE:** 20 MIN.
MAKES: 3 DOZEN

Mincemeat is just so classic for holiday desserts. Even people who say they don't care for the taste will love these tender chocolate bars—I promise.
—Darlene Berndt, South Bend, IN

- ½ cup shortening
- 1 cup sugar
- 3 large eggs, room temperature
- 2 cups all-purpose flour
- 2 tsp. baking soda
- 1¾ cups mincemeat
- 2 cups semisweet chocolate chips
  Confectioners' sugar

1. Preheat oven to 375°. In a large bowl, cream shortening and sugar until light and fluffy, 5-7 minutes. Add eggs, 1 at a time, beating well after each addition. Combine flour and baking soda; gradually add to the creamed mixture and mix well. Beat in mincemeat. Stir in chocolate chips.

2. Spread into a greased 15x10x1-in. baking pan. Bake for 15-20 minutes or until dark golden brown. Cool on a wire rack. Cut into bars. Dust with confectioners' sugar.

1 BAR: 142 cal., 6g fat (2g sat. fat), 18mg chol., 80mg sod., 21g carb. (15g sugars, 1g fiber), 2g pro.

Raisin Sweet Potato Cookies

PREP: 25 MIN. • **BAKE:** 10 MIN./BATCH
MAKES: 5 DOZEN

Cozy up to the fire with a plate of satisfyingly sweet cookies that taste like home. Pair them with a mug of hot chai or ice-cold milk, and no one will be able to resist.
—Jacque Sue Meyer, Lohman, MO

- 1 cup butter, softened
- 1 cup sugar
- 1 large egg, room temperature
- 1 cup mashed sweet potato
- 1 tsp. vanilla extract
- 2 cups all-purpose flour
- 1 tsp. baking powder
- 1 tsp. ground cinnamon
- ½ tsp. baking soda
- ½ tsp. salt
- ½ tsp. ground allspice
- 1 cup chopped pecans
- 1 cup raisins

1. Preheat oven to 375°. In a large bowl, cream butter and sugar until light and fluffy, 5-7 minutes. Beat in the egg, sweet potato and vanilla. Combine the flour, baking powder, cinnamon, baking soda, salt and allspice; gradually add to the creamed mixture and mix well. Fold in pecans and raisins.

Date-Nut Honey Bars

PREP: 45 MIN. • **BAKE:** 25 MIN. + COOLING
MAKES: 2 DOZEN

The flavor combination here reminds me of baklava—without the hours of work! These bars are perfect for gifts, party platters and bake sales...they never fail to impress.
—Anna Wood, Cullowhee, NC

¾ cup butter, softened
⅓ cup sugar
1¾ cups all-purpose flour
½ cup old-fashioned oats
¼ tsp. salt

FILLING

½ cup honey
½ cup apple jelly
2 Tbsp. butter
½ cup packed brown sugar

2 large eggs, lightly beaten
½ tsp. vanilla extract
2 Tbsp. all-purpose flour
½ tsp. baking powder
¼ tsp. salt
¼ tsp. ground cinnamon
1¼ cups chopped walnuts
1¼ cups chopped dates

1. Preheat oven to 350°. In a large bowl, cream butter and sugar until light and fluffy, 5-7 minutes. In a small bowl, whisk flour, oats and salt; gradually add to the creamed mixture, mixing well. Press onto bottom and ½ in. up sides of an ungreased 13x9-in. baking pan. Bake until the edges begin to brown, 16-20 minutes. Cool on a wire rack.

2. For filling, in a large saucepan, combine honey, apple jelly and butter over medium heat; stir until jelly and butter are melted. Remove from heat; whisk in brown sugar, eggs and vanilla. In a small bowl, whisk flour, baking powder, salt and cinnamon; whisk into the honey mixture. Fold in walnuts and dates. Pour over crust; spread evenly.

3. Bake until golden brown, 24-28 minutes. Cool completely in pan on a wire rack. Cut into bars.

1 BAR: 235 cal., 11g fat (5g sat. fat), 33mg chol., 120mg sod., 33g carb. (22g sugars, 1g fiber), 3g pro.

Carrot Spice Thumbprint Cookies

PREP: 30 MIN.
BAKE: 10 MIN./BATCH + COOLING
MAKES: 5 DOZEN

Carrot cake is a family favorite, and these delicious cookies with shredded carrots, dried cranberries, toasted walnuts, cinnamon and cloves taste very similar. They're even topped with a rich cream cheese frosting. With each cookie it feels as if you're eating a piece of carrot cake, but no fork is needed!
—Susan Bickta, Kutztown, PA

- 1 **cup margarine, softened**
- 1 **cup sugar**
- ½ **cup packed brown sugar**
- 2 **large eggs, room temperature**
- 2 **tsp. vanilla extract**
- 3 **cups all-purpose flour**
- 1½ **tsp. ground cinnamon**
- 1 **tsp. baking powder**
- ¾ **tsp. salt**
- ½ **tsp. baking soda**
- ⅛ **tsp. ground cloves**
- 1½ **cups shredded carrots**
- ⅔ **cup chopped walnuts, toasted**
- ½ **cup dried cranberries**

FROSTING
- ½ **cup butter, softened**
- 4 **oz. cream cheese, softened**
- 2 **cups confectioners' sugar**
- 1 **tsp. vanilla extract**
  Additional confectioners' sugar

1. Preheat oven to 375°. In a large bowl, cream together margarine and sugars until light and fluffy, 5-7 minutes. Beat in eggs and vanilla. In another bowl, whisk flour, cinnamon, baking powder, salt, baking soda and cloves; gradually beat into the creamed mixture. Stir in carrots, walnuts and cranberries.

2. Drop dough by rounded tablespoonfuls 2 in. apart onto parchment-lined baking sheets. Press a deep indentation in the center of each with the back of a ½-tsp. measuring spoon.

3. Bake until the edges begin to brown, 10-12 minutes. Reshape indentations as needed. Cool on pans 5 minutes before removing to wire racks to cool completely.

4. For frosting, beat butter, cream cheese, confectioners' sugar and vanilla until blended. To serve, fill each cookie with about 1½ tsp. frosting; sprinkle with the additional confectioners' sugar. Refrigerate any leftover filled cookies.

1 COOKIE: 167 cal., 9g fat (3g sat. fat), 17mg chol., 146mg sod., 21g carb. (14g sugars, 1g fiber), 2g pro.

Coconut Nutella Brownies

PREP: 15 MIN. • **BAKE:** 25 MIN. + COOLING
MAKES: 2 DOZEN

My parents were coming over for dinner, and I wanted to create a fast go-to brownie. My mom loves coconut and chocolate, so I thought this would be the perfect treat. And since everyone always seems to be watching what they eat, I decided to lighten them a bit, too. Win-win!
—Danielle Lee, West Palm Beach, FL

- ½ cup butter, softened
- 1⅓ cups sugar
- ½ cup Nutella
- 4 large eggs, room temperature
- 1 tsp. vanilla extract
- 1 cup all-purpose flour
- ½ cup whole wheat flour
- ⅔ cup Dutch-processed cocoa
- ½ cup flaked coconut
- ½ cup old-fashioned oats

1. Preheat oven to 350°. In a large bowl, beat butter, sugar and Nutella until blended. Add eggs, 1 at a time, beating well after each addition. Beat in vanilla. In another bowl, whisk flours and cocoa; gradually beat into butter mixture, mixing well. Fold in coconut and oats. Spread into a greased 13x9-in. baking pan.

2. Bake until a toothpick comes out with moist crumbs (do not overbake), 22-25 minutes. Cool completely in pan on a wire rack. Cut into bars.

1 BROWNIE: 186 cal., 9g fat (5g sat. fat), 41mg chol., 50mg sod., 26g carb. (16g sugars, 4g fiber), 4g pro.

Buttery Potato Chip Cookies

PREP: 15 MIN. • **BAKE:** 10 MIN./BATCH
MAKES: 4½ DOZEN

Can't decide whether to bring chips or cookies to the tailgate? These crisp and buttery cookies make plenty for the crowd and will keep people guessing the secret ingredient.
—Rachel Roberts, Lemoore, CA

- 2 **cups butter, softened**
- 1 **cup sugar**
- 1 **tsp. vanilla extract**
- 3½ **cups all-purpose flour**
- 2 **cups crushed potato chips**
- ¾ **cup chopped walnuts**

1. Preheat oven to 350°. In a large bowl, cream the butter and the sugar until light and fluffy, 5-7 minutes. Beat in vanilla. Gradually add flour to the creamed mixture and mix well. Stir in potato chips and walnuts.

2. Drop mixture by rounded tablespoonfuls 2 in. apart onto ungreased baking sheets. Bake 10-12 minutes or until lightly browned. Cool 2 minutes before removing from the pans to wire racks.

1 COOKIE: 126 cal., 9g fat (5g sat. fat), 18mg chol., 67mg sod., 11g carb. (4g sugars, 0 fiber), 1g pro.

Cinnamon Pecan Bars

PREP: 10 MIN. • **BAKE:** 25 MIN.
MAKES: 2 DOZEN

I'm a special education teacher and we bake these bars in my life skills class. It is an easy recipe that my special-needs students have fun preparing.
—Jennifer Peters, Adams Center, NY

- 1 **pkg. butter pecan cake mix (regular size)**
- ½ **cup packed dark brown sugar**
- 2 **large eggs, room temperature**
- ½ **cup butter, melted**
- ½ **cup chopped pecans**
- ½ **cup cinnamon baking chips**

1. Preheat oven to 350°. In a large bowl, combine cake mix and brown sugar. Add eggs and melted butter; mix well. Stir in pecans and baking chips. Spread into a greased 13x9 in. baking pan.
2. Bake until golden brown, 25-30 minutes. Cool in pan on a wire rack. Cut into bars.
1 BAR: 185 cal., 9g fat (4g sat. fat), 26mg chol., 190mg sod., 25g carb. (17g sugars, 0 fiber), 2g pro.

Caramel-Apple Shortbread Cookies

PREP: 35 MIN. + CHILLING
BAKE: 10 MIN./BATCH + COOLING
MAKES: 3 DOZEN

There is nothing like seeing my friends almost melt to the floor when they bite into something I made. I use an apple-shaped cookie cutter, but you can use whatever shape you like. These cookies never fail to elicit oohs and aahs.
—Amber Taylor, Lenoir City, TN

- 1 **cup butter, softened**
- ⅔ **cup confectioners' sugar**
- 2¼ **tsp. ground cinnamon, divided**
- 2 **cups all-purpose flour**
- ⅓ **cup finely chopped dried apple chips**
- 15 **caramels**
- 2 **Tbsp. heavy whipping cream**
  Additional finely chopped dried apple chips, optional

1. In a large bowl, beat softened butter, confectioners' sugar and 2 tsp. cinnamon until blended. Gradually beat in flour. Stir in ⅓ cup apple chips.
2. Divide dough in half. Shape each half into a disk; wrap and refrigerate for 1 hour or until firm enough to roll.
3. Preheat oven to 350°. On a lightly floured surface, roll each portion of dough to ¼ in. thickness. Cut with a floured 2-in. shaped cookie cutter. Place 1 in. apart on greased baking sheets.
4. Bake 9–11 minutes or until light brown. Remove from pans to wire racks to cool completely
5. In a small saucepan, melt the caramels with cream and remaining cinnamon over medium heat, stirring frequently. Drizzle over the cookies. If desired, sprinkle with additional apple chips. Let stand until set.
1 COOKIE: 110 cal., 6g fat (4g sat. fat), 15mg chol., 53mg sod., 13g carb. (6g sugars, 0 fiber), 1g pro.

Filbertines

PREP: 15 MIN. + CHILLING • **BAKE:** 15 MIN.
MAKES: 3 DOZEN

Hazelnuts, or filberts, are by far the most important nut crop grown commercially here in the Pacific Northwest. This tasty cookie showcases their goodness so well.
—Hollis Mattson, Puyallup, WA

- ½ **cup butter, softened**
- ½ **cup sugar**
- 1 **large egg, room temperature**
- 1⅓ **cups all-purpose flour**
- ½ **tsp. baking soda**
- ⅛ **tsp. ground cardamom**
- ½ **cup finely chopped hazelnuts**

1. In a small bowl, cream butter and sugar until light and fluffy, 5-7 minutes. Beat in egg. Combine the flour, baking soda and cardamom; add to creamed mixture and mix well. Cover and refrigerate for 1 hour.
2. Preheat oven to 350°. Shape dough into 1-in. balls; roll in chopped nuts. Place 2 in. apart on greased baking sheets.
3. Bake for 15-18 minutes or until lightly browned. Remove from pans to wire racks to cool.
1 COOKIE: 62 cal., 4g fat (2g sat. fat), 12mg chol., 40mg sod., 7g carb. (3g sugars, 0 fiber), 1g pro.

Julie Peterson

Blue Springs, MO

My family and I love apples any time of the year, but in fall, they are always crisp, juicy and absolutely perfect! I found a blondie recipe similar to this and did a little bit of tweaking to make it my own.

Apple-Peanut Blondies

PREP: 15 MIN.
BAKE: 25 MIN. + COOLING
MAKES: 9 SERVINGS

- 1 **cup packed brown sugar**
- ½ **cup butter, melted**
- 1 **large egg,**
  room temperature
- 1 **tsp. vanilla extract**
- 1 **cup all-purpose flour**
- ½ **tsp. baking powder**
- ¼ **tsp. baking soda**
- ¼ **tsp. salt**
- 2 **small apples**
  (about 9 oz.),
  peeled and sliced
- ½ **cup chopped**
  salted peanuts

1. Preheat oven to 350°. Beat brown sugar and butter until light and fluffy, 5-7 minutes. Add egg and vanilla; beat until smooth. In a separate bowl, whisk together flour, baking powder, baking soda and salt; gradually beat into brown sugar mixture just until combined (batter will be thick).

2. Spread all but ¼ cup batter into a greased and floured 8-in. square baking dish. Layer with apple slices; dot with remaining batter. Sprinkle with peanuts.

3. Bake 22-28 minutes or until top is golden brown and center is set. Cool on a wire rack.

1 BLONDIE: 302 cal., 15g fat (7g sat. fat), 48mg chol., 256mg sod., 39g carb. (26g sugars, 1g fiber), 4g pro.

Egg Yolk Cookies

PREP: 20 MIN. + CHILLING
BAKE: 15 MIN./BATCH + COOLING
MAKES: 6 DOZEN

*Simple and truly melt-in-your-mouth
due to the hard-boiled eggs, this is not
a thick cookie, but thin, just like the
recipe my grandma used to make.*
—Kathy Gagliardi, Holmdel, NJ

- 4 hard-boiled large egg yolks
- 1 cup unsalted butter, softened
- ½ cup sugar
- 1 Tbsp. vanilla extract
- 2½ cups all-purpose flour
  Dash salt
- 1 raw large egg yolk, lightly beaten

1. Press hard-boiled egg yolks through a
fine-mesh strainer into a bowl. In a large
bowl, cream butter and sugar until light
and fluffy, 5-7 minutes. Beat in strained
egg yolks and vanilla. In another bowl,
whisk flour and salt; gradually beat into
the creamed mixture. Divide dough in half.
Shape each into a disk; wrap. Refrigerate
30 minutes or until firm enough to roll.
2. Preheat the oven to 350°. On a lightly
floured surface, roll each portion of dough
to ¼-in. thickness. Cut with a floured 2-in.
fluted cookie cutter. Place 1 in. apart on
parchment-lined baking sheets. Brush
with beaten egg yolk.
3. Bake until cookies are lightly browned,
12-14 minutes. Remove from pans to wire
racks to cool completely.
1 COOKIE: 46 cal., 3g fat (2g sat. fat),
19mg chol., 3mg sod., 5g carb. (1g
sugars, 0 fiber), 1g pro.

Caramel Whiskey Cookies

PREP: 30 MIN. • **BAKE:** 10 MIN./BATCH
MAKES: 4 DOZEN

Yogurt replaces part of the butter in this traditional cookie, but you would never know. I get a lot of requests for these and can't make a cookie tray without them.
—Priscilla Yee, Concord, CA

- ½ **cup butter, softened**
- ½ **cup sugar**
- ½ **cup packed brown sugar**
- ¼ **cup plain Greek yogurt**
- 2 **Tbsp. canola oil**
- 1 **tsp. vanilla extract**
- 2½ **cups all-purpose flour**
- 2 **tsp. baking powder**
- 1 **tsp. baking soda**
- ¼ **tsp. salt**

TOPPING
- 24 **caramels**
- 1 **Tbsp. whiskey**
- 3 **oz. semisweet chocolate, melted**
- ½ **tsp. kosher salt, optional**

1. Preheat oven to 350°. In a large bowl, beat butter and sugars until crumbly. Beat in yogurt, oil and vanilla. In another bowl, whisk flour, baking powder, baking soda and salt; gradually beat into the sugar mixture.

2. Shape dough into 1-in. balls; place 2 in. apart on ungreased baking sheets. Flatten with bottom of a glass dipped in flour. Bake until the edges are light brown, 7-9 minutes. Cool on pans 2 minutes. Remove to wire racks to cool completely.

3. For the topping, in a microwave, melt caramels with whiskey; stir until smooth. Spread over the cookies. Drizzle with chocolate; sprinkle with salt if desired. Let stand until set. Store in an airtight container.

1 COOKIE: 93 cal., 4g fat (2g sat. fat), 6mg chol., 83mg sod., 14g carb. (9g sugars, 0 fiber), 1g pro.

Chocolate Chunk Walnut Blondies

PREP: 15 MIN. • **BAKE:** 30 MIN. + COOLING
MAKES: 2 DOZEN

Put these beauties out at a potluck and you'll find only crumbs on your platter when it's time to head home. Everyone will ask who made those scrumptious blondies, so take copies of the recipe!
—*Peggy Woodward, Shullsburg, WI*

- 1 cup butter, melted
- 2 cups packed brown sugar
- 2 tsp. vanilla extract
- 2 large eggs, room temperature
- 2 cups all-purpose flour
- ½ cup ground walnuts
- 1 tsp. baking powder
- ½ tsp. salt
- ⅛ tsp. baking soda
- 1 cup chopped walnuts, toasted
- 1 cup semisweet chocolate chunks

1. Preheat oven to 350°. Line a greased 13x9-in. pan with parchment, letting ends extend up sides; grease paper. Mix butter, brown sugar and vanilla until blended. Add eggs, 1 at a time; whisk to blend after each addition. In another bowl, mix flour, ground walnuts, baking powder, salt and baking soda; stir into the butter mixture. Fold in walnuts and chocolate chunks.

2. Spread batter into prepared pan. Bake until a toothpick inserted in center comes out clean, 30-35 minutes (do not overbake). Cool completely in pan on a wire rack. Lifting with parchment, remove from pan. Cut into bars. Store in an airtight container.

1 BAR: 260 cal., 15g fat (7g sat. fat), 38mg chol., 140mg sod., 32g carb. (22g sugars, 1g fiber), 3g pro.

Scottish Shortbread

PREP: 15 MIN. + CHILLING
BAKE: 20 MIN./BATCH + COOLING
MAKES: 4 DOZEN

My mother, who is of Scottish heritage, passed this recipe, along with most of my favorite recipes, on to me. When I entered it at our local fair, it won a red ribbon.
—*Rose Mabee, Selkirk, MB*

- 2 cups butter, softened
- 1 cup packed brown sugar
- 4 to 4½ cups all-purpose flour

1. Preheat oven to 325°. Cream butter and brown sugar until light and fluffy, 5-7 minutes. Add 3¾ cups flour; mix well. Turn dough onto a floured surface; knead for 5 minutes, adding enough remaining flour to form a soft dough.

2. On a sheet of parchment, roll dough to a 16x9-in. rectangle. Transfer to a baking sheet and cut into 3x1-in. strips. Prick each cookie multiple times with a fork. Refrigerate at least 30 minutes or overnight.

3. Separate cookies and place 1 in. apart on ungreased baking sheets. Bake until lightly browned, 20-25 minutes. Transfer from pan to wire racks to cool completely.

1 COOKIE: 123 cal., 8g fat (5g sat. fat), 20mg chol., 62mg sod., 12g carb. (5g sugars, 0 fiber), 1g pro.

TEST KITCHEN TIP
You can use either salted or unsalted butter for this recipe, whichever you prefer. Salted butter will make a slightly less sweet cookie.

SEE HOW IT'S DONE
Why prick shortbread with a fork? Find out the reason, plus lots of other tips—just hover your camera here!

Triple-Ginger Gingersnaps

PREP: 35 MIN. + CHILLING
BAKE: 10 MIN./BATCH
MAKES: 5 DOZEN

These crunchy treats feature fresh, ground and crystallized ginger, making them a bit more special than a traditional gingersnap. They are always a hit around the holidays.
—Jessica Follen, Waunakee, WI

⅔ cup butter, softened
1 cup packed brown sugar
¼ cup molasses
1 large egg, room temperature
2 tsp. minced fresh gingerroot
1 cup all-purpose flour
¾ cup whole wheat flour
3 tsp. ground ginger
1½ tsp. baking soda
½ tsp. fine sea salt or kosher salt
½ tsp. ground nutmeg
¼ tsp. ground cloves
3 Tbsp. finely chopped crystallized ginger
¼ cup sugar
1½ tsp. ground cinnamon

1. In a large bowl, cream butter and brown sugar until light and fluffy, 5-7 minutes. Beat in molasses, egg and fresh ginger.
2. Combine flours, ground ginger, baking soda, salt, nutmeg and cloves; gradually add to the creamed mixture and mix well. Stir in the crystallized ginger. Cover and refrigerate until easy to handle, about 1 hour.
3. Preheat oven to 350°. In a small bowl, combine sugar and cinnamon. Shape dough into 1-in. balls; roll in the sugar mixture. Place 3 in. apart on parchment-lined baking sheets.
4. Bake until set, 10-12 minutes. Cool for 2 minutes before removing from pans to wire racks. Store in an airtight container.

1 COOKIE: 54 cal., 2g fat (1g sat. fat), 8mg chol., 65mg sod., 9g carb. (6g sugars, 0 fiber), 1g pro. **DIABETIC EXCHANGES:** ½ starch, ½ fat.

Butter Pecan Cookies

PREP: 25 MIN. + CHILLING
BAKE: 10 MIN./BATCH
MAKES: 4 DOZEN

When my daughter was a teen, these cookies earned her blue ribbons from two county fairs. Then a few years ago, her own daughter took home a blue ribbon for the same cookie. Needless to say, these mouthwatering morsels are proven winners!
—Martha Thefield, Cedartown, GA

- 1¾ cups chopped pecans
- 1 Tbsp. plus 1 cup butter, softened, divided
- 1 cup packed brown sugar
- 1 large egg, separated, room temperature
- 1 tsp. vanilla extract
- 2 cups self-rising flour
- 1 cup pecan halves

1. Preheat oven to 325°. Place chopped pecans and 1 Tbsp. butter in a baking pan. Bake 5-7 minutes or until the pecans are toasted and browned, stirring frequently. Set aside to cool.

2. In a large bowl, cream brown sugar and remaining 1 cup butter until light and fluffy, 5-7 minutes. Beat in egg yolk and vanilla. Gradually add flour and mix well. Cover dough and refrigerate for 1 hour or until easy to handle.

3. Preheat oven to 375°. Roll dough into 1-in. balls, then roll balls in toasted pecans, pressing nuts into dough. Place 2 in. apart on ungreased baking sheets. Beat egg white until foamy. Dip pecan halves in egg white, then gently press 1 into each ball.

4. Bake for 10-12 minutes or until golden brown. Cool on pans for 2 minutes before removing to wire racks.

NOTE: As a substitute for each cup of self-rising flour, place 1½ tsp. baking powder and ½ tsp. salt in a measuring cup. Add all-purpose flour to measure 1 cup.
2 COOKIES: 233 cal., 18g fat (6g sat. fat), 31mg chol., 208mg sod., 18g carb. (9g sugars, 1g fiber), 3g pro.

TEST KITCHEN TIP

For extra toasty flavor, try browning your butter. Heat butter in a large saucepan over medium heat until golden brown, 7-9 minutes (do not let it burn). Pour the brown butter into a glass dish and allow it to cool in the refrigerator until solidified. Follow the rest of the recipe as directed.

Pistachio-Cherry S'more Bars

PREP: 15 MIN. • **BAKE:** 30 MIN. + COOLING
MAKES: 2 DOZEN

Surprise! These treats have all the chewy, sticky fun of a traditional s'more plus tart cherries, rich pistachios and a citrusy zing. Make a couple of batches—folks will be lining up to sneak more than one.
—Jeanne Holt, St. Paul, MN

- 1½ cups graham cracker crumbs
- 2 Tbsp. brown sugar
- ½ tsp. ground cinnamon
- ½ cup butter, melted

TOPPING
- ¾ cup dried tart cherries, chopped
- 1 cup white baking chips
- 1 cup dark chocolate chips
- 1 cup pistachios, coarsely chopped
- 1 cup sweetened condensed milk
- 1 tsp. grated orange zest
- 3 cups miniature marshmallows

1. Preheat oven to 350°. Line a 13x9-in. pan with foil, letting ends extend up sides; grease foil.

2. Mix cracker crumbs, brown sugar and cinnamon; stir in melted butter. Press onto bottom of prepared pan. Sprinkle evenly with cherries, chips and pistachios. In a small bowl, mix milk and orange zest; drizzle over top. Bake 20 minutes.

3. Top with marshmallows; bake until top is golden brown, 10-12 minutes longer. Cool in pan on a wire rack. Lifting with foil, remove from pan. Cut into bars.

1 BAR: 219 cal., 10g fat (4g sat. fat), 6mg chol., 82mg sod., 33g carb. (26g sugars, 2g fiber), 4g pro.

Candy Corn Cookies

PREP: 35 MIN. + CHILLING
BAKE: 10 MIN./BATCH
MAKES: 5 DOZEN

Get a head start on these buttery cookies by shaping and chilling the homemade dough ahead of time. When you're ready, just slice and bake the tricolor treats.
—Taste of Home *Test Kitchen*

- 1½ **cups butter, softened**
- 1½ **cups sugar**
- ½ **tsp. vanilla extract**
- 3 **cups all-purpose flour**
- 1 **tsp. baking soda**
- ½ **tsp. salt**
  Yellow and orange paste food coloring

1. Cream butter and sugar until light and fluffy, 5-7 minutes. Beat in vanilla. In another bowl, whisk together flour, baking soda and salt; gradually beat into the creamed mixture.

2. Divide dough in half. Tint 1 portion yellow. Divide the remaining dough into two-thirds and one-third portions. Color the larger portion orange; leave the smaller portion plain.

3. Shape each portion of dough into two 8-in. logs. Flatten top and push sides in at a slight angle. Place orange logs on yellow logs; push sides in at a slight angle. Top with the plain logs, forming a slightly rounded top. Wrap and refrigerate until firm, about 4 hours.

4. Preheat oven to 350°. Unwrap and cut dough into ¼-in. slices. Place 2 in. apart on ungreased baking sheets.

5. Bake until set, 10-12 minutes. Remove from pans to wire racks to cool.

1 COOKIE: 83 cal., 5g fat (3g sat. fat), 12mg chol., 77mg sod., 10g carb. (5g sugars, 0 fiber), 1g pro.

SEE HOW IT'S DONE
Learn how to color, stack and shape the dough for these cookies. Just hover your camera here.

White Chocolate-Cranberry Biscotti

PREP: 15 MIN. • **BAKE:** 35 MIN. + COOLING
MAKES: 2½ DOZEN

The original version of this recipe was handed down from my great-aunt. Through the years, my mother and I tried different flavor combinations—this one has become a favorite.
—*Brenda Keith, Talent, OR*

- ½ cup butter, softened
- 1 cup sugar
- 4 large eggs, room temperature
- 1 tsp. vanilla extract
- 3 cups all-purpose flour
- 1 Tbsp. baking powder
- ¾ cup dried cranberries
- ¾ cup vanilla or white chips

1. Preheat oven to 350°. In a large bowl, cream butter and sugar until light and fluffy, 5-7 minutes. Add eggs, 1 at a time, beating well after each addition. Beat in vanilla. Combine the flour and baking powder; gradually add to creamed mixture and mix well. Stir in cranberries and vanilla chips. Divide dough into 3 portions.

2. On ungreased baking sheets, shape each portion into a 10x2-in. rectangle. Bake until lightly browned, 20-25 minutes. Cool for 5 minutes.

3. Transfer to a cutting board; cut diagonally with a serrated knife into 1-in. slices. Place cut side down on ungreased baking sheets. Bake until golden brown, 15-20 minutes. Remove to wire racks to cool. Store in an airtight container.

2 COOKIES: 281 cal., 10g fat (6g sat. fat), 75mg chol., 167mg sod., 43g carb. (17g sugars, 1g fiber), 5g pro.

Maple Butterscotch Brownies

PREP: 15 MIN. • **BAKE:** 30 MIN. + COOLING
MAKES: 16 BROWNIES

I often make a double batch of these brownies—they go fast no matter where I take them! I've baked them for family dinners and church suppers, and I always come back with an empty pan. They are easy to make and freeze well.
—*Grace Vonhold, Rochester, NY*

- 1½ cups all-purpose flour
- 1 tsp. baking powder
- 1¼ cups packed brown sugar
- ½ cup butter, melted
- 1½ tsp. maple flavoring
- 2 large eggs, room temperature
- 1 cup chopped walnuts
  Confectioners' sugar, optional

1. Preheat oven to 350°. Whisk together flour and baking powder.

2. In a large bowl, mix brown sugar, melted butter and maple flavoring. Beat in eggs, 1 at a time, mixing well after each addition. Stir in the flour mixture and walnuts. Spread into a greased 9-in. square baking pan.

3. Bake until a toothpick inserted in the center comes out clean, 27-32 minutes. Cool completely in pan on a wire rack. If desired, dust with confectioners' sugar. Cut into bars.

1 BROWNIE: 216 cal., 11g fat (4g sat. fat), 42mg chol., 98mg sod., 27g carb. (17g sugars, 1g fiber), 4g pro.

Big Soft Ginger Cookies

PREP: 20 MIN. • **BAKE:** 10 MIN./BATCH
MAKES: 2½ DOZEN

These nicely spiced, soft gingerbread cookies are perfect for folks who like the flavor of ginger but don't care for crunchy gingersnaps.
—Barbara Gray, Boise, ID

¾ cup butter, softened
1 cup sugar
1 large egg, room temperature
¼ cup molasses
2¼ cups all-purpose flour
2 tsp. ground ginger
1 tsp. baking soda
¾ tsp. ground cinnamon
½ tsp. ground cloves
¼ tsp. salt
   Additional sugar

1. Preheat oven to 350°. In a large bowl, cream butter and sugar until light and fluffy, 5-7 minutes. Beat in the egg and molasses. Combine the flour, ginger, baking soda, cinnamon, cloves and salt; gradually add to the creamed mixture and mix well.

2. Roll dough into 1½-in. balls, then roll in sugar. Place balls 2 in. apart on ungreased baking sheets. Bake until puffy and lightly browned, 10-12 minutes. Remove to wire racks to cool.

1 COOKIE: 111 cal., 5g fat (3g sat. fat), 19mg chol., 98mg sod., 16g carb. (8g sugars, 0 fiber), 1g pro.

TEST KITCHEN TIP

The difference between these soft ginger cookies and the crispy kind has to do with the leavening agent (think yeast, baking soda or baking powder). If you leave out the baking soda in this recipe, the cookies will come out hard and crisp.

Fruit-Filled Spritz Cookies

PREP: 30 MIN.
BAKE: 15 MIN./BATCH + COOLING
MAKES: ABOUT 7½ DOZEN

From the first time I baked these, they've been a divine success. Old-fashioned and attractive, they make a perfect pastry— for the holidays or any time at all.
—Ingeborg Keith, Newark, DE

- 1½ **cups chopped dates**
- 1 **cup water**
- ½ **cup sugar**
- 2 **tsp. orange juice**
- 2 **tsp. grated orange zest**
- 1 **cup maraschino cherries, chopped**
- ½ **cup sweetened shredded coconut**
- ½ **cup ground nuts**

DOUGH

- 1 **cup butter, softened**
- 1 **cup sugar**
- ½ **cup packed brown sugar**
- 3 **large eggs, room temperature**
- ½ **tsp. almond extract**
- ½ **tsp. vanilla extract**
- 4 **cups all-purpose flour**
- ½ **tsp. baking soda**
- ½ **tsp. salt**
  Confectioners' sugar, optional

1. Preheat oven to 375°. In a small saucepan, combine first 5 ingredients; bring to a boil, stirring constantly. Reduce heat; cook and stir for 8 minutes or until thickened. Cool completely. Stir in the cherries, coconut and nuts; set aside.

2. In a large bowl, cream butter and sugars until light and fluffy, 5-7 minutes. Beat in eggs and extracts. Combine the flour, baking soda and salt; gradually add to creamed mixture and mix well.

3. Using a cookie press fitted with a bar disk, press a 12-in.-long strip of dough onto an ungreased baking sheet. Spread fruit filling over dough. Press another strip over the filling. Cut into 1-in. pieces (there is no need to separate the pieces). Repeat with remaining dough and filling.

4. Bake for 12-15 minutes or until edges are golden. Recut into pieces if necessary. Remove from pan to wire racks to cool completely. Dust with confectioners' sugar if desired.

1 COOKIE: 77 cal., 3g fat (2g sat. fat), 12mg chol., 45mg sod., 12g carb. (7g sugars, 0 fiber), 1g pro.

Maple & Bacon Bars

PREP: 15 MIN. • **BAKE:** 20 MIN. + COOLING
MAKES: 9 SERVINGS

This is the perfect treat when you're craving both salty and sweet. The aroma will tantalize you while the bars are baking.
—Taste of Home *Test Kitchen*

- ½ cup butter, softened
- ¾ cup packed brown sugar
- 2 large eggs, room temperature
- 1 Tbsp. 2% milk
- 1 tsp. vanilla extract
- ¾ cup all-purpose flour
- ¾ cup quick-cooking oats
- ½ tsp. baking powder
- ¼ tsp. salt
- 4 bacon strips, cooked and crumbled
- ⅓ cup chopped pecans, toasted

MAPLE GLAZE

- 1 cup confectioners' sugar
- 2 Tbsp. maple syrup
- ½ to 1 tsp. maple flavoring, optional

1. Preheat oven to 350°. In a large bowl, cream butter and brown sugar until light and fluffy, 5-7 minutes. Beat in eggs, milk and vanilla. Combine flour, oats, baking powder and salt; gradually add to creamed mixture. Fold in bacon and pecans.

2. Spread into a greased 9-in. square baking pan. Bake until a toothpick inserted in the center comes out clean, 20-25 minutes. Cool on a wire rack. For glaze, in a small bowl, mix confectioners' sugar, syrup and, if desired, maple flavoring. Drizzle over bars; let stand until set.

1 BAR: 351 cal., 16g fat (8g sat. fat), 72mg chol., 261mg sod., 48g carb. (34g sugars, 1g fiber), 5g pro.

Warren's Oatmeal Jam Squares

PREP: 20 MIN. • **BAKE:** 25 MIN. + COOLING
MAKES: 16 SQUARES

At 102, I still love to bake. I make these bars in my toaster oven for my fellow residents at our assisted living home.
—Warren Patrick, Townshend, VT

- 1¼ **cups quick-cooking oats**
- 1¼ **cups all-purpose flour**
- ½ **cup sugar**
- ½ **tsp. baking soda**
- ¼ **tsp. salt**
- ¾ **cup butter, melted**
- 2 **tsp. vanilla extract**
- 1 **jar (10 oz.) seedless raspberry jam or jam of your choice**
- 4 **whole graham crackers, crushed**

1. Preheat oven to 350°. In a large bowl, mix the first 5 ingredients. In a small bowl, mix melted butter and vanilla; add to the oat mixture, stirring until crumbly.

2. Reserve 1 cup oat mixture; press remaining mixture onto bottom of a greased 9-in. square baking pan. Spread jam over top to within ½ in. of edges. Add crushed graham crackers to the reserved oat mixture; sprinkle over jam.

3. Bake 25-30 minutes or until the edges are golden brown. Cool in pan on a wire rack. Cut into squares.

1 SQUARE: 220 cal., 9g fat (6g sat. fat), 23mg chol., 161mg sod., 33g carb. (18g sugars, 1g fiber), 2g pro.

Banana Nut Brownies

PREP: 10 MIN. • **BAKE:** 40 MIN. + COOLING
MAKES: 16 SERVINGS

*Any time there are ripe bananas around
our house, it's banana brownies time!
People are always surprised to learn there
are bananas in the brownies. This recipe
comes from my Grandma Schlientz.*
—Christine Mol, Grand Rapids, MI

 ½ cup butter, melted, cooled
  1 cup sugar
  3 Tbsp. baking cocoa
  2 large eggs, room temperature,
    lightly beaten
  1 Tbsp. 2% milk
  1 tsp. vanilla extract
 ½ cup all-purpose flour
  1 tsp. baking powder
 ¼ tsp. salt
  1 cup mashed ripe bananas
    (2½ to 3 medium)
 ½ cup chopped walnuts
    Confectioners' sugar, optional

1. Preheat oven to 350°. Combine butter,
sugar and cocoa. Stir in eggs, milk and
vanilla. Blend in flour, baking powder and
salt. Stir in bananas and nuts.
2. Pour into a greased 9-in. square baking
pan. Bake until a toothpick comes out with
moist crumbs, 40-45 minutes. Cool on a
wire rack. Just before serving, dust with
confectioners' sugar if desired.
1 BROWNIE: 163 cal., 9g fat (4g sat. fat),
42mg chol., 128mg sod., 20g carb. (15g
sugars, 1g fiber), 3g pro.

Honey-Peanut Butter Cookies

PREP: 15 MIN. • **BAKE:** 10 MIN./BATCH
MAKES: 5 DOZEN

*It's not unusual for my husband to request
these cookies by name. You'll love 'em.*
—Lucile Proctor, Panguitch, UT

 ½ cup shortening
  1 cup creamy peanut butter
  1 cup honey
  2 large eggs, room temperature,
    lightly beaten
  3 cups all-purpose flour
  1 cup sugar
 1½ tsp. baking soda
  1 tsp. baking powder
 ½ tsp. salt

1. Preheat oven to 350°. Mix shortening,
peanut butter and honey. Add eggs; mix
well. Combine flour, sugar, baking soda,
baking powder and salt; add to peanut
butter mixture and mix well.
2. Roll into 1-1½-in. balls; place on
ungreased baking sheets. Flatten with
a fork dipped in flour. Bake 8-10 minutes
or until set. Remove to wire racks to cool.
1 COOKIE: 95 cal., 4g fat (1g sat. fat),
6mg chol., 80mg sod., 14g carb. (8g
sugars, 0 fiber), 2g pro.

Almond Chocolate Biscotti

PREP: 20 MIN. • **BAKE:** 40 MIN. + COOLING
MAKES: 3½ DOZEN

These white chocolate-drizzled cookies are a cinch to make, so I'm always happy to whip up a batch. This is good because my neighbors always look forward to them!
—Ginger Chatfield, Muscatine, IA

- 1 pkg. chocolate cake mix (regular size)
- 1 cup all-purpose flour
- ½ cup butter, melted
- 2 large eggs, room temperature
- ¼ cup chocolate syrup
- 1 tsp. vanilla extract
- ½ tsp. almond extract
- ½ cup slivered almonds
- ½ cup miniature semisweet chocolate chips
- 1 cup white baking chips
- 1 Tbsp. shortening

1. Preheat oven to 350°. In a large bowl, beat cake mix, flour, butter, eggs, chocolate syrup and extracts until well blended. Stir in almonds and chocolate chips.

2. Divide dough in half. On ungreased baking sheets, shape each portion into a 12x2-in. log. Bake 30-35 minutes or until firm to the touch. Carefully remove to wire racks; cool 20 minutes.

3. Transfer baked logs to a cutting board. Using a serrated knife, cut diagonally into ½-in. slices. Place on ungreased baking sheets, cut side down. Bake until firm, 10-15 minutes longer. Remove from pans to wire racks to cool completely.

4. In a microwave, melt baking chips and shortening; stir until smooth. Drizzle over biscotti; let stand until set. Store between pieces of waxed paper in airtight containers.

FREEZE OPTION: Freeze undrizzled cookies in freezer containers. To use, thaw in covered containers. Drizzle with baking chip mixture as directed.

1 COOKIE: 126 cal., 6g fat (3g sat. fat), 16mg chol., 117mg sod., 17g carb. (10g sugars, 1g fiber), 2g pro.

Butterscotch Sandwich Cookies

PREP: 45 MIN. + CHILLING
BAKE: 5 MIN./BATCH + COOLING
MAKES: ABOUT 6½ DOZEN

Butterscotch lovers will go crazy for these cookie-jar classics. The brickle toffee bits in the filling are a deliciously fun surprise.
—Taste of Home *Test Kitchen*

- 3 cups butter, softened
- 1½ cups packed brown sugar
- 6 cups all-purpose flour
  Sugar

FILLING
- 3 cups packed brown sugar
- 1 cup 2% milk
- ⅓ cup butter, cubed
- ¼ tsp. salt
- 1½ cups confectioners' sugar
- 3 Tbsp. heavy whipping cream
- 3 tsp. vanilla extract
- ¾ cup brickle toffee bits
- ⅓ cup semisweet chocolate, melted, optional

1. In a large bowl, cream butter and brown sugar until light and fluffy, 5-7 minutes. Gradually beat in flour. Refrigerate at least 1 hour.

2. Preheat oven to 375°. Shape dough into 1-in. balls; place 2 in. apart on ungreased baking sheets. Flatten cookies with the bottom of a glass dipped in sugar. Bake 5-7 minutes or until set. Remove from pans to wire racks to cool completely.

3. For filling, in a large saucepan, combine brown sugar, milk, butter and salt. Bring to a boil over medium heat, stirring constantly. Cook and stir until a candy thermometer reads 234° (soft-ball stage). Remove from heat; cool to room temperature.

4. Transfer mixture to a large bowl; beat in confectioners' sugar, cream and vanilla until mixture reaches spreading consistency. Stir in toffee bits. Carefully spread on bottoms of half the cookies; cover with remaining cookies. If desired, drizzle with melted chocolate.

FREEZE OPTION: Freeze cookies, before filling, in freezer containers. To use, thaw cookies in covered containers. Fill as directed.

1 SANDWICH COOKIE: 159 cal., 8g fat (5g sat. fat), 20mg chol., 78mg sod., 21g carb. (14g sugars, 0 fiber), 1g pro.

White Chocolate Chip Hazelnut Cookies

PREP: 15 MIN. • **BAKE:** 10 MIN./BATCH
MAKES: 3 DOZEN

This is a cookie you will want to make again and again. I like to take it to church get-togethers and family reunions. It's very delicious—crispy on the outside and chewy on the inside.
—Denise DeJong, Pittsburgh, PA

- 1¼ **cups whole hazelnuts, toasted, divided**
- 9 **Tbsp. butter, softened, divided**
- ½ **cup sugar**
- ½ **cup packed brown sugar**
- 1 **large egg, room temperature**
- 1 **tsp. vanilla extract**
- 1½ **cups all-purpose flour**
- ½ **tsp. baking soda**
- ½ **tsp. salt**
- 1 **cup white baking chips**

1. Preheat oven to 350°. Coarsely chop ½ cup hazelnuts; set aside. Melt 2 Tbsp. butter. In a food processor, combine the melted butter and remaining ¾ cup hazelnuts. Cover and process until the mixture forms a crumbly paste; set aside.

2. In a bowl, cream the remaining 7 Tbsp. butter. Beat in the sugars. Add egg and vanilla; beat until light and fluffy, about 5 minutes. Beat in ground hazelnut mixture until blended. Combine the flour, baking soda and salt; add to batter and mix just until combined. Stir in chips and reserved chopped hazelnuts.

3. Drop dough by rounded tablespoonfuls 2 in. apart onto greased baking sheets. Bake until lightly browned, 10-12 minutes. Remove from pans to wire racks to cool.

1 COOKIE: 132 cal., 8g fat (3g sat. fat), 14mg chol., 80mg sod., 14g carb. (9g sugars, 1g fiber), 2g pro.

Cranberry Bog Bars

PREP: 25 MIN. • **BAKE:** 25 MIN.
MAKES: 2 DOZEN

Sweet and chewy, these fun bars combine the flavors of oats, cranberries, brown sugar and pecans. I like to sprinkle the squares with confectioners' sugar before serving them.
—Sally Wakefield, Gans, PA

1¼ **cups butter, softened, divided**
1½ **cups packed brown sugar, divided**
3½ **cups old-fashioned oats, divided**
 1 **cup all-purpose flour**
 1 **can (14 oz.) whole-berry cranberry sauce**
½ **cup finely chopped pecans**

1. Preheat oven to 375°. In a large bowl, cream 1 cup butter and 1 cup brown sugar until light and fluffy, 5-7 minutes.
2. Combine 2½ cups oats and the flour. Gradually add to the creamed mixture until crumbly. Press into a greased 13x9-in. baking pan. Spread with cranberry sauce.
3. In a microwave-safe bowl, melt remaining ¼ cup butter; stir in the pecans and remaining ½ cup brown sugar and 1 cup oats. Sprinkle over cranberry sauce. Bake until lightly browned, 25-30 minutes. Cool in pan on a wire rack. Cut into bars.
1 BAR: 239 cal., 12g fat (6g sat. fat), 25mg chol., 88mg sod., 32g carb. (18g sugars, 2g fiber), 2g pro.

Chocolate-Stuffed Peanut Butter Skillet Cookie

PREP: 20 MIN. • **BAKE:** 35 MIN. + COOLING
MAKES: 12 SERVINGS

A surprise chocolate filling makes this dessert extra delicious! Serve warm from the oven with a scoop of your favorite ice cream.
—Andrea Price, Grafton, WI

- 1 cup creamy peanut butter
- ¾ cup butter, softened
- 1¼ cups plus 1 Tbsp. sugar, divided
- 1 large egg, room temperature
- 1 tsp. vanilla extract
- 1½ cups all-purpose flour
- ½ tsp. baking soda
- ½ tsp. salt
- 1 cup milk chocolate chips
  Vanilla ice cream, optional

1. Preheat oven to 350°. In a large bowl, cream peanut butter, butter and 1¼ cups sugar until blended. Beat in the egg and vanilla. In another bowl, whisk flour, baking soda and salt; gradually beat into the creamed mixture.

2. Press half the dough into a well-greased 10-in. cast-iron or other ovenproof skillet. Sprinkle chocolate chips over dough in skillet to within ½ in. of edges. Drop the remaining dough over chocolate chips; spread until even. Sprinkle the remaining 1 Tbsp. sugar over top.

3. Bake until a toothpick inserted in center comes out with moist crumbs, 35-40 minutes. Cool completely on a wire rack. If desired, serve with vanilla ice cream.

1 PIECE: 453 cal., 27g fat (12g sat. fat), 49mg chol., 351mg sod., 47g carb. (32g sugars, 2g fiber), 8g pro.

Ultimate Double Chocolate Brownies

PREP: 15 MIN. • **BAKE:** 35 MIN.
MAKES: 3 DOZEN

We live in the city—but within just a block of our house, we can see cattle grazing in a grassy green pasture. It's a sight I never tire of. As someone who grew up in the country, I love home-style recipes like these brownies.
—Carol Prewett, Cheyenne, WY

- ¾ cup baking cocoa
- ½ tsp. baking soda
- ⅔ cup butter, melted, divided
- ½ cup boiling water
- 2 cups sugar
- 2 large eggs, room temperature
- 1⅓ cups all-purpose flour
- 1 tsp. vanilla extract
- ¼ tsp. salt
- ½ cup coarsely chopped pecans
- 2 cups (12 oz.) semisweet chocolate chunks

1. Preheat oven to 350°. In a large bowl, combine cocoa and baking soda; blend in ⅓ cup melted butter. Add boiling water; stir until well blended. Stir in sugar, eggs and the remaining ⅓ cup melted butter. Add flour, vanilla and salt. Stir in pecans and chocolate chunks.

2. Pour into a greased 13x9-in. baking pan. Bake 35-40 minutes or until brownies begin to pull away from sides of pan. Cool.

1 BROWNIE: 159 cal., 8g fat (4g sat. fat), 21mg chol., 73mg sod., 22g carb. (17g sugars, 1g fiber), 2g pro.

Grandma's Pecan Rum Bars

PREP: 20 MIN. • **BAKE:** 1 HOUR + COOLING
MAKES: 2 DOZEN

*My grandmother handed down the recipe
for these gooey bars, which we all love.
The candied cherries are a must—don't
be tempted to skip them!*
—Deborah Pennington, Falkville, AL

4 **cups chopped pecans, divided**
1 **cup butter, softened**
2¼ **cups packed brown sugar**
4 **large eggs, room temperature**
2 **Tbsp. vanilla extract**
1 **cup all-purpose flour**
2¼ **cups red candied cherries**
1½ **cups chopped candied pineapple**
½ **cup chopped candied citron**
⅓ **cup rum**

1. Preheat oven to 350°. Sprinkle 3 cups
pecans over a greased 15x10x1-in. baking
pan; set aside.

2. In a large bowl, cream butter and brown
sugar until light and fluffy, 5-7 minutes.
Add eggs, 1 at a time, beating well after
each addition. Beat in vanilla. Gradually
add flour to creamed mixture, beating well.

3. Spread the batter into prepared pan.
Combine candied fruit and the remaining
1 cup pecans. Spread fruit and pecans
evenly over creamed mixture; press gently
to help mixtures adhere.

4. Bake until a toothpick inserted in center
comes out clean, about 1 hour. Sprinkle
rum over the top; cool completely in pan
on a wire rack. Cut into bars. Store in an
airtight container.

1 BAR: 401 cal., 22g fat (6g sat. fat), 51mg
chol., 123mg sod., 49g carb. (40g sugars,
2g fiber), 4g pro.

TEST KITCHEN TIP

This rich treat tastes like a cross between
rum cake, fruitcake and pecan pie. For
an even more decadent twist, serve the
bars over a swirl of creme anglaise or
vanilla sauce.

Baklava Thumbprint Cookies

PREP: 30 MIN. + CHILLING
BAKE: 15 MIN./BATCH • **MAKES:** 2 DOZEN

The topping on my sister-in-law's peach cobbler was so delicious that I asked for the recipe; then I used it to top a cookie I developed with the flavors of baklava. My adult son tried one and immediately ate two more—which is unusual for him! It's a good recipe to mix up the night before and bake fresh the next day for company.
—Sharon Eshelman, Harrington, DE

- 1 **cup sugar**
- ½ **cup butter, softened**
- 2 **large eggs, room temperature**
- 1 **tsp. almond extract**
- 1 **tsp. vanilla extract**
- 2¼ **cups all-purpose flour**
- 1 **tsp. baking powder**
- ½ **tsp. salt**

TOPPING
- 3 **Tbsp. sugar**
- 2 **tsp. ground cinnamon**
- ½ **cup honey**
- ¾ **cup chopped walnuts**

1. In a large bowl, cream sugar and butter until blended. Beat in eggs, 1 at a time, and extracts. In another bowl, whisk flour, baking powder and salt; gradually beat into the creamed mixture. Wrap dough; refrigerate until firm enough to form into balls, about 30 minutes.

2. Preheat oven to 375°. For topping, combine sugar and cinnamon; set aside. Shape dough into 1-in. balls; refrigerate again if dough becomes too warm. Place balls 2½ in. apart on parchment-lined baking sheets. Bake 8 minutes. Press a deep indentation in the center of each cookie with the back of a rounded teaspoon. Fill each indentation with honey and walnuts; sprinkle with cinnamon sugar. Return to oven and bake until edges begin to brown, 7-9 minutes longer. Cool on pans for 1 minute before removing to wire racks to cool. Store in an airtight container.

1 COOKIE: 168 cal., 7g fat (3g sat. fat), 26mg chol., 106mg sod., 25g carb. (16g sugars, 1g fiber), 2g pro.

PIES & TARTS

ALL DESSERTS ARE GRAND, BUT THERE'S JUST
SOMETHING ABOUT PIE! THESE WINNERS SHOW OFF
LATE-SUMMER FRUIT AND HARVEST FLAVORS.

NANTUCKET CRANBERRY
TARTS, P. 165

Bread Pudding Pie

PREP: 15 MIN. • **BAKE:** 55 MIN. + CHILLING
MAKES: 8 SERVINGS

This unique dessert is a bread pudding-pie combo. It was created by my paternal grandmother's family. They had a farm and made their own bread, which made this a low-cost dessert.
—Kelly Barnes, Lexington, IN

Dough for single-crust pie (left)
- 1 **cup cubed bread**
- 2 **large eggs, room temperature**
- 2 **cups 2% milk**
- ¾ **cup sugar**
- ½ **tsp. vanilla extract**
- ¼ **tsp. ground nutmeg**
- 2 **tsp. butter**

1. Preheat oven to 425°. On a lightly floured surface, roll dough to a ⅛-in.-thick circle; transfer to a 9-in. pie plate. Trim crust to ½ in. beyond rim of plate; flute edge.
2. Arrange bread in bottom of pie crust. In a large bowl, whisk eggs, milk, sugar and vanilla; pour over bread. Sprinkle with nutmeg and dot with butter. Bake 10 minutes.
3. Reduce oven setting to 350°. Bake until a knife inserted in the center comes out clean, 45-50 minutes longer. Cover edge loosely with foil during the last 15 minutes if needed to prevent overbrowning. Remove foil. Cool on a wire rack 1 hour. Refrigerate for at least 3 hours before serving.
1 PIECE: 314 cal., 15g fat (9g sat. fat), 84mg chol., 230mg sod., 39g carb. (22g sugars, 1g fiber), 6g pro.

Classic Butter Pie Crust

PREP: 10 MIN. + CHILLING
MAKES: CRUST FOR ONE 9-IN. PIE

This all-butter dough makes a flavorful, flaky pie crust that's easy to handle and bakes up golden brown and beautiful. It's just like Mom's, only better! You can use this for any recipe that calls for dough for a single- or double-crust pie—or use your own favorite crust recipe.
—Taste of Home *Test Kitchen*

INGREDIENTS FOR SINGLE-CRUST PIE
- 1¼ **cups all-purpose flour**
- ¼ **tsp. salt**
- ½ **cup cold butter, cubed**
- 3 **to 4 Tbsp. ice water**

INGREDIENTS FOR DOUBLE-CRUST PIE
- 2½ **cups all-purpose flour**
- ½ **tsp. salt**
- 1 **cup cold butter, cubed**
- ⅓ **to ⅔ cup ice water**

1. Combine flour and salt; cut in butter until crumbly. Gradually add ice water, tossing with a fork until the dough holds together when pressed.
2. For a single-crust pie, shape into a disk; wrap and refrigerate 1 hour or overnight. For a double-crust pie, divide dough in half, with 1 piece slightly larger than the other. Shape into 2 disks. Wrap individually and refrigerate 1 hour or overnight.
3. Roll out dough, fill pies, and bake according to specific pie recipe directions.
1 PIECE SINGLE-CRUST DOUGH: 173 cal., 12g fat (7g sat. fat), 31mg chol., 165mg sod., 15g carb. (0 sugars, 1g fiber), 2g pro.

Cranberry Apple Sheet Pie

PREP: 45 MIN. +CHILLING
BAKE: 45 MIN. + COOLING
MAKES: 24 SERVINGS

My husband loves pie, so I made this one. I even bend the rules and let the grandkids have it for breakfast!
—*Brenda R Smith, Curran, MI*

Dough for 2 double-crust pies (p. 154)
2¼ cups sugar
⅓ cup all-purpose flour
7 medium tart apples, peeled and sliced (about 8 cups)
3 cups fresh or frozen cranberries
2 tsp. grated orange zest
1½ tsp. ground nutmeg
1½ tsp. ground cinnamon
6 cups frozen or fresh raspberries
Optional: Egg wash, additional sugar or coarse sugar, and whipped cream

1. Divide dough into 2 portions so that 1 is slightly larger; wrap and refrigerate 1 hour or overnight.

2. Roll out the larger portion of dough and place in a 15x10x1-in. baking pan (instructions at right); chill crust while preparing the filling.

3. In a Dutch oven, mix sugar and flour; stir in apples, cranberries, orange zest and spices. Bring to a boil over medium-high heat. Reduce heat; simmer, uncovered, 10-12 minutes or until apples are tender and juices are thickened, stirring occasionally. Remove from heat; stir in raspberries. Cool completely; add to prepared crust.

4. On a well-floured surface, roll remaining dough into a ⅛-in.-thick rectangle; cut into 1½-in.-wide strips. Arrange strips over the filling, sealing the ends to bottom crust. If desired, brush crust with egg wash; sprinkle with additional sugar or coarse sugar.

5. Bake at 375° on lowest oven rack for 45-50 minutes or until the crust is golden brown and the filling is bubbly. Set on a wire rack to cool. If desired, serve with whipped cream.

1 PIECE: 352 cal., 16g fat (10g sat. fat), 40mg chol., 207mg sod., 51g carb. (25g sugars, 4g fiber), 4g pro.

HOW-TO
MAKE A SHEET-PAN PIE CRUST

1. Roll out the larger portion of dough between 2 pieces of waxed paper into an 18x13-in rectangle.

2. Remove the top sheet of waxed paper; place the baking pan upside down over the crust. Check the size; if necessary, roll the crust out farther so that it is larger than the pan on all sides.

3. Lifting with the waxed paper, carefully invert the pan and the crust so that the crust settles into the pan. Remove waxed paper.

4. Press crust onto the bottom and up the sides of pan. Fold edge inward and shape as desired.

5. Let the filling cool completely before adding it to the crust; this keeps the butter from melting.

6. Chilling the dough gives the gluten time to relax, the dough easier to work and the crust more tender. Remove the dough from the refrigerator a few minutes before rolling, to let it soften.

7. If you don't have a pastry cutter, a pizza cutter also works well for cutting strips.

Shoofly Chocolate Pie

PREP: 20 MIN. • **BAKE:** 45 MIN. + COOLING
MAKES: 8 SERVINGS

*If you like traditional shoofly pie, I think
the chocolate version is even better!
I sometimes serve it topped with vanilla
ice cream, but it's just as good on its own.*
—Gwen Brounce Widdowson,
Fleetwood, PA

　　　 Dough for single-crust pie (p. 154)
½　cup semisweet chocolate chips
1½　cups all-purpose flour
½　cup packed brown sugar
3　Tbsp. butter-flavored shortening
1　tsp. baking soda
1½　cups water
1　large egg, room temperature,
　　　 lightly beaten
1　cup molasses

1. Preheat oven to 350°. Roll out dough to
fit a 9-in. deep-dish pie plate or cast-iron
skillet. Trim to ½ in. beyond rim of plate;
flute edge. Sprinkle chocolate chips into
crust; set aside.
2. In a large bowl, combine flour and brown
sugar; cut in shortening until crumbly. Set
aside 1 cup for topping. Add baking soda,
water, egg and molasses to the remaining
crumb mixture and mix well. Pour over
chocolate chips. Sprinkle with the reserved
crumb mixture.
3. Bake until a knife inserted in the center
comes out clean, 45-55 minutes. Let stand
on a wire rack for 15 minutes before
cutting. Serve warm.
1 PIECE: 526 cal., 20g fat (10g sat. fat),
53mg chol., 341mg sod., 83g carb. (49g
sugars, 2g fiber), 6g pro.

Apricot-Almond Tartlets

PREP: 25 MIN. • **BAKE:** 20 MIN. + COOLING
MAKES: 2 DOZEN

*These delicate, buttery tarts melt in your mouth.
With their jeweled apricot tops, they make a
pretty presentation on a cookie tray or nestled
next to a cup of coffee.*
—*Julie Dunsworth, Oviedo, FL*

  1   **cup all-purpose flour**
  3   **Tbsp. confectioners' sugar**
  ⅓   **cup cold butter**
  1   **large egg yolk**
  1   **to 2 Tbsp. water**

FILLING
  ½   **cup almond paste**
  ¼   **cup butter, softened**
  1   **large egg white**
  ¼   **tsp. almond extract**
  ½   **cup apricot preserves**

1. Preheat oven to 350°. In a large bowl, combine flour and confectioners' sugar; cut in butter until the mixture resembles coarse crumbs. Add egg yolk and water; stir until dough forms a ball. Roll into twenty-four 1-in. balls. Press onto the bottoms and up the sides of greased miniature muffin cups.

2. In a small bowl, beat almond paste and butter until blended; beat in egg white and almond extract. Spoon into the tart shells, about 2 tsp. in each.

3. Bake until golden brown, 20-25 minutes. Cool for 5 minutes before removing from pans to wire racks. Top with apricot preserves.

1 TARTLET: 103 cal., 6g fat (3g sat. fat), 20mg chol., 37mg sod., 12g carb. (5g sugars, 0 fiber), 1g pro.

Lime Divine Tarts

PREP: 30 MIN. + CHILLING
BAKE: 15 MIN. + COOLING • **MAKES:** 2 DOZEN

Tart, but not too tart, sweet but not too sweet—these cute cups filled with luscious lime curd are impressive but easy to make.
—Ann Yri, Lewisville, TX

- 2 **large eggs, room temperature**
- 1 **large egg yolk, room temperature**
- ½ **cup sugar**
- ¼ **cup lime juice**
- 1 **tsp. grated lime zest**
- ¼ **cup unsalted butter, cubed**

TART SHELLS
- ½ **cup unsalted butter, softened**
- 3 **oz. cream cheese, softened**
- 1 **cup all-purpose flour**
  Optional: Grated lime zest and grated white chocolate

1. For curd, in a small heavy saucepan over medium heat, whisk eggs, egg yolk, sugar, lime juice and zest until blended. Add butter; cook, whisking constantly, until mixture is thickened and coats the back of a spoon. Transfer to a small bowl; cool. Cover and refrigerate until chilled.

2. In a small bowl, cream butter and cream cheese until smooth. Gradually add flour; mix well. Cover and refrigerate 1 hour or until easy to handle.

3. Preheat oven to 375°. Shape dough into 1-in. balls; press onto the bottom and up sides of 24 ungreased miniature muffin cups. Prick bottoms with a fork. Bake until golden brown, 13-15 minutes. Cool 5 minutes before removing from pans to wire racks to cool completely.

4. Fill shells with lime curd. Garnish as desired. Refrigerate leftovers.

1 TART: 107 cal., 8g fat (5g sat. fat), 45mg chol., 18mg sod., 9g carb. (4g sugars, 0 fiber), 2g pro.

Walnut-Date Pumpkin Pie

PREP: 10 MIN. • **BAKE:** 1 HOUR + COOLING
MAKES: 8 SERVINGS

I'm always looking for a little something extra to enhance a favorite recipe. In this case, crunchy walnuts and chewy dates take traditional pumpkin pie to a new level.
—Edna Hoffman, Hebron, IN

- 1 **cup all-purpose flour**
- ½ **cup cold butter, cubed**
- 1 **cup packed light brown sugar, divided**
- 2 **large eggs, room temperature**
- 1 **tsp. ground cinnamon**
- ¼ **tsp. ground cloves**
- 1 **cup canned pumpkin**
- 1 **cup evaporated milk**
- ½ **cup finely chopped dates**
- ¼ **cup chopped walnuts, toasted**
  Whipped cream

1. Preheat oven to 350°. In a food processor, combine the flour, butter and ⅓ cup brown sugar. Cover and pulse until the mixture resembles coarse crumbs. Press onto the bottom and up the sides of a 9-in. pie plate. Bake for 5 minutes; cool on a wire rack.

2. In a bowl, beat the eggs, cinnamon, cloves and remaining ⅔ cup brown sugar. Beat in the pumpkin and milk. Stir in the dates and walnuts. Pour into the crust. Cover edge loosely with foil.

3. Bake for 55-60 minutes or until a knife inserted in the center comes out clean. Cool for 2 hours on a wire rack. Refrigerate until serving. Serve with whipped cream. Refrigerate leftovers.

1 PIECE: 389 cal., 18g fat (9g sat. fat), 94mg chol., 173mg sod., 52g carb. (38g sugars, 2g fiber), 7g pro.

Coconut-Pecan German Chocolate Pie

PREP: 50 MIN. + CHILLING
BAKE: 35 MIN. + CHILLING
MAKES: 8 SERVINGS

This delectable, indulgent pie combines the ingredients everyone loves from its classic cake cousin. It's so silky and smooth, you won't be able to put your fork down until you've finished the very last bite.
—Anna Jones, Coppell, TX

1¼ cups all-purpose flour
¼ tsp. salt
6 Tbsp. cold lard
3 to 4 Tbsp. ice water

FILLING
4 oz. German sweet chocolate, chopped
2 oz. unsweetened chocolate, chopped
1 can (14 oz.) sweetened condensed milk
4 large egg yolks
1 tsp. vanilla extract
1 cup chopped pecans

TOPPING
½ cup packed brown sugar
½ cup heavy whipping cream
¼ cup butter, cubed
2 large egg yolks
1 cup sweetened shredded coconut
1 tsp. vanilla extract
¼ cup chopped pecans

1. Mix flour and salt; cut in lard until crumbly. Gradually add ice water, tossing with a fork until dough holds together when pressed. Shape into a disk; cover and refrigerate 30 minutes or overnight.

2. Preheat oven to 400°. On a lightly floured surface, roll dough to a ⅛-in.-thick circle; transfer to a 9-in. pie plate. Trim crust to ½ in. beyond rim of plate; flute edge. Line unpricked crust with a double thickness of foil. Fill with pie weights, dried beans or uncooked rice.

3. Bake 11-13 minutes or until bottom is lightly browned. Remove foil and weights; bake 6-8 minutes longer or until light brown. Cool on a wire rack. Reduce oven setting to 350°.

4. In a microwave, melt chocolates in a large bowl; stir until smooth. Cool slightly. Whisk in milk, egg yolks and vanilla; stir in pecans. Pour into crust. Bake 16-19 minutes or until set. Cool 1 hour on a wire rack.

5. For topping, in a small heavy saucepan, combine brown sugar, cream and butter. Bring to a boil over medium heat, stirring to dissolve sugar. Remove from heat.

6. Whisk a small amount of the hot mixture into egg yolks; return all to pan, whisking constantly. Cook 2-3 minutes or until mixture thickens and a thermometer reads 160°; stir constantly. Remove from heat. Stir in coconut and vanilla; cool 10 minutes.

7. Pour over filling; sprinkle with pecans. Refrigerate 4 hours or until cold.

1 PIECE: 801 cal., 54g fat (24g sat. fat), 215mg chol., 227mg sod., 75g carb. (53g sugars, 5g fiber), 12g pro.

TEST KITCHEN TIP

To achieve a silky smooth filling and topping, heat the egg yolks slowly and gently; cook them too fast and you'll scramble them.

Cranberry Pecan Pie

PREP: 25 MIN. + CHILLING
BAKE: 45 MIN. + CHILLING
MAKES: 8 SERVINGS

I first prepared this pie at Thanksgiving to share with my co-workers. It was such a success! Now I freeze cranberries while they are in season so that I can make it year-round.
—Dawn Liet Hartman, Miffinburg, PA

- 6 Tbsp. shortening
- 1½ tsp. buttermilk
- 2 Tbsp. hot water
- 1 cup all-purpose flour
- ½ tsp. salt

FILLING

- 3 large eggs
- 1 cup light or dark corn syrup
- ⅔ cup sugar
- ¼ cup butter, melted
- 1 tsp. vanilla extract
- 2 cups fresh or frozen cranberries, thawed
- 1 cup chopped pecans
  Sweetened whipped cream, optional

1. Beat shortening and buttermilk until blended. Gradually add water, beating until light and fluffy. Beat in flour and salt. Shape into a disk; cover and refrigerate 4 hours or overnight.

2. Preheat oven to 425°. On a lightly floured surface, roll dough to a ⅛-in.-thick circle; transfer to a 9-in. pie plate. Trim crust to ½ in. beyond edge of plate; flute edge.

3. In a large bowl, whisk the first 5 filling ingredients until blended. Stir in cranberries and pecans. Pour into crust.

4. Bake on a lower oven rack 10 minutes. Reduce oven setting to 350°; bake until filling is almost set, 35-40 minutes. Cool completely on a wire rack. Refrigerate, covered, overnight before serving. If desired, serve with whipped cream.

NOTE: To toast nuts, bake in a shallow pan in a 350° oven for 5-10 minutes or cook in a skillet over low heat until lightly browned, stirring occasionally.

1 PIECE: 514 cal., 27g fat (7g sat. fat), 85mg chol., 250mg sod., 68g carb. (52g sugars, 3g fiber), 50g pro.

Orange Chocolate Ricotta Pie

PREP: 20 MIN. • **BAKE:** 40 MIN. + COOLING
MAKES: 8 SERVINGS

Orange and chocolate make a classic pairing in this pie—a traditional Italian dessert served during holidays and for special occasions.
—Trisha Kruse, Eagle, ID

- 2 cartons (15 oz. each) whole-milk ricotta cheese
- 2 large eggs, lightly beaten
- ½ cup dark chocolate chips
- ⅓ cup sugar
- 1 Tbsp. grated orange zest
- 2 Tbsp. orange liqueur, optional
  Dough for double-crust pie (p. 154)

1. Preheat oven to 425°. In a large bowl, combine ricotta cheese, eggs, chocolate chips, sugar, orange zest and, if desired, orange liqueur.
2. On a floured surface, roll out 1 portion of the dough to fit a 9-in. pie plate; transfer to pie plate. Fill with ricotta mixture.
3. Roll out the remaining dough into an 11-in. circle; cut into 1-in.-wide strips. Lay half the strips across the pie, about 1 in. apart. Fold back every other strip halfway. Lay another strip across center of pie at a right angle. Unfold strips over center strip. Fold back the alternate strips; place a second strip across the pie. Continue to add strips until pie is covered with lattice. Trim, seal and flute edge.
4. Bake until the crust is golden brown, 40-45 minutes. Refrigerate leftovers.

1 PIECE: 525 cal., 31g fat (16g sat. fat), 106mg chol., 346mg sod., 49g carb. (23g sugars, 0 fiber), 17g pro.

Nantucket Cranberry Tart

PREP: 15 MIN. • **BAKE:** 40 MIN. + COOLING
MAKES: 12 SERVINGS

While everyone is enjoying a bountiful meal, this eye-catching tart can be baking to perfection in the oven. The pretty dessert calls for very few ingredients, and it's a snap to assemble.
—*Jackie Zack, Riverside, CT*

- 1 **pkg. (12 oz.) fresh or frozen cranberries, thawed**
- 1 **cup sugar, divided**
- ½ **cup sliced almonds**
- 2 **large eggs, room temperature**
- ¾ **cup butter, melted**
- 1 **tsp. almond extract**
- 1 **cup all-purpose flour**
- 1 **Tbsp. confectioners' sugar**

1. In a small bowl, combine the cranberries, ½ cup sugar and almonds. Transfer to a greased 11-in. fluted tart pan with a removable bottom. Place on a baking sheet.

2. In a small bowl, beat the eggs, butter, extract and remaining ½ cup sugar. Beat in the flour just until moistened (batter will be thick). Spread evenly over the berries.

3. Bake at 325° for 40-45 minutes or until a toothpick inserted in the center comes out clean. Cool in pan on a wire rack. Dust with confectioners' sugar. Refrigerate leftovers.

1 PIECE: 255 cal., 14g fat (8g sat. fat), 65mg chol., 93mg sod., 30g carb. (19g sugars, 2g fiber), 3g pro.

TEST KITCHEN TIP

The tart may ooze from the pan a little bit as it bakes. If you'd like, try placing the tart pan on a 15x10x1-in. baking sheet while baking.

Ginger Plum Tart

PREP: 15 MIN. • **BAKE:** 20 MIN. + COOLING
MAKES: 8 SERVINGS

Sweet cravings, begone: This free-form plum tart is done in only 35 minutes. Plus, it's extra-awesome when served warm.
—Taste of Home *Test Kitchen*

    1 **sheet refrigerated pie crust**
3½ **cups sliced fresh plums**
        (about 10 medium)
    3 **Tbsp. plus 1 tsp. coarse sugar,**
        divided
    1 **Tbsp. cornstarch**
    2 **tsp. finely chopped**
        crystallized ginger
    1 **large egg white**
    1 **Tbsp. water**

1. Preheat oven to 400°. On a work surface, unroll crust. Roll to a 12-in. circle. Transfer to a parchment-lined baking sheet.
2. In a large bowl, toss plums with 3 Tbsp. sugar and cornstarch. Arrange plums on crust to within 2 in. of edge; sprinkle with ginger. Fold crust edge over plums, pleating as you go.
3. In a small bowl, whisk egg white and water; brush over folded crust. Sprinkle with remaining sugar.
4. Bake until the crust is golden brown, 20-25 minutes. Cool in pan on a wire rack. Serve warm or at room temperature.
1 PIECE: 190 cal., 7g fat (3g sat. fat), 5mg chol., 108mg sod., 30g carb. (14g sugars, 1g fiber), 2g pro. **DIABETIC EXCHANGES:** 1½ starch, 1 fat, ½ fruit.

Mixed Nut & Fig Pie

PREP: 30 MIN. • **BAKE:** 1 HOUR + COOLING
MAKES: 8 SERVINGS

Can't decide on a favorite nut? My recipe settles the question by calling for deluxe mixed nuts. A hint of orange enhances this sweet, crunchy pie.
—Barbara Estabrook, Appleton, WI

        Dough for single-crust pie (p. 154)
    ½ **cup chopped dried figs**
    3 **Tbsp. water**
    2 **Tbsp. orange marmalade**
    ¾ **cup packed brown sugar**
    1 **Tbsp. cornstarch**
    1 **cup corn syrup**
    3 **large eggs**
    6 **Tbsp. butter, melted**
    2 **tsp. vanilla extract**
1½ **cups deluxe mixed nuts**
TOPPING
    1 **cup heavy whipping cream**
    2 **Tbsp. sugar**
    1 **Tbsp. orange marmalade**

1. Preheat oven to 450°. Roll out dough to fit a 9-in. pie plate; transfer to pie plate, then trim and flute edge. Line crust with a double thickness of heavy-duty foil. Bake for 8 minutes. Remove foil; bake 5 minutes longer. Cool on a wire rack. Reduce heat to 300°.
2. In a small saucepan, combine figs and water. Cook and stir over low heat until water is absorbed. Remove from the heat; stir in marmalade. In a large bowl, combine brown sugar and cornstarch. Add the corn syrup, eggs, butter, vanilla and fig mixture; stir in nuts. Pour into crust.
3. Bake at 300° for 1-1¼ hours or until set. Cover edge with foil during the last 30 minutes to prevent overbrowning if necessary. Cool on a wire rack.
4. For topping, in a small bowl, beat cream until it begins to thicken. Add sugar and marmalade; beat until soft peaks form. Serve with pie. Refrigerate leftovers.
1 PIECE: 749 cal., 40g fat (17g sat. fat), 148mg chol., 321mg sod., 95g carb. (52g sugars, 4g fiber), 9g pro.

Sweet Potato Pie

PREP: 30 MIN. • **BAKE:** 50 MIN. + COOLING
MAKES: 8 SERVINGS

This creamy sweet potato pie is subtly spiced and slices beautifully! We suggest baking up a few sweet potato pies around the holidays to give to friends and family.
—*North Carolina Sweet Potato Commission*

Dough for single-crust pie (p. 154)
2 **medium sweet potatoes (about 1½ lbs.), peeled and cubed**
⅓ **cup butter, softened**
½ **cup sugar**
2 **large eggs, lightly beaten**
¾ **cup evaporated milk**
1 **tsp. vanilla extract**
½ **tsp. ground cinnamon**
½ **tsp. ground nutmeg**
¼ **tsp. salt**

1. Preheat oven to 425°. On a lightly floured surface, roll dough to a ⅛-in.-thick circle; transfer to a 9-in. pie plate. Trim crust to ½ in. beyond rim of plate; flute edge. Refrigerate while preparing filling.

2. Place sweet potatoes in a medium saucepan; add water to cover. Bring to a boil. Reduce heat; cook, uncovered, until tender, 13-15 minutes. Drain potatoes; return to pan. Mash until very smooth; cool to room temperature.

3. In a bowl, cream butter and sugar. Add eggs; mix well. Add milk, 2 cups mashed sweet potatoes, vanilla, cinnamon, nutmeg and salt; mix well. Pour into crust. Bake for 15 minutes. Reduce heat to 350°; bake until set or a knife inserted in the center comes out clean, 35-40 minutes. Cool on a wire rack. Refrigerate leftover.

1 PIECE: 372 cal., 18g fat (9g sat. fat), 86mg chol., 300mg sod., 48g carb. (25g sugars, 2g fiber), 6g pro.

SEE HOW IT'S DONE
Watch the whole process of making this pie by hovering your camera here.

Gingersnap Crumb Pear Pie

PREP: 35 MIN. + CHILLING
BAKE: 1 HOUR + COOLING
MAKES: 8 SERVINGS

My grandmother used this basic recipe for making crumble pies from fresh fruit. She simply used oats, gingersnaps or vanilla wafers depending on which fruit she was using. Pear was always my favorite. I added the ginger and caramel to this recipe to give it a new twist.
—Fay Moreland, Wichita Falls, TX

Dough for single-crust pie (p. 154)

TOPPING
- 1 **cup crushed gingersnap cookies (about 16 cookies)**
- ¼ **cup all-purpose flour**
- ¼ **cup packed brown sugar**
  Pinch salt
- ½ **cup cold butter, cubed**

FILLING
- ⅔ **cup sugar**
- ⅓ **cup all-purpose flour**
- ½ **tsp. ground ginger**
- ¼ **tsp. salt**
- 2½ **lbs. ripe pears (about 4 medium), peeled and thinly sliced**
- 1 **Tbsp. lemon juice**
- 1 **tsp. vanilla extract**
  Hot caramel ice cream topping, optional

1. On a lightly floured surface, roll dough to a ⅛-in.-thick circle; transfer to a 9-in. pie plate. Trim crust to ½ in. beyond rim of plate; flute edge. Refrigerate 30 minutes. Preheat oven to 400°.

2. Line unpricked crust with a double thickness of foil. Fill with pie weights, dried beans or uncooked rice. Bake on a lower oven rack until the edge is light golden brown, 15-20 minutes. Remove foil and weights; bake until bottom is golden brown, 3-6 minutes longer. Cool on a wire rack. Reduce oven setting to 350°.

3. For topping, in a food processor, combine the crushed cookies, flour, brown sugar and salt. Add butter; pulse until crumbly.

4. For filling, in a large bowl, mix sugar, flour, ginger and salt. Add pears, lemon juice and vanilla; toss gently to combine. Transfer to crust; cover with topping.

5. Place pie on a baking sheet; bake until topping is lightly browned and pears are tender, 60-70 minutes. Cover pie loosely with foil during last 15 minutes if needed to prevent overbrowning. Remove the foil. Cool on a wire rack at least 1 hour before serving. If desired, drizzle pie with caramel topping.

NOTE: Let pie weights cool before storing. Beans and rice may be reused for pie weights, but not for cooking.

1 PIECE: 530 cal., 25g fat (15g sat. fat), 61mg chol., 394mg sod., 76g carb. (39g sugars, 5g fiber), 4g pro.

Rustic Chocolate Raspberry Tart

PREP: 20 MIN. + CHILLING
BAKE: 45 MIN. + COOLING
MAKES: 8 SERVINGS

Here's a delectable dessert that all ages will enjoy. With its raspberries and Nutella-covered homemade crust, you won't be able to get enough of this.
—Christina Seremetis, Rockland, MA

- 5 oz. cream cheese, softened
- 6 Tbsp. butter, softened
- 1½ cups all-purpose flour

FILLING
- 2 cups fresh raspberries
- 2 Tbsp. sugar
- 1 tsp. cornstarch
- ⅓ cup Nutella

1. Process cream cheese and butter in a food processor until blended. Add flour; process just until a dough forms. Shape into a disk; wrap and refrigerate 1 hour or overnight.

2. Preheat oven to 350°. In a small bowl, toss raspberries, sugar and cornstarch with a fork, mashing some of the berries slightly.

3. On a lightly floured surface, roll dough into a 14x8-in. rectangle. Transfer to a parchment-lined baking sheet. Spread with Nutella to within 1 in. of edge. Top with the raspberry mixture. Fold the crust edge toward the center of the tart, pleating and pinching as needed.

4. Bake until the crust is golden brown, 45-50 minutes. Transfer to a wire rack to cool.

1 PIECE: 315 cal., 19g fat (10g sat. fat), 41mg chol., 130mg sod., 34g carb. (12g sugars, 3g fiber), 5g pro.

Becky Ruff
McGregor, IA

In fall or any time of year, this nutty, rich and delicious pecan pie recipe is one I am proud to serve. While it seems very special, this caramel-pecan spin on cheesecake is a snap to make.

Caramel-Pecan Cheesecake Pie

PREP: 15 MIN.
BAKE: 35 MIN. + CHILLING
MAKES: 8 SERVINGS

- 1 **sheet refrigerated pie crust**
- 1 **pkg. (8 oz.) cream cheese, softened**
- ½ **cup sugar**
- 4 **large eggs, room temperature**
- 1 **tsp. vanilla extract**
- 1¼ **cups chopped pecans**
- 1 **jar (12¼ oz.) fat-free caramel ice cream topping**
  Additional fat-free caramel ice cream topping, optional

1. Preheat oven to 375°. Line a 9-in. deep-dish pie plate or cast-iron skillet with crust. Trim and flute edge. In a small bowl, beat cream cheese, sugar, 1 egg and vanilla until smooth. Spread into crust; sprinkle with pecans.
2. In a small bowl, whisk the remaining 3 eggs; gradually whisk in the caramel topping until blended. Pour slowly over the pecans
3. Bake for 35-40 minutes or until lightly browned (loosely cover edge with foil after 20 minutes if pie browns too quickly). Cool on a wire rack 1 hour. Refrigerate 4 hours or overnight before slicing. If desired, garnish with additional caramel ice cream topping.
1 PIECE: 502 cal., 33g fat (11g sat. fat), 142mg chol., 277mg sod., 45g carb. (26g sugars, 2g fiber), 8g pro.

Apple Butter Pumpkin Pie

PREP: 25 MIN. • **BAKE:** 50 MIN. + COOLING
MAKES: 8 SERVINGS

The addition of apple butter gives this pumpkin pie a slightly fruity flavor. I'm always happy to share reliable recipes like this.
—Edna Hoffman, Hebron, IN

Dough for single-crust pie (p. 154)
- 3 **large eggs, lightly beaten**
- 1 **cup canned pumpkin**
- 1 **cup apple butter**
- ¾ **cup packed brown sugar**
- 1 **can (5 oz.) evaporated milk**
- ⅓ **cup 2% milk**
- 1 **tsp. vanilla extract**
- ½ **tsp. salt**
- ½ **tsp. ground cinnamon**
- ⅛ **tsp. each ground ginger, cloves and nutmeg**
- **Whipped cream, optional**

1. Preheat oven to 400°. On a lightly floured surface, roll dough to a ⅛-in.-thick circle; transfer to a 9-in. pie plate. Trim crust to ½ in. beyond rim of plate; flute edge. In a large bowl, combine the eggs, pumpkin, apple butter, brown sugar, evaporated milk, 2% milk and vanilla. Whisk in salt and spices until well blended; pour into crust.
2. Bake until a knife inserted in the center comes out clean, 50-55 minutes. Cover the edge loosely with foil during the last 20 minutes if necessary. Cool on a wire rack. If desired, garnish with whipped cream. Refrigerate leftovers.
NOTE: This recipe was tested with commercially prepared apple butter.
1 PIECE: 328 cal., 10g fat (5g sat. fat), 92mg chol., 304mg sod., 53g carb. (37g sugars, 2g fiber), 5g pro.

Almond Macaroon Tart

PREP: 25 MIN. • **BAKE:** 30 MIN. + COOLING
MAKES: 16 SERVINGS

My husband loves his aunt's special almond cake, but she's secretive about her recipe. So I used that idea to create something new—a nutty, golden-brown tart.
—Elisa Thoresen, Englishtown, NJ

- 1 **cup slivered almonds**
- 1 **cup sweetened shredded coconut**
- 2¼ **cups all-purpose flour**
- 1 **cup sugar**
- 1 **cup butter, softened**

FILLING
- 1¼ **cups confectioners' sugar**
- ¾ **cup sweetened shredded coconut, divided**
- 1 **pkg. (7 oz.) almond paste, crumbled**
- 1 **tsp. almond extract**
- 2 **large egg whites**

1. Preheat oven to 350°. Place almonds and coconut in a food processor; process until finely ground. Add flour and sugar; pulse to combine. Add butter; pulse until crumbly. Reserve 1½ cups of the crumb mixture for topping. Press the remaining mixture onto bottom and up sides of a greased 11-in. fluted tart pan with removable bottom.
2. For filling, place confectioners' sugar, ½ cup coconut, almond paste and extract in food processor; pulse until fine crumbs form. Add the egg whites; process until blended. Spread into crust; sprinkle with the reserved topping.
3. Bake 25-30 minutes or until golden brown. Sprinkle with remaining coconut; bake 5-8 minutes longer or until coconut is lightly browned. Cool completely on a wire rack.
1 PIECE: 401 cal., 22g fat (11g sat. fat), 31mg chol., 127mg sod., 48g carb. (31g sugars, 2g fiber), 5g pro.

Pumpkin Pie Tartlets with Maple Pecan Crust

PREP: 45 MIN. + COOLING
BAKE: 35 MIN+ COOLING • **MAKES:** 1½ DOZEN

I came up with this recipe after discovering multiple food sensitivities were affecting my health. It was important to me to still participate in family holidays and events where food was being served, so I began developing dishes that would be safe for me, but that others would enjoy, too. These mini pumpkin pie tarts are so delicious, you would never suspect they're free of gluten, egg and dairy!
—Chantale Michaud, Guelph, ON

- 2 **cups old-fashioned oats**
- 4 **cups chopped pecans**
- ½ **cup maple syrup**
- 2 **tsp. ground cinnamon**
- 1 **tsp. sea salt**
- 1 **tsp. vanilla extract**
- ¼ **tsp. ground cloves**

FILLING
- ½ **cup maple syrup**
- 3 **Tbsp. cornstarch**
- 2¼ **cups canned pumpkin or homemade pumpkin puree**
- ¼ **cup cream of coconut, warmed**
- 2 **tsp. vanilla extract**
- 2 **tsp. ground cinnamon**
- ½ **tsp. sea salt**
- ½ **tsp. ground nutmeg**
- ¼ **tsp. ground ginger**
- ¼ **tsp. ground cloves**

TOPPING
- ½ **cup chopped pecans**
- 2 **tsp. maple syrup**
   Dash sea salt

1. Preheat oven to 350°. Process oats in a food processor until a fine powder forms. Add pecans; pulse until nuts are chopped. Add next 5 ingredients; pulse until mixture is moistened. Remove from processor.

2. Fill 18 greased muffin cups with ⅓ cup oat mixture each. Using a wet 1 Tbsp. measure, press mixture onto bottom and up sides of the muffin cups. Bake until lightly browned, about 10 minutes. Cool on a wire rack.

3. For filling, whisk together maple syrup and cornstarch. In another bowl, mix the remaining filling ingredients, then add the maple syrup mixture. Spoon about 3 Tbsp. into each crust.

4. Combine topping ingredients; spoon about 1 tsp. onto each tartlet. Bake until dark golden and set, 35-40 minutes. Cool for 10 minutes before removing tartlets to a wire rack; cool 1 hour. If desired, refrigerate before serving.

1 TARTLET: 302 cal., 21g fat (2g sat. fat), 0 chol., 173mg sod., 28g carb. (16g sugars, 5g fiber), 4g pro.

Apple Frangipane Phyllo Tart

PREP: 30 MIN. • **BAKE:** 40 MIN.
MAKES: 16 SERVINGS

*An almond-flavored frangipane creates
a nutty bottom layer for my apple tart.
Golden phyllo dough creates a delicate
and crispy melt-in-your-mouth crust.*
—Jessie Sarrazin, Livingston, MT

10	sheets phyllo dough (14x9 in.)
	Butter-flavored cooking spray
1¼	cups blanched almonds
⅓	cup sugar
2	Tbsp. all-purpose flour
2	Tbsp. butter, softened
⅛	tsp. salt
3	large egg yolks
1	Tbsp. plus 2 tsp. amaretto
⅛	tsp. almond extract
4	small apples, peeled
2	Tbsp. apple jelly, warmed

1. Preheat oven to 375°. Place 1 sheet of phyllo dough on a work surface; coat with cooking spray. Gently press phyllo into a 9-in. tart pan, allowing ends to extend over edge of pan.

2. Layer with the remaining phyllo, spraying with cooking spray after each layer; arrange in pan, rotating phyllo so corners do not overlap. Fold in the overhanging phyllo to form a shell.

3. Place almonds and sugar in a food processor; cover and process until finely ground. Add the flour, butter and salt; pulse until blended.

4. Add egg yolks, amaretto and almond extract; cover and pulse to blend well. Spread filling over bottom of phyllo shell.

5. Halve and core apples; thinly slice widthwise. Arrange the apple slices in a pinwheel pattern over the filling.

6. Bake 40-50 minutes or until apples are tender. Cover edge with foil during the last 15 minutes to prevent overbrowning if necessary. Remove to a wire rack and cool slightly. Brush warmed jelly over apples. Serve warm. Refrigerate any leftovers.

1 PIECE: 175 cal., 9g fat (2g sat. fat), 38mg chol., 91mg sod., 20g carb. (9g sugars, 2g fiber), 4g pro. **DIABETIC EXCHANGES:** 2 fat, 1 starch.

TEST KITCHEN TIP

While working with each sheet of phyllo dough, always keep the remaining phyllo covered with a damp towel to prevent it from drying out.

Rum-Raisin Pumpkin Pie

PREP: 20 MIN. • **BAKE:** 35 MIN. + COOLING
MAKES: 8 SERVINGS

This recipe is a fantastic way to change up a classic dessert. Try it and see how many compliments you receive from friends and family!
—Gertrudis Miller, Evansville, IN

       Dough for single-crust pie (p. 154)
½   cup raisins
¼   cup rum
¼   cup boiling water
2   large eggs
¾   cup packed brown sugar
1   Tbsp. all-purpose flour
½   tsp. salt
½   tsp. ground ginger
½   tsp. ground cinnamon
¼   tsp. ground nutmeg
¼   tsp. ground cloves
1   can (15 oz.) pumpkin
1   cup evaporated milk

1. Preheat oven to 400°. On a lightly floured surface, roll dough to a ⅛-in.-thick circle; transfer to a 9-in. pie plate. Trim crust to ½ in. beyond rim of plate; flute edge.
2. Place raisins and rum in a small bowl. Cover with boiling water; let stand for 5 minutes. Meanwhile, in a large bowl, combine the eggs, brown sugar, flour, salt and spices. Stir in pumpkin and the raisin mixture. Gradually add milk. Pour into crust.
3. Bake until a knife inserted in the center comes out clean (cover edge with foil during the last 15 minutes if necessary to prevent overbrowning), 35-40 minutes. Cool on a wire rack. Refrigerate leftovers.
1 PIECE: 322 cal., 11g fat (5g sat. fat), 68mg chol., 305mg sod., 48g carb. (32g sugars, 3g fiber), 6g pro.

Turtle Praline Tart

PREP: 35 MIN. + CHILLING
MAKES: 16 SERVINGS

This rich dessert is my own creation, and I'm very proud of it. It's easy enough to make for everyday meals but special enough to serve guests or take to a potluck.
—Kathy Specht, Clinton, MT

1	**sheet refrigerated pie crust**
36	**caramels**
1	**cup heavy whipping cream, divided**
3½	**cups pecan halves**
½	**cup semisweet chocolate chips, melted**

1. Preheat oven to 450°. Unroll pie crust on a lightly floured surface. Transfer to an 11-in. fluted tart pan with removable bottom; trim edge.

2. Line unpricked pie crust with a double thickness of heavy-duty foil. Bake 8 minutes. Remove foil; bake until light golden brown, 5-6 minutes longer. Cool on a wire rack.

3. In a large saucepan, combine caramels and ½ cup cream. Cook and stir over medium-low heat until caramels are melted. Stir in pecans. Spread filling evenly into crust. Drizzle with melted chocolate.

4. Refrigerate until set, about 30 minutes. Whip remaining ½ cup cream; serve with tart.

1 PIECE: 335 cal., 24g fat (4g sat. fat), 4mg chol., 106mg sod., 31g carb. (19g sugars, 3g fiber), 4g pro.

3. Bake for 25 minutes. Reduce heat to 350°; bake 25-30 minutes longer or until the filling is bubbly and topping is golden. Cool on a wire rack. Refrigerate leftovers.

1 PIECE: 299 cal., 11g fat (6g sat. fat), 22mg chol., 126mg sod., 49g carb. (28g sugars, 2g fiber), 4g pro.

Rustic Cranberry Tarts

PREP: 15 MIN. • **BAKE:** 20 MIN./BATCH
MAKES: 2 TARTS (6 SERVINGS EACH)

For gatherings with family and friends, we love a dessert with a splash of red. These beautiful tarts are filled with cranberry and citrus flavor and are easy to make and serve.
—Holly Bauer, West Bend, WI

- 1 **cup orange marmalade**
- ¼ **cup sugar**
- ¼ **cup all-purpose flour**
- 4 **cups fresh or frozen cranberries, thawed**
- 2 **sheets refrigerated pie crust**
- 1 **large egg white, lightly beaten**
- 1 **Tbsp. coarse sugar**

1. Preheat oven to 425°. In a large bowl, mix marmalade, sugar and flour; stir in the cranberries.

2. Unroll 1 pie crust onto a parchment-lined baking sheet. Spoon half of the cranberry mixture over crust to within 2 in. of edge. Fold edge over the filling, pleating as you go and leaving a 5-in. opening in the center. Brush the folded crust with egg white; sprinkle with half of the coarse sugar. Repeat with the remaining ingredients to make a second tart.

3. Bake 18-22 minutes or until crust is golden and filling is bubbly. Transfer tarts to wire racks to cool.

1 PIECE: 260 cal., 9g fat (4g sat. fat), 6mg chol., 144mg sod., 45g carb. (24g sugars, 2g fiber), 2g pro.

Creamy Apple Crumb Pie

PREP: 20 MIN. • **BAKE:** 50 MIN. + COOLING
MAKES: 8 SERVINGS

I found a vintage apple pie recipe in a church cookbook, and made a few revisions to make it my own. I knew the recipe was a keeper when my mother-in-law asked for a copy!
—Linda Pawelski, Milwaukee, WI

- **Dough for single-crust pie (p. 154)**
- ⅓ **cup sugar**
- 3 **Tbsp. cornstarch**
- 1 **tsp. ground cinnamon**
- ¼ **tsp. ground allspice**
- 6 **cups diced peeled tart apples (about 6 medium)**
- 1 **cup reduced-fat sour cream**
- 1 **tsp. vanilla extract**
- **TOPPING**
- ½ **cup all-purpose flour**
- ¼ **cup packed brown sugar**
- ½ **tsp. ground cinnamon**
- 2 **Tbsp. cold butter**

1. Preheat oven to 400°. Unroll the crust into a 9-in. deep-dish pie plate or cast-iron skillet; flute edge. In a large bowl, combine sugar, cornstarch, cinnamon and allspice. Fold in the apples. Combine sour cream and vanilla; stir into apple mixture. Spoon into crust.

2. For topping, combine the flour, brown sugar and cinnamon in a bowl; cut in butter until the mixture resembles coarse crumbs. Sprinkle over filling.

Salted Caramel Walnut Tart

PREP: 20 MIN. + CHILLING
BAKE: 20 MIN. + COOLING
MAKES: 12 SERVINGS

It took me a while to figure out a way to convert one of my favorite ice cream flavors into one of my favorite desserts— pie! The result took quite a few tries, but in the end, it was so worth it.
—*Ruth Ealy, Plain City, OH*

- 2 **large eggs, lightly beaten**
- ¼ **cup plus 2 Tbsp. heavy whipping cream**
- ¾ **cup packed light brown sugar**
- ¼ **cup plus 2 Tbsp. golden syrup or light corn syrup**
- 3 **Tbsp. unsalted butter, cubed**
- 1½ **tsp. vanilla extract**
- ¾ **tsp. sea salt**
- 1 **sheet refrigerated pie crust**
- 1 **cup chopped walnuts, toasted**

1. Let eggs stand at room temperature for 30 minutes. In a microwave, heat cream on high for 20 seconds. Keep warm.

2. Meanwhile, in a large, heavy saucepan over medium heat, combine sugar and syrup, stirring frequently. Bring to a boil; cook, stirring constantly, for 1 minute. Remove from heat. Slowly pour cream into pan; continue stirring constantly (cream may spatter) until well blended. Gradually add butter, stirring until melted. Add vanilla and sea salt; stir until smooth. Cool.

3. Unroll crust into a 9-in. tart pan; trim edge. Refrigerate 30 minutes. Line unpricked crust with a double thickness of foil. Fill with pie weights, dried beans or uncooked rice. Bake at 400° on a lower oven rack until edge are golden brown, 10-12 minutes. Remove foil and weights; bake until bottom is golden brown, 3-5 minutes longer. Cool on a wire rack.

4. Reduce oven setting to 350°. Whisk eggs into caramel mixture; stir in walnuts. Add filling to crust. Bake until center is just set (mixture will jiggle), 20-25 minutes. Cool completely. Refrigerate leftovers.

1 PIECE: 293 cal., 17g fat (6g sat. fat), 50mg chol., 238mg sod., 32g carb. (23g sugars, 1g fiber), 3g pro.

TEST KITCHEN TIP

If you don't like walnuts, try substituting pecans, almonds or even mixed nuts. For testing, we used Lyle's Golden Syrup. It adds a subtle caramel flavor that's just right with walnuts. If you can't find it, simply use regular corn syrup.

Butterscotch Pie

PREP: 30 MIN. + CHILLING
BAKE: 15 MIN. + COOLING
MAKES: 8 SERVINGS

*This creamy pudding-like pie filling is
crowned with golden peaks of meringue.*
—Cary Letsche, Brandenton, FL

	Dough for single-crust pie (p. 154)
6	Tbsp. butter
6	Tbsp. all-purpose flour
1½	cup packed brown sugar
2	cups whole milk
¼	tsp. salt
3	large egg yolks, room temperature, beaten
1	tsp. vanilla extract

MERINGUE

3	large egg whites, room temperature
¼	tsp. cream of tartar
½	cup sugar

1. On a lightly floured surface, roll dough to a ⅛-in.-thick circle; transfer to a 9-in. pie plate. Trim to ½ in. beyond rim of plate; flute edge. Refrigerate 30 minutes.

2. Preheat oven to 425°. Line unpricked crust with a double thickness of foil. Fill with pie weights, dried beans or uncooked rice. Bake on a lower oven rack until edge is light golden brown, 15-20 minutes. Remove foil and weights; bake until the bottom is golden brown, 3-6 minutes longer. Cool on a wire rack. Reduce oven setting to 350°.

3. In a saucepan, melt butter. Remove from the heat; add flour and stir until smooth. Stir in brown sugar. Return to heat; stir in milk and salt until blended. Cook and stir over medium-high heat until thickened and bubbly. Reduce heat; cook and stir 2 minutes longer. Remove from the heat.

4. Stir about 1 cup hot filling into egg yolks; return all to pan, stirring constantly. Bring to a gentle boil; cook and stir for 2 minutes longer. Remove from the heat. Gently stir in vanilla. Pour into crust.

5. For meringue, beat egg whites and cream of tartar in a small bowl on medium speed until soft peaks form. Gradually beat in sugar, about 1 Tbsp. at a time, on high speed until stiff glossy peaks form and sugar is dissolved. Spread evenly over hot filling, sealing edge to crust.

6. Bake until meringue is golden brown, 12-15 minutes. Cool on a wire rack for 1 hour. Refrigerate at least 3 hours before serving. Refrigerate leftovers.

1 PIECE: 487 cal., 20g fat (10g sat. fat), 116mg chol., 330mg sod., 73g carb. (56g sugars, 0 fiber), 6g pro.

SEE HOW IT'S DONE

See how to make this sweet pie—including perfect meringue—by hovering your phone here.

Orange Gingerbread Tassies

PREP: 20 MIN. + CHILLING
BAKE: 15 MIN. + COOLING • **MAKES:** 2 DOZEN

With the gingerbread and orange, these little tarts have a delicious flavor—plus they're really easy to make! They're also yummy made with lemon zest, if you prefer.
—*Elisabeth Larsen, Pleasant Grove, UT*

- ½ cup butter, softened
- 4 oz. cream cheese, softened
- ¼ cup molasses
- 1 tsp. ground ginger
- ½ tsp. ground cinnamon
- ½ tsp. ground allspice
- ¼ tsp. ground cloves
- 1 cup all-purpose flour
- ½ cup white baking chips
- ¼ cup heavy whipping cream
- 2 Tbsp. butter
- 4 tsp. grated orange zest
  Candied orange peel, optional

1. Beat the first 7 ingredients until light and fluffy. Gradually beat in flour. Refrigerate, covered, until mixture is firm enough to shape, about 1 hour.

2. Preheat oven to 350°. Shape dough into 1-in. balls; press evenly onto bottom and up sides of ungreased mini-muffin cups. Bake until golden brown, 15-18 minutes. Press centers with the handle of a wooden spoon to reshape as necessary. Cool completely in pan before removing to wire rack.

3. In a microwave-safe bowl, heat baking chips, cream and butter until blended, stirring occasionally. Stir in orange zest; cool completely. Spoon filling into crusts. Refrigerate until soft-set. If desired, garnish with candied orange peel.

1 TASSIE: 91 cal., 6g fat (4g sat. fat), 13mg chol., 43mg sod., 9g carb. (5g sugars, 0 fiber), 1g pro.

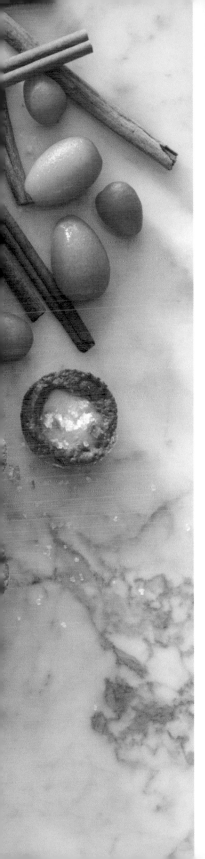

TEST KITCHEN TIP
Using a food mill or potato ricer to mash the potatoes will produce a very smooth filling.

Mom-Mom's White Potato Pie

PREP: 35 MIN. • **BAKE:** 50 MIN+ COOLING
MAKES: 2 PIES (8 SERVINGS EACH)

My Mom-Mom Beatrice taught me how to make a white potato pie when I was 12 years old. I always remembered the recipe and I make it every holiday for parties. The staff at work has fallen in love with it—so much that they actually order pies from me every holiday season!
—Loretta Hooks, Dover, DE

¾ **cup plus 1 Tbsp. sugar, divided**
3½ **tsp. ground cinnamon, divided**
2 **frozen deep-dish pie crusts (9 in.)**
3 **lbs. potatoes, peeled and cubed**
½ **cup butter, softened**
3 **large eggs**
½ **cup sweetened condensed milk**
⅛ **tsp. vanilla extract**
¾ **cup evaporated milk**
1½ **tsp. ground nutmeg**
    Confectioners' sugar, optional

1. Preheat oven to 350°. In a small bowl, combine 1 Tbsp. sugar and ½ tsp. cinnamon. Sprinkle half the mixture in the bottoms of both pie crusts; set the rest aside. Bake crust until lightly browned, 7-10 minutes.

2. Meanwhile, place potatoes in a large saucepan; add water to cover. Bring to a boil. Reduce heat; cook, uncovered, until potatoes are tender, about 10-15 minutes, stirring occasionally. Drain.

3. In a large bowl, mash potatoes with butter; beat until fluffy. Add eggs, condensed milk and vanilla; mix well. Stirring continuously, slowly add evaporated milk; mix until smooth. Add nutmeg and remaining ¾ cup sugar and 3 tsp. cinnamon; mix well. Pour potato mixture into prepared crusts; do not over-fill. Sprinkle with remaining cinnamon sugar mixture. Bake until pie is set or until a knife inserted in the center comes out clean, about 45 minutes. Cool on a wire rack 1 hour before serving. If desired, sprinkle with confectioner's sugar.

1 PIECE: 308 cal., 13g fat (6g sat. fat), 57mg chol., 168mg sod., 43g carb. (17g sugars, 2g fiber), 6g pro.

Oatmeal Pie

PREP: 10 MIN. • **BAKE:** 45 MIN.
MAKES: 8 SERVINGS

The recipe for this delicious pie came from my mother. My husband especially enjoys it during the holidays. I have shared the pie crust with many others because it's flaky and so easy to roll out. We even use it at our children's school when apple pies are made for a fundraiser.
—Ruth Gritter, Grand Rapids, MI

- ½ cup sugar
- ½ cup light or dark corn syrup
- ¾ cup old-fashioned oats
- ½ cup sweetened shredded coconut
- ½ cup butter, melted
- 2 large eggs, room temperature, beaten
- 1 tsp. vanilla extract
- 1 sheet refrigerated pie crust
- 1 pkg. (3 oz.) pecan halves

1. Preheat oven to 350°. Unroll crust into a 9-in. pie plate; flute edge. In a large bowl, combine sugar, corn syrup, oats, coconut, butter, eggs and vanilla. Pour into crust.
2. Bake 15 minutes. Arrange pecans on top of pie; bake until well browned, about 30 minutes more. Cool completely on a wire rack.

1 PIECE: 483 cal., 30g fat (13g sat. fat), 82mg chol., 238mg sod., 52g carb. (34g sugars, 2g fiber), 5g pro.

Lemon Tart with Almond Crust

PREP: 40 MIN. • **BAKE:** 10 MIN. + COOLING
MAKES: 8 SERVINGS

Our state produces an abundance of lemons, and everyone is always looking for new ways to use them. This beautiful tart is my delicious solution to the excess-lemon problem!
—Lois Kinneberg, Phoenix, AZ

- 1 cup all-purpose flour
- ½ cup sliced almonds, toasted
- ¼ cup sugar
- 6 Tbsp. cold butter
- ½ tsp. almond extract
- ¼ tsp. salt
- 2 to 3 Tbsp. cold water

FILLING

- 3 large eggs
- 3 large egg yolks
- 1 cup sugar
- ¾ cup lemon juice
- 2 Tbsp. grated lemon zest
  Dash salt
- 6 Tbsp. butter, cubed

1. Preheat oven to 400°. Place the flour, almonds, sugar, butter, extract and salt in a food processor. Cover and pulse until blended. Gradually add water, 1 Tbsp. at a time, pulsing until the mixture forms a soft dough.
2. Press onto the bottom and up the sides of a greased 9-in. fluted tart pan with a removable bottom. Bake for 15-20 minutes or until golden brown. Cool on a wire rack. Reduce oven setting to 325°.
3. In a small heavy saucepan over medium heat, whisk the eggs, egg yolks, sugar, lemon juice, peel and salt until blended. Add butter; cook, whisking constantly, until mixture is thickened and coats the back of a spoon. Pour into crust.
4. Bake for 8-10 minutes or until set. Cool on a wire rack. Refrigerate leftovers.

1 PIECE: 419 cal., 24g fat (12g sat. fat), 185mg chol., 424mg sod., 47g carb. (32g sugars, 1g fiber), 6g pro.

Spiced Upside-Down Apple Pie

PREP: 20 MIN. • **BAKE:** 50 MIN. + COOLING
MAKES: 8 SERVINGS

My grandma taught me to make this pie when I was 4. Over the years I've kept it about the same with just a few changes. Flip it out the second it stops bubbling. The glaze it makes looks like stained glass.
—Francine Bryson, Pickens, SC

SEE HOW IT'S DONE
Watch how this decadent dessert is built, from the top down! Just hover your camera here.

2 cups pecan halves
½ cup butter, melted
1 cup packed brown sugar
Dough for double-crust pie (p. 154)
½ cup sugar
3 Tbsp. all-purpose flour
1 Tbsp. apple pie spice
½ tsp. ground nutmeg
6 cups thinly sliced peeled tart apples
2 Tbsp. lemon juice
1 tsp. vanilla extract

1. Preheat oven to 450°. Arrange pecans, rounded sides facing down, on the bottom of a 9-in. deep-dish pie plate; drizzle with butter. Sprinkle with the brown sugar; press lightly.

2. Roll out 1 portion of dough to fit the pie plate; place over brown sugar and pecans. Press the crust firmly against the nuts and the sides of pie plate. Trim edge.

3. In a large bowl, combine sugar, flour, pie spice and nutmeg. Add the apples, lemon juice and vanilla; toss to coat. Fill crust. Roll out the remaining dough to fit top of pie; place over filling. Trim, seal and flute edge. Cut slits in crust.

4. Place a foil-lined baking sheet on a rack below the pie to catch any spills. Bake for 10 minutes. Reduce heat to 350°. Bake until the top is golden brown and the apples are tender, 40-45 minutes longer. Cool for 10 minutes before inverting onto a serving plate. Serve warm.

1 PIECE: 825 cal., 53g fat (23g sat. fat), 91mg chol., 409mg sod., 87g carb. (50g sugars, 5g fiber), 7g pro.

TEST KITCHEN TIP

Don't wait too long before inverting the pie onto a serving plate. If it cools off too much, it might be difficult to remove from the pan.

Mile-High Cranberry Meringue Pie

PREP: 1 HOUR • **BAKE:** 25 MIN. + CHILLING
MAKES: 8 SERVINGS

Your dinner guests will be blown away when they see this pie with towering meringue on top. Let it sit in your refrigerator for at least 4 hours for best results.
—Marcia Whitney, Gainesville, FL

- 4 **large eggs, separated**
  Dough for single-crust pie (p. 154)
- 4 **cups fresh or frozen cranberries, thawed**
- 2¼ **cups sugar, divided**
- ¾ **cup water**
- 2 **Tbsp. all-purpose flour**
- ¼ **tsp. salt**
- 2 **Tbsp. butter**
- 2 **tsp. vanilla extract, divided**
- ½ **tsp. cream of tartar**

1. Let egg whites stand 30 minutes at room temperature. Preheat oven to 425°.

2. On a lightly floured surface, roll dough to a ⅛-in.-thick circle; transfer to a 9-in. pie plate. Trim crust to ½ in. beyond rim of plate; flute edge. Refrigerate 30 minutes.

3. Line unpricked crust with a double thickness of foil. Fill with pie weights, dried beans or uncooked rice. Bake on a lower oven rack for 15-20 minutes or until edge is light golden brown. Remove foil and weights; bake 3-6 minutes longer or until bottom is golden brown. Cool on a wire rack. Reduce heat to 325°.

4. In a large saucepan, combine cranberries, 1½ cups sugar and the water. Bring to a boil, stirring to dissolve sugar. Reduce heat to medium; cook, uncovered, 4-6 minutes or until the berries stop popping, stirring occasionally. Remove from heat.

5. In a small bowl, whisk egg yolks, ¼ cup sugar, flour and salt until blended. Gradually whisk in ½ cup of hot cranberry liquid; return all to saucepan, stirring constantly. Bring to a gentle boil; cook and stir for 2 minutes. Remove from heat; stir in the butter and 1 tsp. vanilla.

6. For meringue, beat egg whites with cream of tartar and remaining 1 tsp. vanilla on medium speed until foamy. Add the remaining ½ cup sugar, 1 Tbsp. at a time, beating on high after each addition until sugar is dissolved. Continue beating until stiff glossy peaks form. Transfer hot filling to crust. Spread meringue evenly over hot filling, sealing to edge of crust. Bake for 25-30 minutes or until golden brown. Cool 1 hour on a wire rack. Refrigerate at least 4 hours before serving.

1 PIECE: 486 cal., 17g fat (10g sat. fat), 131mg chol., 289mg sod., 80g carb. (59g sugars, 3g fiber), 6g pro.

CAKES & CUPCAKES

LAYER CAKE, BUNDT CAKE, COFFEE CAKE,
CUPCAKES—IS THERE ANY DAY THAT CAN'T
BE MADE EVEN BETTER WITH CAKE?

SALTED CARAMEL
CUPCAKES, P. 202

10 minutes before inverting onto a serving plate. Combine whipped topping and yogurt; serve with gingerbread.

1 PIECE WITH 2 TBSP. YOGURT CREAM: 289 cal., 7g fat (5g sat. fat), 42mg chol., 284mg sod., 53g carb. (28g sugars, 2g fiber), 4g pro.

Graham Streusel Coffee Cake

PREP: 20 MIN. • **BAKE:** 40 MIN. + COOLING
MAKES: 16 SERVINGS

I use this sweet coffee cake recipe often because it's quick and easy to make and it never fails to please.
—Blanche Whytsell, Arnoldsburg, WV

- 1½ cups graham cracker crumbs
- ¾ cup packed brown sugar
- ¾ cup chopped pecans
- 1½ tsp. ground cinnamon
- ⅔ cup butter, melted
- 1 pkg. yellow cake mix (regular size)
- ½ cup confectioners' sugar
- 1 Tbsp. milk

1. Preheat oven to 350°. In a small bowl, combine the cracker crumbs, brown sugar, pecans and cinnamon. Stir in butter; set aside. Prepare cake mix according to package directions.
2. Pour half of the batter into a greased 13x9-in. baking pan. Sprinkle with half the graham cracker mixture. Carefully spoon remaining batter on top. Sprinkle with the remaining graham cracker mixture.
3. Bake 40-45 minutes or until a toothpick inserted in center comes out clean. Cool on a wire rack.
4. Combine confectioners' sugar and milk; drizzle over cooled coffee cake.

1 PIECE: 329 cal., 15g fat (6g sat. fat), 21mg chol., 332mg sod., 46g carb. (30g sugars, 2g fiber), 3g pro.

Cran-Apple Praline Gingerbread

PREP: 25 MIN. • **BAKE:** 30 MIN. + COOLING
MAKES: 8 SERVINGS

Start with a spice-rich batter baked atop apples and cranberries in a creamy caramel sauce, then invert when done for a topsy-turvy dessert that's a real beauty. The old-time taste will delight family and friends!
—Jeanne Holt, St. Paul, MN

- ⅔ cup fat-free caramel ice cream topping
- 2 medium tart apples, peeled and thinly sliced
- ⅔ cup fresh or frozen cranberries
- ¼ cup butter, softened
- ¼ cup sugar
- 1 large egg
- 6 Tbsp. molasses
- ¼ cup unsweetened applesauce
- 1½ cups all-purpose flour
- ¾ tsp. baking soda
- ½ tsp. ground ginger
- ½ tsp. apple pie spice
- ¼ tsp. salt
- ¼ cup hot water

YOGURT CREAM
- ¾ cup reduced-fat whipped topping
- ½ cup fat-free vanilla yogurt

1. Preheat oven to 350°. Coat a 9-in. round baking pan with cooking spray. Pour caramel topping into pan and tilt to coat bottom evenly. Arrange apples and cranberries in a single layer over caramel.
2. In a large bowl, beat butter and sugar until crumbly, about 2 minutes. Add egg; mix well. Beat in molasses and applesauce (mixture may appear curdled). Combine the flour, baking soda, ginger, pie spice and salt; add to butter mixture just until moistened. Stir in hot water.
3. Pour over fruit; smooth top. Bake for 30-35 minutes or until a toothpick inserted in the center comes out clean. Cool for

Pumpkin Cake Roll

PREP: 25 MIN. • **BAKE:** 15 MIN. + CHILLING
MAKES: 10 SERVINGS

*This cake is a slice of heaven—
especially if you like the combination
of cream cheese and pumpkin. It's
worth considering as a fancy alternative
to traditional pumpkin pie as your
Thanksgiving dessert.*
—Elizabeth Montgomery, Allston, MA

- 3 **large eggs**
- 1 **cup sugar**
- ⅔ **cup canned pumpkin**
- 1 **tsp. lemon juice**
- ¾ **cup all-purpose flour**
- 2 **tsp. ground cinnamon**
- 1 **tsp. baking powder**
- ½ **tsp. salt**
- ¼ **tsp. ground nutmeg**
- 1 **cup finely chopped walnuts**

CREAM CHEESE FILLING
- 6 **oz. cream cheese, softened**
- 1 **cup confectioners' sugar**
- ¼ **cup butter, softened**
- ½ **tsp. vanilla extract**
  Additional confectioners' sugar

**SEE HOW
IT'S DONE**
To see how to
make this cake
and get that
perfect roll,
hover your
camera here.

1. Preheat oven to 375°. In a large
bowl, beat eggs on high for 5 minutes.
Gradually beat in sugar until thick and
lemon-colored. Add pumpkin and lemon
juice. Combine the flour, cinnamon,
baking powder, salt and nutmeg; fold
into the pumpkin mixture.

2. Grease a 15x10x1-in. baking pan and
line with parchment. Grease and flour
the parchment. Spread batter into the
pan; sprinkle with walnuts. Bake for
15 minutes or until cake springs back
when lightly touched.

3. Immediately turn out onto a clean dish
towel dusted with confectioners' sugar.
Peel off parchment and roll cake up in
towel, starting with a short end. Cool.

4. Meanwhile, in a large bowl, beat the cream
cheese, sugar, butter and vanilla until fluffy.
Carefully unroll the cake. Spread filling over
cake to within 1 in. of edges. Roll up again.
Cover and chill until serving. Dust with
confectioners' sugar.

1 PIECE: 365 cal., 20g fat (8g sat. fat), 85mg
chol., 279mg sod., 44g carb. (33g sugars, 2g
fiber), 6g pro.

DID YOU KNOW

Cutting a slight angle on the short ends
of the cake before spreading the filling
will give you a more elegant-looking roll,
with a tapered point rather than a blunt
end in the center, and a smoother seam
on the outside.

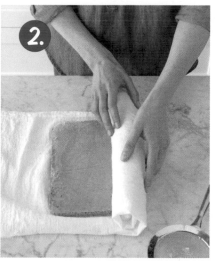

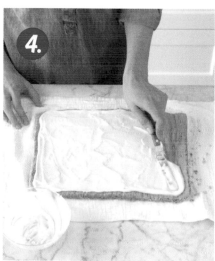

MAKE A CAKE ROLL

1. Sprinkle the clean towel with powdered sugar to keep the cake from sticking to it.

2. Use the towel to guide the roll; this keeps it straight and even, and prevents tearing the warm cake.

3. Let the cake cool in its roll; this will help it keep this shape even once you unroll it.

4. When adding the filling, leave a ½ in. border of plain cake on each side. This will prevent the filling from being pushed out the seam and ends and will make the center of the roll neater.

5. When you roll the cake up again, use the cloth to push the cake into each turn, then peel the cloth back rather than including it in the roll. Because the cake has cooled in a rounded shape, it should not crack.

Apple Bavarian Torte

PREP: 20 MIN. • **BAKE:** 45 MIN. + COOLING
MAKES: 16 SERVINGS

Layer a cream cheese filling, apples and almonds on a cookie-like crust for a picture-perfect torte that's ideal for autumn.
—Sheila Swift, Dobson, NC

- ½ cup butter, softened
- ⅓ cup sugar
- 1 cup all-purpose flour
- ¼ tsp. vanilla extract

FILLING

- 1 pkg. (8 oz.) cream cheese, softened
- ¼ cup plus ⅓ cup sugar, divided
- 1 large egg, lightly beaten
- ½ tsp. vanilla extract
- 5½ cups thinly sliced peeled tart apples (about 6 medium)
- ½ tsp. ground cinnamon
- ¼ cup sliced almonds

1. Preheat oven to 450°. In a small bowl, cream butter and sugar. Beat in flour and vanilla until blended. Press onto the bottom of a greased 9-in. springform pan.

2. For filling, in a large bowl, beat cream cheese and ¼ cup sugar until fluffy. Beat in egg and vanilla. Pour over crust. In another large bowl, toss apples with cinnamon and the remaining sugar. Spoon over the cream cheese layer.

3. Bake 10 minutes. Reduce the oven setting to 400°; bake 25 minutes longer. Sprinkle almonds over top; bake 10-15 minutes longer or until lightly browned and a toothpick inserted in the center comes out clean. Cool on a wire rack. Remove side of pan before slicing. Store in the refrigerator.

1 PIECE: 213 cal., 12g fat (7g sat. fat), 44mg chol., 87mg sod., 25g carb. (17g sugars, 1g fiber), 3g pro.

Olive Oil Cake

PREP: 15 MIN. • **BAKE:** 45 MIN. + COOLING
MAKES: 16 SERVINGS

A good olive oil cake isn't overly sweet, so it can just as easily be a breakfast treat or an afternoon snack as it can be a dessert. For a flavor variation, try this cake with ground pistachios and lemon zest instead.
—Lisa Kaminski, Wauwatosa, WI

  3 **large eggs**
1½ **cups sugar**
 ¾ **cup extra virgin olive oil**
 ¾ **cup ground almonds**
 ½ **cup 2% milk**
  4 **tsp. grated orange zest**
  1 **tsp. vanilla extract**
1¾ **cups all-purpose flour**
  2 **tsp. baking powder**
 ½ **tsp. salt**
 ¾ **cup confectioners' sugar**
  2 **to 3 Tbsp. orange juice**
      Sliced almonds, toasted, optional

1. Preheat oven to 350°. Grease and flour a 10-in. fluted tube pan. In a large bowl, beat eggs on high speed for 3 minutes. Gradually add the sugar, beating until thick and lemon-colored. Gradually beat in oil. Beat in the ground almonds, milk, orange zest and vanilla.

2. In another bowl, whisk flour, baking powder and salt; fold into the egg mixture. Transfer batter to prepared pan, spreading evenly. Bake until a toothpick inserted near the center comes out clean, 45-50 minutes. Cool in pan 15 minutes before removing to a wire rack to cool completely.

3. For icing, whisk the confectioners' sugar and enough orange juice to reach a drizzling consistency. Drizzle over cake. If desired, sprinkle with almonds.

1 PIECE: 279 cal., 14g fat (2g sat. fat), 35mg chol., 152mg sod., 37g carb. (25g sugars, 1g fiber), 4g pro.

TEST KITCHEN TIP
To ensure that cakes come out easily, use solid shortening to grease plain and decoratively fluted tube pans.

Contest-Winning Chocolate Potato Cake

PREP: 40 MIN. • **BAKE:** 25 MIN. + COOLING
MAKES: 12 SERVINGS

I won grand champion honors in a potato festival baking contest with this moist chocolate cake. Double the icing recipe if you're making it for real sweet tooths.
—Catherine Hahn, Winamac, IN

- 1 cup butter, softened
- 2 cups sugar
- 2 large eggs, room temperature
- 1 cup cold mashed potatoes (without added milk and butter)
- 1 tsp. vanilla extract
- 2 cups all-purpose flour
- ½ cup baking cocoa
- 1 tsp. baking soda
- 1 cup whole milk
- 1 cup chopped walnuts or pecans

CARAMEL ICING
- ½ cup butter, cubed
- 1 cup packed brown sugar
- ¼ cup evaporated milk
- 2 cups confectioners' sugar
- ½ tsp. vanilla extract

1. Preheat oven to 350°. In a large bowl, cream butter and sugar until light and fluffy, 5-7 minutes. Add eggs, 1 at a time, beating well after each addition. Add potatoes and vanilla. Combine the flour, cocoa and baking soda; gradually add to creamed mixture alternately with milk, beating well after each addition. Stir in nuts.

2. Pour batter into 2 greased and floured 9-in. round baking pans. Bake until a toothpick inserted in the center comes out clean, 25-30 minutes. Cool 10 minutes before removing from pans to wire racks to cool completely.

3. For icing, in a saucepan over low heat, cook butter and brown sugar until butter is melted and mixture is smooth. Stir in evaporated milk; bring to a boil, stirring constantly. Remove from the heat; cool to room temperature. Stir in confectioners' sugar and vanilla until smooth. Spread between layers and over top of cake.

1 PIECE: 671 cal., 31g fat (15g sat. fat), 101mg chol., 374mg sod., 94g carb. (71g sugars, 2g fiber), 8g pro.

Frosted Harvest Cake

PREP: 15 MIN. • **BAKE:** 20 MIN. + COOLING
MAKES: 3½ DOZEN

Craving brownies but want something just a little bit different? Indulge in this fall-flavored version topped with a delectable cream cheese frosting.
—Iola Egle, Bella Vista, AR

- 1 can (15 oz.) pumpkin
- 4 large eggs, room temperature
- ¾ cup canola oil
- 2 tsp. vanilla extract
- 2 cups all-purpose flour
- 2 cups sugar
- 1 Tbsp. pumpkin pie spice
- 2 tsp. ground cinnamon
- 2 tsp. baking powder
- 1 tsp. baking soda
- ½ tsp. salt

FROSTING
- 6 Tbsp. butter, softened
- 3 oz. cream cheese, softened
- 1 tsp. vanilla extract
- 1 tsp. 2% milk
- ⅛ tsp. salt
- 1½ to 2 cups confectioners' sugar

1. Preheat oven to 350°. In a large bowl, beat the pumpkin, eggs, oil and vanilla until blended. Combine the dry ingredients; gradually stir into pumpkin mixture.

2. Pour into a greased 15x10x1-in. baking pan. Bake until a toothpick inserted in the center comes out clean, 20-25 minutes. Cool in pan on a wire rack.

3. In a small bowl, beat the butter, cream cheese, vanilla, milk and salt until smooth. Gradually add confectioners' sugar until smooth. Frost cake; cut into bars. Store in the refrigerator.

1 PIECE: 83 cal., 4g fat (1g sat. fat), 16mg chol., 66mg sod., 11g carb. (8g sugars, 0 fiber), 1g pro.

Maple Tree Cake

PREP: 25 MIN. • **BAKE:** 30 MIN. + COOLING
MAKES: 16 SERVINGS

Here's a colorful dessert—perfect for fall. You could use dried fruit instead of frosting to make the leaves of the chocolate tree on this scrumptious maple-flavored cake.
—Lorraine Tishmack, Casselton, ND

- 4 **large eggs**
- 2 **cups sugar**
- 2 **cups sour cream**
- 2 **tsp. maple flavoring**
- 2½ **cups all-purpose flour**
- 2 **tsp. baking soda**
  Dash salt
- ½ **cup chopped pecans**

FROSTING

- 6 **Tbsp. butter, softened**
- 4½ **cups confectioners' sugar**
- ¾ **cup plus 2 Tbsp. maple syrup**
- ¼ **cup semisweet chocolate chips**
- ¼ **cup peanut butter chips**
- ½ **tsp. red paste food coloring**
- ¼ **tsp. yellow paste food coloring**

1. Preheat oven to 350°. In a large bowl, beat eggs and sugar. Add sour cream and maple flavoring. Combine flour, baking soda and salt; add to the sour cream mixture and mix well. Fold in pecans.

2. Pour batter into 2 greased and floured 9-in. round baking pans. Bake until a toothpick inserted in the center comes out clean, 30 minutes. Cool 10 minutes before removing from pans to wire racks to cool completely.

3. For frosting, in a bowl, cream butter and confectioners' sugar. Add syrup; mix well. Set aside ⅔ cup frosting for decoration; spread the remaining frosting between layers and over top and side of cake.

4. In a microwave-safe bowl, melt chocolate and peanut butter chips; stir until smooth. Transfer to a pastry bag fitted with a round tip or tip of your choice. Pipe a tree trunk and branches on the top of the cake.

5. For decorative leaves, divide the reserved frosting between 2 small bowls. Add red food coloring to 1 bowl; stir to combine. Add yellow food coloring to the other bowl; stir to combine. Cut a small hole in the tip of a pastry bag; insert a #21 star tip. Spoon the frostings alternately into the bag. Pipe frosting on top of cake to resemble leaves on the tree.

1 PIECE: 475 cal., 11g fat (5g sat. fat), 54mg chol., 205mg sod., 90g carb. (72g sugars, 1g fiber), 6g pro.

1. Grease a 13x9-in. baking pan; set aside. Microwave buttermilk just until warmed, 30-45 seconds. Stir in the coffee granules until dissolved.

2. In a large bowl, cream the butter and brown sugar until light and fluffy, 5-7 minutes. Add eggs, 1 at a time, beating well after each addition. Beat in vanilla. Combine flour, cornstarch, baking powder, baking soda, salt and nutmeg; add to the creamed mixture alternately with buttermilk mixture, beating well after each addition.

3. Transfer batter to prepared pan; bake at 350° until a toothpick inserted in the center comes out clean, 20-25 minutes. Cool on a wire rack for 5 minutes.

4. Using the end of a wooden spoon handle, poke holes in cake 2 in. apart. Pour ½ cup caramel topping into the holes. Spoon the remaining ¼ cup caramel topping over cake. Cool completely.

5. For frosting, in a small bowl, stir cocoa and coffee granules into boiling water until dissolved; cool to room temperature. In a small bowl, cream the butter and confectioners' sugar until light and fluffy. Stir in the melted chocolate and cocoa mixture until well combined. Frost cake.

1 PIECE: 335 cal., 16g fat (10g sat. fat), 61mg chol., 338mg sod., 47g carb. (22g sugars, 1g fiber), 4g pro.

Cuppa Joe Caramel Cake

PREP: 30 MIN. • **BAKE:** 20 MIN. + COOLING
MAKES: 15 SERVINGS

I get compliments on this wherever I take it. Adults really love the hint of coffee that goes perfectly with the brown sugar and caramel flavors.
—Leigh Doutt, Pueblo West, CO

- 1 cup buttermilk
- 4 tsp. instant coffee granules
- ½ cup butter, softened
- 1 cup packed brown sugar
- 2 large eggs, room temperature
- 1 tsp. vanilla extract
- 2 cups all-purpose flour
- 2 Tbsp. cornstarch
- 1½ tsp. baking powder
- ½ tsp. baking soda
- ½ tsp. salt
- ¼ tsp. ground nutmeg
- ¾ cup caramel ice cream topping, divided

FROSTING
- 1 Tbsp. baking cocoa
- 2 tsp. instant coffee granules
- ¼ cup boiling water
- ½ cup butter, softened
- ¼ cup confectioners' sugar
- ¾ cup semisweet chocolate chips, melted

Hot Chocolate Pumpkin Cake

PREP: 20 MIN.
BAKE: 55 MINUTES + COOLING
MAKES: 16 SERVINGS

Hot chocolate is my go-to cool-weather indulgence. To go with it, I like this moist pumpkin cake dusted with cocoa for an extra chocolate boost.
—Colleen Delawder, Herndon, VA

- 1 can (15 oz.) pumpkin
- 2 cups sugar
- 3 large eggs
- ½ cup packed brown sugar
- ½ cup butter, melted
- ½ cup canola oil
- 1 Tbsp. vanilla extract
- 3 cups all-purpose flour
- 2 tsp. baking soda
- 2 tsp. ground cinnamon
- ¼ tsp. ground nutmeg
- ¼ tsp. ground chipotle pepper
- ½ tsp. salt
- 1 pkg. (10 oz.) miniature semisweet chocolate chips
  Optional: Baking cocoa or confectioners' sugar

1. Preheat oven to 350°. Generously grease and flour a 10-in. fluted tube pan.
2. Beat the first 7 ingredients until well blended. In another bowl, whisk together the flour, baking soda, spices and salt; gradually beat into the pumpkin mixture. Stir in chocolate chips.
3. Add batter to prepared pan. Bake until a toothpick inserted in center comes out clean, 55-65 minutes. Let cool in pan for 30 minutes before removing to a wire rack; cool completely. If desired, dust with cocoa.

1 PIECE: 450 cal., 20g fat (8g sat. fat), 50mg chol., 298mg sod., 66g carb. (45g sugars, 3g fiber), 5g pro.

Hazelnut Cake Squares

PREP: 10 MIN. • **BAKE:** 25 MIN. + COOLING
MAKES: 15 SERVINGS

Whenever one of my daughters is asked to bring a dish to a church function, party or special occasion, she asks me for this recipe. It is so easy to prepare because it starts with a mix. It doesn't need icing, so it's great for bake sales too.
—Brenda Melancon, McComb, MS

1	**pkg. yellow cake mix (regular size)**
3	**large eggs**
⅔	**cup water**
⅔	**cup Nutella**
¼	**cup canola oil**
½	**cup semisweet chocolate chips**
½	**cup chopped hazelnuts, toasted**

½ **cup brickle toffee bits, optional**
Confectioners' sugar, optional

1. Preheat oven to 350°. Grease a 13x9-in. baking pan; set aside.
2. In a large bowl, combine cake mix, eggs, water, Nutella and oil; beat on low speed for 30 seconds. Beat on medium for 2 minutes. Fold in chocolate chips, hazelnuts and, if desired, toffee bits.
3. Transfer batter to prepared pan. Bake until a toothpick inserted in center comes out clean, 25-30 minutes.
4. Cool completely in pan on a wire rack. Dust with confectioners' sugar if desired.
1 PIECE: 280 cal., 14g fat (3g sat. fat), 37mg chol., 245mg sod., 38g carb. (24g sugars, 2g fiber), 4g pro.

Salted Caramel Cupcakes

PREP: 25 MIN. + CHILLING
BAKE: 20 MIN. + COOLING
MAKES: 10 CUPCAKES

To help balance the sweetness of the brown sugar cupcake, our Test Kitchen experts created a unique salty frosting. It's the best of both worlds!
—Taste of Home *Test Kitchen*

½ cup butter, softened
½ cup packed brown sugar
¼ cup sugar
2 large eggs, room temperature
1 tsp. vanilla extract
1¼ cups all-purpose flour
¾ tsp. baking powder
¼ tsp. salt
½ cup 2% milk

FROSTING
⅓ cup sugar
4 tsp. water
⅛ tsp. salt
1⅓ cups heavy whipping cream
   Optional: Caramel ice cream topping and flaky sea salt

1. Preheat oven to 350°. In a large bowl, cream butter and sugars until light and fluffy, 5-7 minutes. Add eggs, 1 at a time, beating well after each addition. Beat in vanilla. Combine flour, baking powder and salt; add to the creamed mixture alternately with milk, beating well after each addition.

2. Fill 10 paper-lined muffin cups three-fourths full with batter. Bake 18-22 minutes or until a toothpick inserted in the center of a cupcake comes out clean. Cool for 10 minutes before removing from pan to a wire rack to cool completely.

3. For frosting, in a large heavy saucepan, combine sugar, water and salt. Cook over medium-low heat until sugar begins to melt. Gently pull melted sugar to center of pan until the sugar melts evenly. Cook, without stirring, until mixture turns an amber color.

4. Remove from heat; gradually stir in cream until smooth. Transfer to a small bowl; refrigerate, covered, for 4 hours.

5. Beat frosting until stiff peaks form. Frost cupcakes. If desired, top with caramel ice cream topping and sprinkle with sea salt.

1 CUPCAKE: 416 cal., 22g fat (14g sat. fat), 111mg chol., 224mg sod., 52g carb. (39g sugars, 0 fiber), 4g pro.

1. Line the bottom of a greased 9-in. springform pan with parchment; grease the paper. Place pan on a double thickness of heavy-duty foil (about 18 in. square). Securely wrap foil around pan; set aside.

2. In a large heavy saucepan, combine the chocolate, butter and wine over low heat, stirring constantly while melting. Remove from the heat. Cool to room temperature.

3. Meanwhile, in a large bowl, beat the eggs, sugar and vanilla until frothy and doubled in volume, about 5 minutes. Gradually fold into the chocolate mixture, one-third at a time, until well blended. Pour into prepared pan. Place springform pan in a large baking pan; add 1 in. hot water to larger pan.

4. Bake at 350° for 28-32 minutes or until the outer edge is set (center will jiggle). Remove springform pan from water bath. Cool completely on a wire rack.

5. Carefully run a knife around edge of pan to loosen; remove side. Invert onto a serving platter; remove parchment.

6. For the ganache, place chocolate in a small bowl. In a small saucepan, bring cream and rosemary just to a boil. Remove from the heat; discard rosemary. Pour cream over chocolate; whisk until smooth. Cool slightly, stirring occasionally. Pour over cake. Chill until set.

TO MAKE AHEAD: This cake can be made a day in advance. Store, covered, in the refrigerator. Remove from refrigerator 1 hour before serving.

1 PIECE: 435 cal., 35g fat (20g sat. fat), 156mg chol., 121mg sod., 31g carb. (26g sugars, 3g fiber), 7g pro.

Flourless Chocolate Cake with Rosemary Ganache

PREP: 40 MIN. • **BAKE:** 30 MIN. + COOLING
MAKES: 16 SERVINGS

This rich cake is the essence of moist, dense and chocolaty. A silky chocolate ganache infused with rosemary really takes it over the top.
—*Kelly Gardner, Alton, IL*

1 lb. semisweet chocolate, chopped
1 cup butter, cubed
¼ cup dry red wine
8 large eggs
½ cup sugar
1 tsp. vanilla extract

GANACHE
9 oz. bittersweet chocolate, chopped
1 cup heavy whipping cream
2 fresh rosemary sprigs

3. Spread frosting between layers and over top and sides of cake. Sprinkle top with the remaining ½ cup walnuts. Store in the refrigerator.

1 PIECE: 504 cal., 24g fat (8g sat. fat), 49mg chol., 570mg sod., 71g carb. (52g sugars, 2g fiber), 5g pro.

Honey Bun Cake

PREP: 20 MIN. • **BAKE:** 35 MIN.
MAKES: 20 SERVINGS

I carry along recipe cards to hand out whenever I take this moist, fluffy cake to school socials, potlucks and the like. It always goes quickly.
—Kathy Mayo, Winston-Salem, NC

  1 **pkg. yellow or white cake mix (regular size)**
  4 **large egg whites**
  1 **cup sour cream**
 ⅔ **cup unsweetened applesauce**
 ½ **cup packed brown sugar**
  2 **tsp. ground cinnamon**
1½ **cups confectioners' sugar**
  2 **Tbsp. 2% milk**
  1 **tsp. vanilla extract**

1. Grease a 13x9-in baking pan; set aside. Preheat oven to 325°. Combine dry cake mix, egg whites, sour cream and applesauce. Beat on low until moistened. Beat on medium for 2 minutes.

2. Pour half the batter into prepared pan. Combine brown sugar and cinnamon; sprinkle over batter. Cover with remaining batter; cut through with a knife to swirl. Bake until a toothpick comes out clean, 35-40 minutes. Cool on a wire rack.

3. For glaze, combine confectioners' sugar, milk and vanilla until smooth; drizzle over warm cake.

1 PIECE: 185 cal., 4g fat (1g sat. fat), 5mg chol., 198mg sod., 36g carb., 1g fiber), 2g pro.

Dark Chocolate Carrot Cake

PREP: 20 MIN. • **BAKE:** 25 MIN. + COOLING
MAKES: 16 SERVINGS

Carrot cake has a dark side—and it's delicious! Cream cheese and shredded carrots in the batter keep the cake moist, while nuts and cinnamon boost the flavor.
—Darlene Brenden, Salem, OR

  1 **pkg. dark chocolate cake mix (regular size)**
  4 **oz. cream cheese, softened**
  1 **pkg. (3.9 oz.) instant chocolate pudding mix**
  1 **cup 2% milk**
  3 **large eggs**
  1 **tsp. ground cinnamon**
  3 **cups shredded carrots**
  1 **cup chopped walnuts, toasted, divided**
  2 **cans (16 oz. each) cream cheese frosting**

1. Preheat oven to 350°. Combine the cake mix, cream cheese, pudding mix, milk, eggs and cinnamon; beat on low speed for 30 seconds. Beat on medium speed for 2 minutes. Stir in carrots and ½ cup of the walnuts.

2. Pour into 3 greased and floured 8-in. round baking pans. Bake 25-30 minutes or until a toothpick inserted in the center comes out clean. Cool 10 minutes in pans; remove to wire racks to cool completely.

Moist Chocolate Cake

PREP: 15 MIN. • **BAKE:** 25 MIN. + COOLING
MAKES: 12 SERVINGS

The cake reminds me of my grandmother because it was one of her specialties. I bake it often for family parties, and it always brings back fond memories. The cake is light and airy with a delicious chocolate taste. This recipe is a keeper!
—Patricia Kreitz, Richland, PA

- 2 **cups all-purpose flour**
- 1 **tsp. salt**
- 1 **tsp. baking powder**
- 2 **tsp. baking soda**
- ¾ **cup baking cocoa**
- 2 **cups sugar**
- 1 **cup canola oil**
- 1 **cup brewed coffee**
- 1 **cup whole milk**
- 2 **large eggs**
- 1 **tsp. vanilla extract**

ICING

- 1 **cup whole milk**
- 5 **Tbsp. all-purpose flour**
- ½ **cup butter, softened**
- ½ **cup shortening**
- 1 **cup sugar**
- 1 **tsp. vanilla extract**
  Additional baking cocoa, optional

1. Preheat oven to 325°. Grease and flour two 9-in. round baking pans; set aside. In a bowl, sift together dry ingredients. Add oil, coffee and milk; mix at medium speed 1 minute. Add eggs and vanilla; beat 2 minutes longer. (Batter will be thin.)

2. Pour batter into prepared pans; bake until a toothpick inserted in the center comes out clean, 25-30 minutes. Cool 10 minutes before removing from pans to cool on wire racks.

3. Meanwhile, for icing, combine milk and flour in a saucepan; cook until thick. Cover and refrigerate.

4. In a bowl, beat butter, shortening, sugar and vanilla until creamy. Add chilled milk mixture and beat 10 minutes. Frost cooled cake. If desired, dust with additional cocoa.

1 PIECE: 636 cal., 37g fat (10g sat. fat), 61mg chol., 549mg sod., 73g carb. (51g sugars, 2g fiber), 6g pro.

TEST KITCHEN TIP

You can use this same recipe to make a smaller layer cake and a suite of cupcakes. Instead of using two 9-in. pans, use two 8-in. round pans and six muffin cups.

SEE HOW IT'S DONE
Watch the simple steps of creating this classic cake. Just hover your camera here.

Cranberry-Filled Orange Pound Cake

PREP: 25 MIN. • **BAKE:** 50 MIN. + COOLING
MAKES: 12 SERVINGS

I made this for a holiday dinner with my family. Everyone loved the cran-orange flavor and the sweet glaze drizzled on top. For a fun variation, include ⅔ cup flaked sweetened coconut when adding the orange juice to the batter, and sprinkle the finished cake with toasted coconut.
—Patricia Harmon, Baden, PA

- 1 **cup butter, softened**
- 1 **pkg. (8 oz.) reduced-fat cream cheese**
- 2 **cups sugar**
- 6 **large eggs, room temperature**
- 3 **Tbsp. orange juice, divided**
- 4 **tsp. grated orange zest**
- 3 **cups all-purpose flour**
- 1 **tsp. baking powder**
- ½ **tsp. baking soda**
- ½ **tsp. salt**
- 1 **can (14 oz.) whole-berry cranberry sauce**
- ½ **cup dried cherries**

GLAZE
- 1 **cup confectioners' sugar**
- ¼ **tsp. grated orange zest**
- 4 **to 5 tsp. orange juice**

1. Preheat oven to 350°. Grease and flour a 10-in. fluted tube pan; set aside. In a large bowl, cream the butter, cream cheese and sugar until light and fluffy. Add 1 egg at a time, beating well after each addition. Beat in 2 Tbsp. orange juice and the orange zest. In another bowl, whisk the flour, baking powder, baking soda and salt; gradually add to the creamed mixture, beating just until combined.

2. In a small bowl, mix cranberry sauce, cherries and the remaining 1 Tbsp. orange juice. Spoon two-thirds of the batter into the prepared pan. Spread with cranberry mixture. Top with remaining batter.

3. Bake 50-60 minutes or until a toothpick inserted in center comes out clean. Loosen sides from pan with a knife. Let cool in pan for 10 minutes before removing to a wire rack to cool completely.

4. For the glaze, mix confectioners' sugar, orange zest and enough orange juice to reach desired consistency. Pour over the top of the cake, allowing some to flow over the sides.

1 PIECE: 573 cal., 22g fat (13g sat. fat), 147mg chol., 447mg sod., 87g carb. (57g sugars, 2g fiber), 9g pro.

Carrot Cupcakes

PREP: 15 MIN. • **BAKE:** 20 MIN.
MAKES: 2 DOZEN

To try to get my family to eat more vegetables, I often hide nutritional foods inside sweet treats. Now we can have our cake and eat our vegetables, too!
—Doreen Kelly, Rosyln, PA

- 4 **large eggs**
- 2 **cups sugar**
- 1 **cup canola oil**
- 2 **cups all-purpose flour**
- 2 **tsp. ground cinnamon**
- 1 **tsp. baking soda**
- 1 **tsp. baking powder**
- 1 **tsp. ground allspice**
- ½ **tsp. salt**
- 3 **cups grated carrots**

CHUNKY FROSTING

- 1 **pkg. (8 oz.) cream cheese, softened**
- ¼ **cup butter, softened**
- 2 **cups confectioners' sugar**
- ½ **cup sweetened shredded coconut**
- ½ **cup chopped pecans**
- ½ **cup chopped raisins**

1. Preheat oven to 325°. In a large bowl, beat the eggs, sugar and oil. In a second bowl, combine flour, cinnamon, baking soda, baking powder, allspice and salt; gradually add to egg mixture. Stir in carrots.

2. Fill 24 greased or paper-lined muffin cups two-thirds full. Bake until a toothpick inserted in the center comes out clean, 20-25 minutes. Cool 5 minutes before removing from pans to wire racks.

3. For frosting, in a large bowl, beat cream cheese and butter until fluffy. Gradually beat in confectioners' sugar until smooth. Stir in coconut, pecans and raisins. Frost cupcakes. Store in the refrigerator.

1 CUPCAKE: 326 cal., 18g fat (5g sat. fat), 51mg chol., 187mg sod., 40g carb. (30g sugars, 1g fiber), 3g pro.

Nancy Heishman

Las Vegas, NY

My favorite apple cake is made with a shot of apple brandy and drizzled with caramel to set off the wonderful flavors. If alcohol is a no-go in your house, use orange juice instead. If you'd rather follow a chocolate route, add mini chocolate chips to the cake and use chocolate ice cream topping for the drizzle.

Apple Brandy Pecan Cake

PREP: 20 MIN.
BAKE: 40 MIN. + COOLING
MAKES: 20 SERVINGS

- ½ cup butter, softened
- 1 cup packed brown sugar
- 3 large eggs, room temperature
- 2 cups unsweetened applesauce
- 2 Tbsp. apple brandy
- 3 cups all-purpose flour
- 1 tsp. salt
- ½ tsp. baking soda
- 1 tsp. ground cinnamon
- ¾ tsp. ground allspice
- ¼ tsp. ground nutmeg
- 3 medium tart apples, peeled cored and chopped, about 3 cups
- 1 cup chopped pecans
  Hot caramel ice cream topping, optional

1. Preheat oven to 350°. Lightly grease a 13x9-in. baking pan.

2. In a large bowl, beat butter and sugar until well blended, about 3 minutes. Add 1 egg at a time, beating well after each addition. Beat in applesauce and brandy. In another bowl, whisk the flour, salt, baking soda, cinnamon, allspice and nutmeg; gradually add to butter mixture. Fold in apples and pecans.

3. Transfer batter to prepared pan. Bake until a toothpick inserted in the center comes out clean, 40-50 minutes. Cool completely. If desired, top with caramel topping.

1 PIECE: 223 cal., 10g fat (4g sat. fat), 40mg chol., 201mg sod., 31g carb. (15g sugars, 2g fiber), 4g pro.

Red Wine & Chocolate Cupcakes

PREP: 15 MIN. • **BAKE:** 20 MIN. + COOLING
MAKES: 2 DOZEN

Red wine and chocolate make an amazing pairing, especially in these rich, elegant cupcakes I make each year for my mother's birthday. She adores them!
—Candace Cheney, Fort McMurray, AB

- ½ cup baking cocoa
- 4 oz. bittersweet chocolate, chopped
- ½ cup boiling water
- 1 cup butter, softened
- 1½ cups sugar
- 4 large eggs, room temperature
- 1¾ cups all-purpose flour
- 1½ tsp. baking powder
- 1 tsp. salt
- ½ cup dry red wine

MASCARPONE ICING

- 2 cartons (8 oz. each) mascarpone cheese
- 2 cups confectioners' sugar
- ¼ tsp. vanilla extract

1. Place cocoa and chocolate in a small bowl; whisk in boiling water until chocolate is melted and mixture is blended.
2. In a large bowl, cream butter and sugar until light and fluffy, 5-7 minutes. Add 1 egg at a time, beating well after each addition. Combine the flour, baking powder and salt; add to creamed mixture alternately with wine and the chocolate mixture, beating well after each addition. Fill 24 paper-lined muffin cups three-fourths full.
3. Bake at 350° for 18-22 minutes or until a toothpick inserted in center comes out clean. Cool for 10 minutes before removing from pans to wire racks to cool completely.
4. For frosting, in a small bowl, beat mascarpone cheese, confectioners' sugar and vanilla extract until creamy. Frost cupcakes. Store in the refrigerator.

1 CUPCAKE: 318 cal., 19g fat (11g sat. fat), 75mg chol., 212mg sod., 31g carb. (23g sugars, 1g fiber), 4g pro.

Apple Pear Cake

PREP: 25 MIN. • **BAKE:** 1 HOUR + COOLING
MAKES: 15 SERVINGS

When my sister Catherine made her apple cake for me, I knew I needed the recipe. For my version, I added some pears from the trees on our acreage. This cake is very moist and so good. Every time I make it, people ask for the recipe.
—Mary Ann Lees, Centreville, AL

- 2 cups shredded peeled tart apples
- 2 cups shredded peeled pears
- 2 cups sugar
- 1¼ cups canola oil
- 1 cup raisins
- 1 cup chopped pecans
- 2 large eggs, lightly beaten
- 1 tsp. vanilla extract
- 3 cups all-purpose flour
- 2 tsp. baking soda
- 2 tsp. ground cinnamon
- ½ tsp. ground nutmeg
- ½ tsp. salt

CREAM CHEESE FROSTING

- 3 oz. cream cheese, softened
- 3 cups confectioners' sugar
- ¼ cup butter, softened
- 2 Tbsp. 2% milk
- ½ tsp. vanilla extract

1. Grease a 13x9-in baking pan; set aside. Preheat oven to 325°. In a large bowl, combine the first 8 ingredients. Combine dry ingredients; stir into the fruit mixture.
2. Pour batter into prepared pan. Bake until a toothpick inserted in the center comes out clean, about 1 hour. Cool completely on a wire rack.
3. For frosting, in a large bowl, beat cream cheese, confectioners' sugar and butter until smooth. Beat in milk and vanilla; frost cake. Store in the refrigerator.

1 PIECE: 613 cal., 30g fat (6g sat. fat), 43mg chol., 306mg sod., 84g carb. (60g sugars, 3g fiber), 5g pro.

Cherry Cola Cake

PREP: 30 MIN. • **BAKE:** 25 MIN. + COOLING
MAKES: 12 SERVINGS

Cherry cola and marshmallows make a zippy chocolate dessert that is simply scrumptious topped with ice cream.
—Cheri Mason, Harmony, NC

- 1½ cups miniature marshmallows
- 2 cups all-purpose flour
- 2 cups sugar
- 1 tsp. baking soda
- 1 cup butter, cubed
- 1 cup cherry-flavored cola
- 3 Tbsp. baking cocoa
- 2 large eggs
- ½ cup buttermilk
- 1 tsp. vanilla extract

FROSTING

- ¾ cup butter, softened
- 1 cup confectioners' sugar
- 1 jar (7 oz.) marshmallow creme
- 2 Tbsp. frozen cherry-pomegranate juice concentrate, thawed
  Fresh sweet cherries with stems

1. Preheat oven to 350°. Line bottoms of 2 greased 9-in. round baking pans with parchment; grease paper. Divide marshmallows between the 2 pans.

2. In a large bowl, whisk flour, sugar and baking soda. In a small saucepan, combine butter, cola and cocoa; bring just to a boil, stirring occasionally. Add to flour mixture, stirring just until moistened.

3. In a small bowl, whisk eggs, buttermilk and vanilla until blended; add to the flour mixture, whisking constantly. Pour into prepared pans, dividing batter evenly. (Marshmallows will float to the top.)

4. Bake 25-30 minutes or until a toothpick inserted in center comes out clean. Cool cake in pans 10 minutes before removing to wire racks; remove paper. Cool completely.

5. For frosting, beat the butter and confectioners' sugar until smooth. Beat in marshmallow creme and the juice concentrate on low just until blended.

6. Place 1 cake layer on a serving plate; spread top with 1 cup frosting. Top with the remaining cake layer; spread with the remaining frosting. Decorate with cherries.

1 PIECE: 587 cal., 28g fat (17g sat. fat), 106mg chol., 335mg sod., 83g carb. (61g sugars, 1g fiber), 4g pro.

Walnut Blitz Torte

PREP: 30 MIN. + CHILLING
BAKE: 35 MIN. + COOLING
MAKES: 16 SERVINGS

This pretty torte is very popular at family gatherings. The cake layers are baked with the "frosting"—crunchy, sweet meringue—already in place, and then assembled with a layer of luscious custard in the center. Whenever I make it, everyone always asks me for the recipe.
—Suzan Stacey, Parsonsfield, ME

2 Tbsp. sugar
4½ tsp. cornstarch
1 cup whole milk
1 large egg yolk, room temperature
1 tsp. vanilla extract

CAKE BATTER
½ cup butter, softened
½ cup sugar
4 large egg yolks, room temperature
1 tsp. vanilla extract
1 cup all-purpose flour
1 tsp. baking powder
¼ tsp. salt
5 Tbsp. whole milk

MERINGUE
5 large egg whites, room temperature
1 cup sugar
2 cups chopped walnuts, divided

1. Preheat oven to 325°. In a small saucepan, combine sugar and cornstarch. Stir in milk until smooth. Cook and stir over medium-high heat until thickened and bubbly. Reduce heat to low; cook and stir 2 minutes longer. Remove from heat. Stir a small amount of the hot filling into egg yolk; return all to the pan, stirring constantly. Bring to a gentle boil; cook and stir for 2 minutes. Remove from heat; stir in the vanilla. Cover and refrigerate.

2. Meanwhile, in a large bowl, cream the butter and sugar until light and fluffy, 5-7 minutes. Beat in egg yolks and vanilla. Combine the flour, baking powder and salt; gradually add to the creamed mixture alternately with milk and mix well. Spread into 2 greased and floured 9-in. round baking pans; set aside.

3. In a small bowl, beat egg whites on medium speed until foamy. Gradually beat in sugar, 1 Tbsp. at a time, on high until stiff glossy peaks form and the sugar is dissolved. Fold in 1 cup nuts. Spread meringue evenly over batter. Sprinkle with the remaining 1 cup nuts.

4. Bake 35-40 minutes or until meringue is browned and crisp. Cool on wire racks for 10 minutes (meringue will crack).

5. Carefully run a knife around edges of pans to loosen. Remove to wire racks; cool with meringue side up. To assemble, place 1 cake with meringue side up on a serving plate; carefully spread with custard. Top with remaining cake, meringue side up. Refrigerate until serving.

1 PIECE: 292 cal., 17g fat (5g sat. fat), 85mg chol., 149mg sod., 30g carb. (21g sugars, 1g fiber), 7g pro.

Pumpkin Streusel Cupcakes

PREP: 25 MIN. • **BAKE:** 20 MIN. + COOLING
MAKES: 2 DOZEN

A delicious crumb filling becomes the center of attention inside these yummy confections that taste like pumpkin bread.
—Donna Gish, Blue Springs, MO

- 1   **pkg. spice cake mix (regular size)**
- 1¼ **cups water**
- 3   **large eggs**
- ½   **cup canned pumpkin**

STREUSEL
- ½   **cup packed brown sugar**
- ½   **tsp. ground cinnamon**
- 1   **Tbsp. butter**

FROSTING
- 1   **pkg. (8 oz.) cream cheese, softened**
- 2   **Tbsp. butter**
- 2   **cups confectioners' sugar**
- ½   **tsp. vanilla extract**

1. Preheat oven to 350°. In a large bowl, combine the cake mix, water, eggs and pumpkin. Beat on low speed just until moistened. Beat on medium for 2 minutes.

2. In a small bowl, combine brown sugar and cinnamon; cut in butter until crumbly. Fill 24 paper-lined muffin cups one-fourth full with batter. Drop streusel by heaping teaspoonfuls into center of each cupcake. Cover with the remaining batter.

3. Bake for 18-20 minutes or until a toothpick inserted in the cake portion comes out clean. Cool for 10 minutes before removing from pans to wire racks to cool completely.

4. In a small bowl, beat cream cheese and butter until fluffy. Add confectioners' sugar and vanilla; beat until smooth. Frost cupcakes. Store in the refrigerator.

1 CUPCAKE: 204 cal., 8g fat (4g sat. fat), 46mg chol., 213mg sod., 31g carb. (23g sugars, 0 fiber), 3g pro.

Chocolate-Peanut Butter Sheet Cake

PREP: 25 MIN. • **BAKE:** 25 MIN. + COOLING
MAKES: 15 SERVINGS

I love peanut butter and chocolate, so I combined a few recipes to blend the two flavors into one heavenly sheet cake.
—Lisa Varner, El Paso, TX

- 2 **cups all-purpose flour**
- 2 **cups sugar**
- 1 **tsp. baking soda**
- ½ **tsp. salt**
- 1 **cup water**
- ½ **cup butter, cubed**
- ½ **cup creamy peanut butter**
- ¼ **cup baking cocoa**
- 3 **large eggs**
- ½ **cup sour cream**
- 2 **tsp. vanilla extract**

FROSTING

- 3 **cups confectioners' sugar**
- ⅓ **cup creamy peanut butter**
- ½ **cup 2% milk**
- ½ **tsp. vanilla extract**
- ½ **cup chopped salted or unsalted peanuts**

1. Preheat oven to 350°. Grease a 13x9-in. baking pan; set aside.

2. In a large bowl, whisk flour, sugar, baking soda and salt. In a small saucepan, combine water, butter, peanut butter and cocoa; bring just to a boil, stirring occasionally. Add to flour mixture, stirring just until moistened.

3. In a small bowl, whisk the eggs, sour cream and vanilla until blended; add to flour mixture, whisking constantly. Transfer to prepared pan. Bake until a toothpick inserted in center comes out clean, 25-30 minutes.

4. Meanwhile, prepare frosting. In a large bowl, beat confectioners' sugar, peanut butter, milk and vanilla until smooth.

5. Remove cake from oven; place pan on a wire rack. Immediately spread cake with frosting; sprinkle with peanuts. Cool completely.

1 PIECE: 482 cal., 20g fat (7g sat. fat), 59mg chol., 337mg sod., 70g carb. (53g sugars, 2g fiber), 9g pro.

Apricot Mud Hen Cake Bars

PREP: 20 MIN. • **BAKE:** 30 MIN. + COOLING
MAKES: 24 SERVINGS

These bars have been in my family for generations. My maternal grandmother gave this recipe to my mother, who shared it with me. I've been told the name comes from the speckled meringue topping that resembles the coloring of hens.
—Kristine Chayes, Smithtown, NY

¾ cup butter, softened
⅓ cup sugar
2 large egg yolks, room temperature
1 tsp. vanilla extract
1½ cups all-purpose flour
⅛ tsp. salt

MERINGUE
2 large egg whites, room temperature
⅛ tsp. cream of tartar
⅓ cup sugar
¾ cup finely chopped pecans
1 cup apricot preserves

1. Preheat oven to 350°. In a large bowl, cream butter and sugar until light and fluffy, 5-7 minutes. Add egg yolks, 1 at a time, beating well after each addition. Beat in vanilla. In another bowl, whisk flour and salt; beat into the creamed mixture. Spread batter into a greased 13x9-in. baking pan. Bake until a toothpick inserted in center comes out clean, 12-15 minutes.

2. Meanwhile, for meringue, with clean beaters, beat egg whites with cream of tartar on medium speed until foamy. Gradually add sugar, 1 Tbsp. at a time, beating on high after each addition until the sugar is dissolved. Continue beating until stiff glossy peaks form; gently fold in pecans.

3. Spread preserves over hot cake. Spread the meringue over the preserves, sealing meringue to edges of pan. Bake until the meringue is golden brown, 15-20 minutes. Cool completely on a wire rack. Refrigerate any leftovers.

1 PIECE: 163 cal., 9g fat (4g sat. fat), 31mg chol., 69mg sod., 21g carb. (12g sugars, 1g fiber), 2g pro.

TEST KITCHEN TIP

Spreading meringue over a hot surface ensures that it seals well, without peeling back during baking. You can also use raspberry, peach or another jam in place of the apricot preserves.

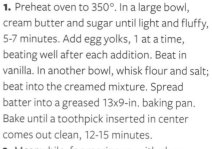

Bee Sting Cake

PREP: 45 MIN. • **BAKE:** 25 MIN. + COOLING
MAKES: 8 SERVINGS

The bee sting cake, or bienenstich, originated in Germany. Its playful name may come from the sweet honey-almond topping. And although the recipe looks daunting, it's worth the effort. Take it step by step—you'll be surprised how easy it is.
—Taste of Home *Test Kitchen*

- ¼ **cup sugar**
- 3 **Tbsp. cornstarch**
- ¼ **tsp. salt**
- 1½ **cups whole milk**
- 3 **large egg yolks**
- 2 **Tbsp. butter, cubed**
- 2 **tsp. vanilla extract**
- ½ **cup heavy whipping cream, whipped**

CAKE
- ¼ **cup sugar**
- 1 **envelope (¼ oz.) active dry yeast**
- ¼ **tsp. salt**
- 2¾ **cups all-purpose flour, divided**
- ¾ **cup whole milk**
- ⅓ **cup butter, cubed**
- 2 **large eggs, room temperature**

ALMOND TOPPING
- ¼ **cup butter**
- 3 **Tbsp. honey**
- 2 **Tbsp. sugar**
- 1 **cup sliced almonds**

1. For custard filling, in a small heavy saucepan, mix sugar, cornstarch and salt. Whisk in milk. Cook and stir over medium heat until thickened and bubbly. Reduce heat to low; cook and stir 2 minutes longer. Remove from heat.

2. In a small bowl, whisk egg yolks. Whisk a small amount of the hot mixture into egg yolks; return all to pan, whisking constantly. Bring to a gentle boil, cook and stir for 2 minutes. Remove from heat. Stir in butter until melted. Immediately transfer to a clean bowl; stir in vanilla. Let cool 30 minutes. Press plastic wrap onto surface of filling; refrigerate until cold.

3. Whisk custard gently. Fold in the whipped cream, half at a time. Cover and refrigerate.

4. While custard is chilling, make dough. In a large bowl, mix sugar, yeast, salt and 1 cup flour. In a small saucepan, heat milk and butter to 120°-130°. Add to the dry ingredients; beat on medium speed for 1 minute. Add eggs; beat on high 1 minute. Stir in enough of the remaining flour to form a soft dough (dough will be sticky).

5. Turn dough onto a well-floured surface; knead until smooth and elastic, 6-8 minutes. Place in a greased bowl, turning once to grease the top. Cover and let rise in a warm place until doubled, about 1 hour.

6. While dough is rising, make almond topping. In a small saucepan over medium heat, melt butter, honey and sugar. Cook and stir until sugar is dissolved. Remove from heat; stir in almonds. Cool slightly and set aside.

7. Punch down dough. Turn onto a lightly floured surface; roll into a 9-in. circle. Transfer to a greased 9-in. springform baking pan, pressing to evenly fill pan with dough. Spoon almond mixture over dough and gently spread to cover entire surface. Cover pan with a kitchen towel; let rise in a warm place until doubled, 25-30 minutes.

8. Preheat oven to 350°. Bake until topping is golden brown, 25-30 minutes. Cool on a wire rack 10 minutes. Loosen sides from pan with a knife. Cool 1 hour longer.

9. Remove cake from base of springform pan. Using a long serrated knife, cut cake horizontally in half; spread the filling over bottom layer. Replace top of cake. Serve immediately. Chill leftovers.

1 PIECE: 548 cal., 32g fat (16g sat. fat), 178mg chol., 314mg sod., 56g carb. (18g sugars, 3g fiber), 11g pro.

Pumpkin Gingerbread with Hard Sauce

PREP: 25 MIN. • **BAKE:** 55 MIN. + COOLING
MAKES: 12 SERVINGS

Cakes are a terrific dessert to take to potlucks because they travel well and feed a lot of people. The slightly sweet hard sauce can also be served with quick breads and scones.
—Iola Egle, Bella Vista, AR

- 1   cup butter, softened
- 1   cup sugar
- ½   cup packed brown sugar
- 4   large eggs, room temperature
- 1   can (15 oz.) pumpkin
- ½   cup molasses
- 3½ cups all-purpose flour
- 3   tsp. baking powder
- ½   tsp. baking soda
- 2½ tsp. ground ginger
- ½   tsp. salt
- ½   tsp. pumpkin pie spice
- 1   cup shredded peeled apple
     Confectioners' sugar

SAUCE
- ½   cup butter, softened
- 2   cups confectioners' sugar
- 1   tsp. vanilla extract

1. Preheat oven to 350°. In a large bowl, cream butter and sugars until light and fluffy, 5-7 minutes. Add eggs, 1 at a time, beating well after each addition. Stir in pumpkin and molasses. Combine the flour, baking powder, baking soda, ginger, salt and pie spice; add to the creamed mixture. Beat just until combined. Fold in apple.

2. Transfer to a greased and floured 10-in. fluted tube pan. Bake for 55-60 minutes or until a toothpick inserted in the center comes out clean. Cool for 10 minutes before removing from pan to a wire rack to cool completely. Dust top of cake with confectioner's sugar.

3. For sauce, in a large bowl, beat the butter, confectioners' sugar and vanilla until smooth. Serve with gingerbread.

1 PIECE: 595 cal., 25g fat (15g sat. fat), 131mg chol., 447mg sod., 89g carb. (55g sugars, 3g fiber), 7g pro.

Hot Milk Cake

PREP: 20 MIN. • **BAKE:** 30 MIN.
MAKES: 16 SERVINGS

When I think back on my mom's delicious meals, her milk cake always comes to mind as the perfect dessert. This simple, old-fashioned treat tastes so good, it will surprise you!
—Rosemary Pryor, Pasadena, MD

- 4   large eggs, room temperature
- 2   cups sugar
- 1   tsp. vanilla extract
- 2¼ cups all-purpose flour
- 2¼ tsp. baking powder
- 1¼ cups 2% milk
- 10 Tbsp. butter, cubed

1. Preheat oven to 350°. In a large bowl, beat eggs on high speed for 5 minutes or until thick and lemon-colored. Gradually add sugar, beating until mixture is light and fluffy. Beat in vanilla. Combine flour and baking powder; gradually add to batter beating on low speed until smooth.

2. In a small saucepan, heat milk and butter just until butter is melted. Gradually add to batter; beat just until combined.

3. Pour into a greased 13x9-in. baking pan. Bake until a toothpick inserted in the center comes out clean, 30-35 minutes. Cool on a wire rack.

1 PIECE: 254 cal., 9g fat (5g sat. fat), 75mg chol., 154mg sod., 39g carb. (26g sugars, 0 fiber), 4g pro.

TEST KITCHEN TIP

Lighter and spongier than a pound cake, this old-fashioned homemade sweet works beautifully in place of a store-bought pound cake or a mix cake in a trifle with berries and cream.

Apple Pie Cupcakes with Cinnamon Buttercream

PREP: 20 MIN. • **BAKE:** 20 MIN. + COOLING
MAKES: 2 DOZEN

*These cupcakes are always a hit! They are
so easy to make and the flavor just screams
fall—of course, they're equally delicious
any other time of year, too.*
—Jennifer Stowell, Deep River, IA

1 pkg. yellow cake mix (regular size)
2 Tbsp. butter
4 medium tart apples, peeled and
   finely chopped (about 4 cups)
¾ cup packed brown sugar
1 Tbsp. cornstarch
1 Tbsp. water

FROSTING

1 cup butter, softened
3 cups confectioners' sugar
2 Tbsp. heavy whipping cream
1 tsp. vanilla extract
1½ tsp. ground cinnamon
   Thin apple slices, optional

1. Prepare and bake cake mix according
to the package directions for 24 cupcakes.
Cool completely.

2. Meanwhile, in a large skillet, heat the
butter over medium heat. Add apples and
brown sugar; cook and stir until the apples
are tender, 10-12 minutes. In a small bowl,
mix the cornstarch and water until smooth;
stir into pan. Bring to a boil; cook and stir
until thickened, 1-2 minutes. Remove from
heat; cool completely.

3. Using a paring knife, cut a 1-in.-wide
cone-shaped piece from the top of each
cupcake; discard removed portion. Fill
each cavity with apple mixture.

4. For frosting, in a large bowl, combine
butter, confectioners' sugar, cream, vanilla
and cinnamon; beat until smooth. Frost
cupcakes. If desired, top with apple slices
to serve.

1 CUPCAKE: 300 cal., 15g fat (7g sat. fat),
48mg chol., 221mg sod., 41g carb. (32g
sugars, 1g fiber), 1g pro.

TEST KITCHEN TIP

Dark brown and light (golden) brown
sugar are generally interchangeable
in recipes. Dark brown contains more
molasses than light brown sugar, so
if you prefer a bolder flavor, choose
dark brown sugar.

Chocolate Ginger Cake

PREP: 40 MIN. • **BAKE:** 40 MIN. + COOLING
MAKES: 12 SERVINGS

Indulge in a dark, decadent cake that showcases the flavors of the season. I stir fresh ginger into the batter and sprinkle chopped crystallized ginger over the velvety ganache.
—Amber Evans, Beaverton, OR

- 6 oz. milk chocolate, cut into ½-in. pieces
- 2⅓ cups all-purpose flour
- ½ cup baking cocoa
- 1 tsp. ground cinnamon
- ½ tsp. salt
- ¼ tsp. ground cloves
- 1 cup canola oil
- 1 cup molasses
- 1 cup sugar
- 1 cup water
- 1½ tsp. baking soda
- 3 Tbsp. grated fresh gingerroot
- 2 large eggs, room temperature
- 2 large egg yolks, room temperature

GANACHE
- 4 oz. bittersweet chocolate, chopped
- ½ cup heavy whipping cream
- 2 Tbsp. chopped crystallized ginger
  Optional: Vanilla ice cream or sweetened whipped cream

1. Preheat oven to 350°. Grease a 9-in. springform pan. Place on a baking sheet.

2. Place milk chocolate in a small bowl. In another bowl, whisk flour, cocoa, cinnamon, salt and cloves; add 1 Tbsp. flour mixture to milk chocolate and toss to coat.

3. In a large bowl, beat oil, molasses and sugar until blended. In a small saucepan, bring water to a boil; stir in baking soda until dissolved, then ginger. Add to oil mixture; beat until blended. Gradually add remaining flour mixture, beating on low speed just until moistened. In a small bowl, lightly beat eggs and egg yolks; stir into batter until combined. Fold in milk chocolate.

4. Transfer batter to prepared pan. Bake 40-50 minutes or until toothpick inserted in center comes out clean. Cool on a wire rack for 30 minutes. Loosen sides from pan with a knife; remove rim from pan. Cool cake completely on wire rack.

5. For ganache, place chocolate in a small bowl. In a small saucepan, bring cream just to a boil. Pour over the chocolate; let stand 2 minutes. Stir with a whisk until smooth; cool slightly, stirring occasionally. Pour over cake; sprinkle with crystallized ginger. If desired, serve with ice cream.

1 PIECE: 596 cal., 32g fat (9g sat. fat), 78mg chol., 289mg sod., 71g carb. (47g sugars, 3g fiber), 7g pro.

Double Butterscotch Coconut Cake

PREP: 20 MIN. • **BAKE:** 40 MIN. + COOLING
MAKES: 16 SERVINGS

I got the basic recipe for this cake from a co-worker years ago, and then changed it a bit by adding a family favorite: butterscotch. It is super easy to throw together and is a perfect accompaniment to coffee or tea.
—Marina Castle-Kelley, Canyon Country, CA

- 1 **pkg. yellow cake mix (regular size)**
- 1 **pkg. (3.4 oz.) instant butterscotch pudding mix**
- 4 **large eggs**
- 1 **cup canned coconut milk**
- ¼ **cup canola oil**
- 1 **cup sweetened shredded coconut**
- ½ **cup butterscotch chips**

GLAZE
- ½ **cup butterscotch chips**
- 2 **Tbsp. heavy whipping cream**
- ⅓ **cup sweetened shredded coconut, toasted**

1. Preheat oven to 350°. Grease and flour a 10-in. fluted tube pan.
2. Combine cake mix, pudding mix, eggs, coconut milk and oil; beat on low speed 30 seconds. Beat on medium speed 2 minutes. Stir in coconut and butterscotch chips. Transfer to prepared pan.
3. Bake until a toothpick inserted near the center comes out clean, 40-45 minutes. Cool in pan 10 minutes before removing to a wire rack to cool completely.
4. For glaze, in a microwave, melt butterscotch chips and cream; stir until smooth. Drizzle over cake; sprinkle with coconut.

1 PIECE: 327 cal., 15g fat (10g sat. fat), 49mg chol., 359mg sod., 42g carb. (30g sugars, 1g fiber), 4g pro.

Dutch Oven Cherry Chocolate Dump Cake

PREP: 5 MIN. • **BAKE:** 35 MIN.
MAKES: 8 SERVINGS

Looking for a super quick dessert that will make people think you spent all day in the kitchen? This easy treat will wow your guests. Feel free to use your favorite pie filling in place of cherry.
—Rashanda Cobbins, Milwaukee, WI

- 1 **can (21 oz.) cherry pie filling**
- 1 **can (12 oz.) evaporated milk**
- 1 **pkg. chocolate cake mix (regular size)**
- ⅓ **cup sliced almonds**
- ¾ **cup butter, melted**
  Vanilla ice cream, optional

Preheat oven to 350°. Line a 4-qt. Dutch oven with parchment; lightly spray with cooking spray. Combine pie filling and evaporated milk; spread mixture into bottom of Dutch oven. Sprinkle with cake mix (unprepared) and almonds; drizzle with butter. Bake, covered, until cake springs back when touched, 35-40 minutes. If desired, serve with ice cream.

1 CUP: 515 cal., 24g fat (15g sat. fat), 61mg chol., 605mg sod., 68g carb. (44g sugars, 3g fiber), 7g pro.

TEST KITCHEN TIP
To make this recipe dairy-free, swap in almond milk for evaporated milk and use dairy-free margarine instead of butter.

PASTRIES & BAKESHOP SWEETS

DROPPING INTO YOUR LOCAL BAKERY TO CHOOSE
JUST THE RIGHT SWEET TREAT IS MAGIC—NOW YOU CAN
MAKE THAT MAGIC AT HOME, ANY TIME!

CHERRY DANISH, P. 231

Puff Pastry Danishes

PREP: 30 MIN. • **BAKE:** 15 MIN.
MAKES: 1½ DOZEN

Even though they're simple to make, these jam-filled pastries are right at home in a holiday brunch spread. They were my dad's favorite, so the recipe will always be close to my heart.
—Chellis Richardson, Jackson Center, OH

- 1 **pkg. (8 oz.) cream cheese, softened**
- ¼ **cup sugar**
- 2 **Tbsp. all-purpose flour**
- ½ **tsp. vanilla extract**
- 2 **large egg yolks**
- 1 **Tbsp. water**
- 1 **pkg. (17.3 oz.) frozen puff pastry, thawed**
- ⅔ **cup seedless raspberry jam or jam of choice**
   Confectioners' sugar, optional

1. Preheat oven to 425°. Beat cream cheese, sugar, flour and vanilla until smooth; beat in 1 egg yolk.
2. Mix water and the remaining egg yolk. On a lightly floured surface, unfold each sheet of puff pastry and roll into a 12-in. square. Cut each into nine 4-in. squares; transfer to parchment-lined baking sheets.
3. Top each square with 1 Tbsp. cream cheese mixture and 1 rounded tsp. jam. Bring 2 opposite corners of pastry over the filling, sealing with yolk mixture. Brush tops with the remaining yolk mixture.
4. Bake until golden brown, 14-16 minutes. Serve warm and, if desired, sprinkle with confectioners' sugar. Refrigerate leftovers.
1 PASTRY: 197 cal., 12g fat (4g sat. fat), 33mg chol., 130mg sod., 20g carb. (3g sugars, 2g fiber), 3g pro.

Pumpkin Cheesecake Empanadas

PREP: 25 MIN. • **BAKE:** 15 MIN.
MAKES: 3 DOZEN

These cute pumpkin empanadas make the perfect treat—and we love that they are baked and not fried!
—Taste of Home *Test Kitchen*

- 1 **large egg white**
- ½ **tsp. vanilla extract**
- 1½ **tsp. packed brown sugar**
- 1½ **tsp. aniseed**
- ¾ **tsp. ground cinnamon**
- ¼ **tsp. ground nutmeg**
   EMPANADAS
- 3 **oz. cream cheese, softened**
- ¼ **cup canned pumpkin pie mix**
- 1 **large egg yolk, room temperature, lightly beaten**
- 1 **Tbsp. finely chopped pecans, toasted**
- 2 **sheets refrigerated pie crust**

1. Preheat oven to 400°. In a small bowl, whisk egg white and vanilla; set aside. In another small bowl combine brown sugar, aniseed, cinnamon and nutmeg; set aside.
2. In a small bowl, beat cream cheese and pie mix until smooth. Add egg yolk; beat on low speed just until blended. Stir in pecans.
3. On a lightly floured surface, roll each crust to ¼-in. thickness. Cut with a floured 3-in. round biscuit cutter. Place circles 2 in. apart on parchment-lined baking sheets. Place 1 tsp. filling on 1 side of each circle. Brush edges of crust with egg white mixture; fold circles in half. With a fork, press edges to seal. Brush with egg white mixture and sprinkle with spice mixture. Bake until golden brown, 15-20 minutes.
FREEZE OPTION: Cover and freeze unbaked empanadas on parchment-lined baking sheets until firm. Transfer to a freezer container; return to freezer. To use, bake empanadas as directed.
NOTE: To toast nuts, bake in a shallow pan in a 350° oven for 5-10 minutes or cook in a skillet over low heat until lightly browned, stirring occasionally.
1 EMPANADA: 69 cal., 4g fat (2g sat. fat), 10mg chol., 56mg sod., 7g carb. (1g sugars, 0 fiber), 1g pro.

Creamy Lemon Almond Pastries

PREP: 30 MIN. + CHILLING • **BAKE:** 15 MIN.
MAKES: 9 SERVINGS

I love lemon-filled doughnuts when I can find them. This recipe brings the concept to a new level by placing the filling into a baked beignet and enhancing it with a bit of almond flavoring and toasted almonds. The result? Sunshine in a bite.
—Arlene Erlbach, Morton Grove, IL

½ cup plus 1 Tbsp. cream cheese, softened (4½ oz.)
⅔ cup confectioners' sugar, divided
2 Tbsp. lemon curd
2 tsp. grated lemon zest
¼ tsp. almond extract
1 sheet frozen puff pastry, thawed
1 large egg, beaten
2 Tbsp. water
2 tsp. lemon juice
2 tsp. 2% milk
3 Tbsp. sliced almonds, toasted

1. Beat the cream cheese, 3 Tbsp. of confectioners' sugar, the lemon curd, lemon zest and almond extract on medium until combined. Refrigerate, covered, for 30 minutes.

2. Preheat oven to 400°. On a lightly floured surface, unfold the puff pastry. Roll into a 12x9-in. rectangle. Using a pastry cutter or sharp knife, cut into 9 rectangles. Spoon a rounded Tbsp. of cream cheese mixture in the center of each rectangle. In a small bowl, whisk egg with water. Brush edges of pastry rectangles with the egg mixture.

3. Wrap puff pastry around filling to cover completely. Pinch edges together to form a ball. Place the balls seam side down 2 in. apart on a parchment-lined baking sheet. Brush tops with the remaining egg mixture. Pierce each once with a fork. Bake until golden brown, 15-18 minutes. Cool on a wire rack for 5 minutes. Loosen pastries from the parchment.

4. Meanwhile, combine lemon juice, milk and the remaining confectioners' sugar. Brush each pastry with lemon glaze and top with sliced almonds. When the glaze is set, in 1-2 minutes, peel off parchment. Serve warm.

NOTE: To toast nuts, bake in a shallow pan in a 350° oven for 5-10 minutes or cook in a skillet over low heat until lightly browned, stirring occasionally.

1 PASTRY: 255 cal., 14g fat (5g sat. fat), 39mg chol., 148mg sod., 29g carb. (12g sugars, 2g fiber), 4g pro.

2. Remove from heat. Stir in the pumpkin, vanilla, cinnamon, ginger and nutmeg. Transfer to a bowl. Press plastic wrap onto the surface of the custard. Refrigerate until cool, 2 hours.

3. Preheat oven to 375°. On a lightly floured surface, roll out pastry into a 12x10-in. rectangle. With a sharp knife, cut into 15 rectangles, 4x2 in. each. Place 1 in. apart on ungreased baking sheets. Bake until puffed and golden brown, 15-20 minutes. Remove to wire racks to cool.

4. To assemble, split the pastries in half horizontally. Place 10 bottom layers on a work surface; spread each with a scant 2 Tbsp. pumpkin custard. Top with 10 pastries, the remaining custard and the remaining 10 pastries. Sprinkle with confectioners' sugar. Refrigerate for 1 2 hours before serving.

1 PASTRY: 286 cal., 12g fat (4g sat. fat), 152mg chol., 137mg sod., 40g carb. (22g sugars, 2g fiber), 6g pro.

TEST KITCHEN TIP

Simple steps ensure custard success. Boil the filling the full 2 minutes, stirring continually, or it won't thicken properly as it chills. Pressing plastic wrap to the surface of the custard prevents it from forming a rubbery skin as it cools and sets.

Pumpkin Napoleons

PREP: 20 MIN. + CHILLING
BAKE: 15 MIN. + CHILLING
MAKES: 10 SERVINGS

This is an outstanding dessert for special fall gatherings. The smooth pumpkin puree pairs well with the crunchy puff pastry.
—Priscilla Weaver, Hagerstown, MD

- ¾ cup plus 2 Tbsp. sugar
- ⅓ cup all-purpose flour
- ⅛ tsp. salt
- 1¾ cups 2% milk
- 8 large egg yolks, room temperature, beaten
- ⅔ cup canned pumpkin
- 1¼ tsp. vanilla extract
- ¼ tsp. ground cinnamon
- ¼ tsp. ground ginger
- ⅛ tsp. ground nutmeg
- 1 sheet frozen puff pastry, thawed
- 2 Tbsp. confectioners' sugar

1. In a large saucepan, combine sugar, flour and salt; stir in milk until smooth. Cook and stir over medium-high heat until thickened and bubbly. Reduce heat; cook and stir 2 minutes. Remove from heat. Stir a small amount of hot filling into egg yolks; return all to the pan, stirring constantly. Bring to a gentle boil; cook and stir 2 minutes longer.

Pecan Kringle Sticks

PREP: 40 MIN. + CHILLING • **BAKE:** 20 MIN.
MAKES: 4 KRINGLES (6 SERVINGS EACH)

*My family loves that this kringle is flaky and
not too sweet—it just melts in your mouth.
And it makes a beautiful presentation on
a cookie platter or tucked next to a cup of
hot coffee.*
—Connie Vjestica, Brookfield, IL

- 2 **cups all-purpose flour**
- 1 **cup cold butter, cubed**
- 1 **cup sour cream**

FILLING

- 1 **large egg white, room temperature**
- 1 **tsp. vanilla extract**
- ½ **cup sugar**
- 1 **cup chopped pecans**

ICING

- 1¼ **cups confectioners' sugar**
- 2 **Tbsp. 2% milk**

1. Place flour in a large bowl; cut in butter
until crumbly. Stir in sour cream. Shape into
a disk (mixture will be crumbly). Wrap and
refrigerate overnight.

2. In a small bowl, beat egg white and vanilla
on medium speed until soft peaks form.
Gradually beat in sugar on high until stiff
peaks form. Fold in pecans.

3. Divide the dough into 4 portions. Roll
1 portion into a 12x6-in. rectangle; place on
an ungreased rimmed baking sheet (keep
the remaining dough refrigerated). Spread
a fourth of the filling lengthwise down the
center. Fold in the sides of the pastry to
meet in the center; pinch seam to seal.
Repeat with remaining dough and filling.

4. Bake at 375° for 18-22 minutes or until
lightly browned. Combine confectioners'
sugar and milk; drizzle over warm pastries.

1 SERVING: 201 cal., 13g fat (6g sat. fat),
27mg chol., 60mg sod., 19g carb. (11g
sugars, 1g fiber), 2g pro.

Cherry Danish

PREP: 30 MIN. + RISING • **BAKE:** 15 MIN.
MAKES: 40 PASTRIES

I won an award when I first made this delicious cherry Danish for a 4-H competition years ago.
—Christie Cochran, Canyon, TX

- 1 **pkg. (¼ oz.) active dry yeast**
- ¼ **cup warm water (110° to 115°)**
- 1 **cup warm 2% milk (110° to 115°)**
- ¾ **cup shortening, divided**
- ⅓ **cup sugar**
- 3 **large eggs, room temperature, divided use**
- 1 **tsp. salt**
- ¼ **tsp. each ground mace, lemon extract and vanilla extract**
- 4 **to 4½ cups all-purpose flour**
- 1 **can (21 oz.) cherry pie filling**

GLAZE
- 1½ **cups confectioners' sugar**
- ½ **tsp. vanilla extract**
- 2 **to 3 Tbsp. 2% milk**
- ⅓ **cup chopped almonds**

1. In a large bowl, dissolve yeast in water. Add the milk, ¼ cup shortening, sugar, 2 eggs, salt, mace, extracts and 2 cups flour; beat until smooth. Add enough remaining flour to form a soft dough.

2. Turn onto a floured surface; knead until smooth and elastic, 6-8 minutes. Place in a greased bowl, turning once to grease top. Cover and let rise in a warm place until doubled, about 1 hour.

3. Punch dough down. On a large floured surface, roll dough out to a 24x16-in. rectangle. Dot half the dough with ¼ cup shortening; fold dough lengthwise. Fold the dough another 3 times lengthwise, then 2 times widthwise, each time dotting with some of the remaining shortening. Place dough in a greased bowl; cover and let rise 20 minutes.

4. On a floured surface, roll the dough into a 16x15-in. rectangle. Cut into 8x¾-in. strips; coil each strip into a spiral shape, tucking the ends underneath. Place spirals in 2 greased 15x10x1-in. baking pans. Cover and let rise in a warm place until doubled, about 1 hour.

5. Preheat oven to 375°. Beat the remaining egg. Make a depression in the center of each roll; brush with egg. Fill each depression with 1 Tbsp. pie filling. Bake 15-18 minutes or until golden brown. Cool on a wire rack.

6. Combine confectioners' sugar, vanilla and milk; drizzle over rolls. Sprinkle with almonds.

1 DANISH: 137 cal., 5g fat (1g sat. fat), 17mg chol., 70mg sod., 21g carb. (10g sugars, 1g fiber), 2g pro.

Palmiers

PREP: 20 MIN. + FREEZING
BAKE: 10 MIN. + COOLING
MAKES: 2 DOZEN

It takes just two ingredients to make these impressive but easy-to-do French pastries, which are often called "palm leaves."
—Taste of Home *Test Kitchen*

 1 **cup sugar, divided**
 1 **sheet frozen puff pastry, thawed**

1. Sprinkle a surface with ¼ cup sugar; unfold puff pastry sheet on surface. Sprinkle with 2 Tbsp. sugar. Roll into a 14x10-in. rectangle. Sprinkle with ½ cup sugar to within ½ in. of edges. Lightly press into pastry.

2. With a knife, very lightly score a line crosswise across the middle of the pastry. Starting at a short side, roll up jelly-roll style, stopping at the score mark in the middle. Starting at the other side, roll up pastry jelly-roll style to score mark. Freeze until firm, 20-30 minutes. Cut into ⅜-in. slices.

3. Place slices cut side up 2 in. apart on parchment-lined baking sheets; sprinkle lightly with 1 Tbsp. sugar. Bake at 425° for 8 minutes. Turn pastries over and sprinkle with remaining sugar. Bake until golden brown and glazed, about 3 minutes longer. Remove to wire racks to cool completely. Store in airtight containers.

1 PASTRY: 83 cal., 3g fat (1g sat. fat), 0mg chol., 34mg sod., 14g carb. (8g sugars, 1g fiber), 1g pro.

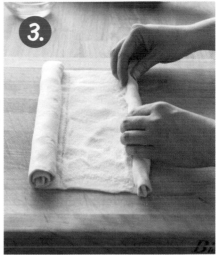

MAKE PALMIERS

1. Sprinkling the puff pastry dough with sugar serves two purposes—it adds sweetness, of course, but it also keeps the pastry from sticking to itself and tearing. You can use demerara sugar to give the palmiers a rich molasses flavor. For a distinct flavor, add just a bit of cinnamon, cardamom or even cayenne to the sugar.

2. Lightly scoring the center of the pastry gives you a guide for rolling each side; take care to score lightly and not cut through the pastry dough.

3. After rolling up one side to the score mark, roll the other side up to meet it. Roll firmly to prevent large gaps in the finished pastry, but don't compress the roll.

4. Freezing the shaped dough before cutting it will ensure clean edges and prevent distorting the shape of the roll.

5. Sprinkling the slices with sugar before baking makes the finished pastry sparkle and creates a crisp exterior. Feel free to use granulated sugar or demerara sugar—or even a special sanding sugar for extra shine.

SCONES GALORE!
Find more scone recipes—sweet and savory—by hovering your camera here.

Hazelnut Chocolate Chip Scones

PREP: 20 MIN. • **BAKE:** 15 MIN.
MAKES: 8 SCONES

With chocolate, hazelnuts and the tangy taste of buttermilk, these delicious scones are easy to make, come together fast and taste so good with your morning coffee.
—Trisha Kruse, Eagle, ID

- 2   cups all-purpose flour
- ¼   cup packed brown sugar
- 1½ tsp. baking powder
- ½   tsp. baking soda
- ½   tsp. salt
- ½   cup cold butter, cubed
- 1   large egg, room temperature
- ½   cup buttermilk
- 1½ tsp. vanilla extract
- 1   cup semisweet chocolate chips
- 1   cup hazelnuts, coarsely chopped

1. Preheat oven to 400°. Whisk together the first 5 ingredients; cut in butter until the mixture resembles coarse crumbs. In another bowl, whisk together the egg, buttermilk and vanilla; stir into the crumb mixture just until moistened. Stir in chocolate chips and hazelnuts.

2. Turn dough onto a lightly floured surface; knead gently 8 times. Pat dough into a 6-in. circle. Cut into 8 wedges; place on a greased baking sheet. Bake until golden brown, 15-20 minutes. Serve warm.

NOTE: To substitute for each cup of buttermilk, use 1 Tbsp. white vinegar or lemon juice plus enough milk to measure 1 cup. Stir, then let stand 5 minutes. Or, use 1 cup plain yogurt or 1¾ tsp. cream of tartar plus 1 cup milk.

1 SCONE: 409 cal., 23g fat (10g sat. fat), 76mg chol., 327mg sod., 47g carb. (20g sugars, 3g fiber), 8g pro.

Caramelized Apple Tarts

PREP: 30 MIN. • **BAKE:** 15 MIN. + COOLING
MAKES: 16 SERVINGS

This recipe cleverly dresses up frozen puff pastry and a no-bake cheesecake mix. Guests will be delighted to be offered their own individual tarts.
—Taste of Home *Test Kitchen*

- 1   pkg. (17.3 oz.) frozen puff pastry, thawed
- 1   pkg. (11.1 oz.) no-bake cheesecake mix
- ½   cup butter, cubed
- 1   cup packed dark brown sugar
- ½   tsp. ground cinnamon
- 5   medium apples, peeled and thinly sliced
- 3   Tbsp. heavy whipping cream

1. Preheat oven to 400°. Unfold pastry sheets on a lightly floured surface. Cut into eight 4-in. circles. Place on greased baking sheets. Bake 15-18 minutes or until lightly browned. Remove to wire racks to cool.

2. Prepare cheesecake filling according to package directions; set aside. (Save packet of crust crumbs for another use.)

3. In a large skillet, melt butter and brown sugar over medium heat; stir in cinnamon. Add half of the apples; cook and stir for 10 minutes or until tender.

4. Remove apples with a slotted spoon to a bowl. Repeat with remaining apples. Drain the cooking juices, reserving ⅓ cup in the skillet; discard remaining juices. Add cream to skillet; cook and stir for 2 minutes.

5. Split each pastry in half horizontally. Top each with 2 heaping Tbsp. of cheesecake filling. Top with apple slices and drizzle with caramel sauce. Refrigerate leftovers.

1 TART: 373 cal., 17g fat (7g sat. fat), 24mg chol., 330mg sod., 52g carb. (29g sugars, 3g fiber), 5g pro.

Tahitian Breakfast Treats

PREP: 35 MIN. + RISING • **BAKE:** 10 MIN.
MAKES: 8 SERVINGS

This is a healthy take on the Tahitian coconut breakfast treat called firi firi, *which is typically fried. My version is baked and rolled in a spicy island sugar mix.*
—Susan Falk, Sterling Heights, MI

¼ cup warm water (110° to 115°)
1 pkg. (¼ oz.) active dry yeast
½ cup warm coconut milk (110° to 115°)
½ cup sweetened shredded coconut
⅓ cup sugar
½ tsp. salt
2 to 2½ cups all-purpose flour
SPICED SUGAR
½ cup sugar
1 tsp. ground cinnamon
½ tsp. ground ginger
½ vanilla bean
¼ cup butter, melted

1. Add yeast to warm water and stir to dissolve; allow to sit until yeast has bubbled, 5-7 minutes. Add yeast mixture to warm coconut milk.

2. In a large bowl, combine coconut, sugar, salt, yeast mixture and 1 cup flour; beat on medium speed until smooth. Stir in enough remaining flour to form a stiff dough (the dough will be sticky).

3. Turn dough onto a floured surface; knead until smooth and elastic, 6-8 minutes. Place in a greased bowl, turning once to grease the top. Cover and let rise in a warm place until doubled, about 1½ hours.

4. Punch down dough. Turn onto a lightly floured surface; divide into 8 portions. Roll each into a 12-in. rope. Curl ends in opposite directions to form a figure 8. Tuck each end under where it meets center of roll and pinch lightly to seal. Place 2 in. apart on a parchment-lined baking sheet. Cover with a kitchen towel; let rise in a warm place until almost doubled, about 30 minutes.

5. Bake at 375° for 10-12 minutes or until light brown. Meanwhile, place the sugar, cinnamon and ginger in a shallow bowl. Split vanilla bean lengthwise. Using the tip of a sharp knife, scrape seeds from the center; stir into sugar mixture. Brush warm pastries with melted butter; roll in the sugar mixture to coat.

1 TREAT: 251 cal., 8g fat (6g sat. fat), 8mg chol., 191mg sod., 42g carb. (18g sugars, 1g fiber), 4g pro.

TEST KITCHEN TIP

Instead of brushing these pastries in butter and rolling them in sugar, try an island-inspired glaze! Combine 1 cup powdered sugar, 3 Tbsp. dark rum and 2 Tbsp. melted butter until smooth (add water, milk or more rum if needed to reach desired consistency); drizzle over pastries.

2. Turn onto a floured surface; knead until smooth and elastic, 6-8 minutes. Place in a greased bowl, turning once to grease top. Cover and let rise in a warm place until doubled, about 1 hour.

3. Punch dough down; turn onto a lightly floured surface. Divide in half; roll each portion into a 15x10-in. rectangle. Spread butter to within ½ in. of edges; spread with strawberry preserves. Combine sugar and cinnamon; sprinkle over preserves.

4. Roll up jelly-roll style, starting with a long side; pinch seams to seal. Cut each roll into 12 slices. Place cut side down in 2 greased 15x10x1-in. baking pans. Cover and let rise until almost doubled, about 30 minutes.

5. Preheat oven to 350°; bake until golden brown, 25-30 minutes. Cool for 20 minutes. For glaze, in a small bowl, beat the cream cheese, confectioners' sugar and extract until smooth. Add enough milk to reach desired consistency; drizzle over rolls. Sprinkle with pecans.

1 ROLL: 202 cal., 6g fat (3g sat. fat), 20mg chol., 139mg sod., 33g carb. (16g sugars, 1g fiber), 4g pro.

Strawberry-Pecan Yeast Rolls

PREP: 40 MIN. + RISING
BAKE: 25 MIN. + COOLING • **MAKES:** 2 DOZEN

These treats are so good! The strawberry filling, creamy glaze and crunchy nuts balance the sweet yeast rolls so perfectly.
—Annie Thomas, Michigan City, MS

- 4 to 4½ cups all-purpose flour
- 1 pkg. (¼ oz.) active dry yeast
- 1 tsp. salt
- 1½ cups 2% milk
- 1 Tbsp. canola oil
- 1 Tbsp. honey
- 1 large egg, room temperature

FILLING
- ¼ cup butter, softened
- ⅔ cup strawberry preserves
- 1 Tbsp. sugar
- ½ tsp. ground cinnamon

GLAZE
- 3 oz. cream cheese, softened
- 1¾ cups confectioners' sugar
- ¼ tsp. almond extract
- 1 to 2 Tbsp. 2% milk
- ½ cup chopped pecans

1. In a large bowl, combine 2 cups flour, yeast and salt. In a small saucepan, heat milk, oil and honey to 120°-130°. Add to dry ingredients; beat just until moistened. Add egg; beat until smooth. Stir in enough remaining flour to form a soft dough.

Mediterranean Apricot Phyllo Bites

PREP: 30 MIN. • **BAKE:** 10 MIN.
MAKES: 2½ DOZEN

*Apricot and almonds make these flaky
little bites a delicious ending to a meal
or a special evening snack.*
—Taste of Home *Test Kitchen*

- ½ cup unblanched almonds
- ½ cup chopped dried apricots
- 1 Tbsp. plus ½ cup butter, melted, divided
- 2 Tbsp. honey
- ¼ tsp. grated lemon zest
- ¼ tsp. almond extract
- 20 sheets phyllo dough (14x9 in.)

1. Place almonds and apricots in a food
processor; cover and process until finely
chopped. In a small bowl, combine 1 Tbsp.
butter, the honey, lemon zest and extract;
add almond mixture and stir until blended.
2. Using the remaining ½ cup butter, lightly
brush 1 sheet of phyllo with butter; place
another sheet of phyllo on top and brush
with butter. (Keep remaining phyllo covered
with a damp towel to prevent it from drying
out.) Cut the 2 layered sheets into three
14x3-in. strips.
3. Place 1½ tsp. filling in lower corner of
each strip. Fold dough over filling, forming a
triangle. Fold triangle up, then fold triangle
over, forming another triangle. Continue
folding, like a flag, until you come to the end
of the strip. Brush end of dough with butter
and press onto triangle to seal. Turn triangle
and brush top with melted butter. Repeat.
4. Place triangles on a greased baking sheet.
Bake at 375° for 10-12 minutes or until
golden brown. Cool on a wire rack. Sprinkle
with confectioners' sugar.
1 PASTRY: 74 cal., 5g fat (2g sat. fat), 9mg
chol., 56mg sod., 7g carb. (3g sugars, 1g
fiber), 1g pro.

Dried Cranberry Scones

PREP: 20 MIN. • **BAKE:** 15 MIN. • **MAKES:** 1 DOZEN

I go on vacation with my best friend to Michigan every July. Her cousin is allowed to come, too—but only if she brings her special cherry scones! In the fall and winter, I make them with cranberries. Don't try to double this recipe. If you need more than 12, make two separate batches of dough.
—Sherry Leonard, Whitsett, NC

- 2 **cups all-purpose flour**
- ¼ **cup sugar**
- 2½ **tsp. baking powder**
- ½ **tsp. salt**
- 6 **Tbsp. cold butter**
- ¾ **cup buttermilk**
- 1 **large egg, room temperature**
- ¾ **cup white baking chips**
- ¾ **cup dried cranberries**
- 1 **Tbsp. turbinado (washed raw) sugar**

1. Preheat oven to 400°. In a large bowl, whisk flour, sugar, baking powder and salt. Cut in butter until the mixture resembles coarse crumbs. In another bowl, whisk buttermilk and egg; stir into the crumb mixture just until moistened. Stir in baking chips and cranberries.

2. Drop dough by ¼ cupfuls 2 in. apart onto parchment-lined baking sheet. Sprinkle with turbinado sugar. Bake until golden brown, 12-15 minutes.

1 SCONE: 247 cal., 10g fat (6g sat. fat), 34mg chol., 290mg sod., 36g carb. (20g sugars, 1g fiber), 4g pro.

Cherry Hand Pies

PREP: 45 MIN. • **BAKE:** 25 MIN. + COOLING
MAKES: 8 SERVINGS

There's nothing better than a sweet, from-scratch delight like traditional cherry pie. These precious little hand pies always go fast when I sell them at my bakery!
—Allison Cebulla, Milwaukee, WI

- 6 Tbsp. water, divided
- 2 Tbsp. sugar
- 2 Tbsp. cherry brandy
- 4½ tsp. cornstarch
- 1½ tsp. lemon juice
- 1 tsp. quick-cooking tapioca
- ¼ tsp. grated lemon zest
  Dash salt
- 2 cups fresh or frozen pitted tart cherries, thawed and halved
- 1 cup fresh or frozen pitted dark sweet cherries, thawed and halved
  Dough for double-crust pie (p.154)
- 1 large egg, room temperature

ICING
- 2⅔ cups confectioners' sugar
- 3 to 4 Tbsp. hot water
- 2 Tbsp. butter, melted
- ½ tsp. almond extract
- ¼ tsp. vanilla extract
  Dash salt
  Freeze-dried strawberries, crushed, optional

1. In a large saucepan, whisk 4 Tbsp. water, sugar, brandy, cornstarch, lemon juice, tapioca, lemon zest and salt until combined. Add cherries. Bring to a boil; cook and stir until thickened, 3-5 minutes. Remove from heat. Set aside to cool.

2. Preheat oven to 400°. On a lightly floured surface, roll half the dough to a 14x9-in. rectangle. Cut dough into eight 3½x4½-in. rectangles. Repeat with remaining dough.

3. Transfer 8 rectangles to parchment-lined baking sheets; spoon about 3 Tbsp. cherry mixture in center of each. Whisk egg and remaining 2 Tbsp. water. Brush edges of crust with egg wash. Top with remaining 8 rectangles; press edges with a fork to seal. Brush tops with egg wash; cut slits in tops.

4. Bake until crust is golden brown and slightly puffed, 25-30 minutes. Remove from pans to wire racks to cool. Combine confectioners' sugar, hot water, melted butter, extracts and salt; drizzle over pies. Garnish with freeze-dried strawberries if desired. Let stand until set.

1 HAND PIE: 589 cal., 27g fat (16g sat. fat), 91mg chol., 380mg sod., 83g carb. (49g sugars, 2g fiber), 6g pro.

Caramel Apple Strudel

PREP: 35 MIN. + COOLING • **BAKE:** 25 MIN.
MAKES: 8 SERVINGS

My father, who was born and raised in Vienna, Austria, would tell us stories about how his mother covered all of the kitchen counters with dough whenever she made apple strudel. This recipe is a modern, delicious way to carry on part of my family's heritage.
—Sarah Haengel, Bowie, MD

- 5 medium apples, peeled and chopped (5 cups)
- ¾ cup apple cider or juice
- ¼ cup sugar
- ½ tsp. ground cinnamon
- ¼ tsp. ground allspice
- ¼ tsp. ground cloves
- 1 frozen puff pastry sheet, thawed
- ¼ cup fat-free caramel ice cream topping
- 1 large egg
- 1 Tbsp. water
- 1 Tbsp. coarse sugar
  Optional: Sweetened whipped cream and additional caramel ice cream topping

1. Preheat the oven to 375°. In a large saucepan, combine first 6 ingredients. Bring to a boil. Reduce heat; simmer, uncovered, for 15-20 minutes or until apples are tender, stirring occasionally. Cool completely.

2. Unfold puff pastry onto a large sheet of parchment; roll into a 16x12-in. rectangle. Transfer parchment and pastry to a baking sheet, placing a short side of the rectangle facing you. Using a slotted spoon, arrange apples on bottom half of pastry to within 1 in. of edges. Drizzle apples with caramel topping. Roll up jelly-roll style, starting with the bottom side. Pinch seams to seal, and tuck ends under.

3. In a small bowl, whisk egg with water; brush over pastry. Sprinkle with coarse sugar. Cut slits in top. Bake 25-30 minutes or until golden brown. If desired, serve with whipped cream and additional caramel ice cream topping.

1 PIECE: 270 cal., 9g fat (2g sat. fat), 26mg chol., 140mg sod., 46g carb. (24g sugars, 4g fiber), 3g pro.

Cinnamon Breakfast Bites

TAKES: 30 MIN.
MAKES: 6 SERVINGS (1½ DOZEN)

These early-morning treats with a sweet, crispy coating are baked in the oven instead of deep-fried.
—Ruth Hastings, Louisville, IL

- 1⅓ cups all-purpose flour
- 1 cup crisp rice cereal, coarsely crushed
- 2 Tbsp. plus ½ cup sugar, divided
- 1 Tbsp. baking powder
- ½ tsp. salt
- ¼ cup butter-flavored shortening
- ½ cup 2% milk
- 1 tsp. ground cinnamon
- ¼ cup butter, melted

1. Preheat oven to 425°. In a large bowl, combine the flour, cereal, 2 Tbsp. sugar, baking powder and salt; cut in shortening until the mixture resembles coarse crumbs. Stir in milk just until moistened. Shape into 1-in. balls.

2. In a shallow bowl, combine the remaining ½ cup sugar and cinnamon. Dip balls in the melted butter, then roll in cinnamon sugar.

3. Arrange in a single layer in an 8-in. cast-iron skillet or round baking pan. Bake until browned and a toothpick inserted in centers comes out clean, 15-18 minutes.

3 BALLS: 352 cal., 17g fat (7g sat. fat), 23mg chol., 527mg sod., 47g carb. (22g sugars, 1g fiber), 4g pro.

Date-Walnut Pinwheels

TAKES: 25 MIN. • **MAKES:** 1 DOZEN

Every time someone drops in for coffee, I bake up a batch of these fruit and nut cookies—I always keep the ingredients in my pantry. The recipe's a cinch to double, too, so it's good for parties and potlucks.
—Lori McLain, Denton, TX

- 3 Tbsp. sugar
- ½ tsp. ground cinnamon
- 1 sheet refrigerated pie crust
- 1 Tbsp. apricot preserves
- ⅔ cup finely chopped pitted dates
- ½ cup finely chopped walnuts

1. Preheat oven to 350°. Mix the sugar and cinnamon. On a lightly floured surface, unroll crust; roll into a 12-in. square. Spread preserves over top; sprinkle with the dates, walnuts and cinnamon-sugar.

2. Roll up jelly-roll style; pinch seam to seal. Cut crosswise into 12 slices, each about 1 in. thick. Place slices 1 in. apart on an ungreased baking sheet. Bake until golden brown, 12-14 minutes. Remove from pan to a wire rack to cool.

1 PINWHEEL: 155 cal., 8g fat (2g sat. fat), 3mg chol., 68mg sod., 21g carb. (11g sugars, 1g fiber), 2g pro.

Pistachio Palmiers

PREP: 30 MIN. + CHILLING
BAKE: 10 MIN./BATCH
MAKES: ABOUT 5 DOZEN

My family loves palmiers from the bakery, so I created my own recipe. These have a Middle Eastern twist with the addition of rosewater, honey and a touch of cardamom. They are light and crisp—a special treat for the holidays.
—Deborah Hinojosa, Saratoga, CA

1½ cups all-purpose flour
¾ cup cake flour
¾ tsp. salt
1¼ cups cold butter, cubed
⅓ cup ice water
1 Tbsp. lemon juice

FILLING
⅓ cup sugar
1 tsp. ground cinnamon
¼ tsp. ground cardamom
¼ cup butter, melted
2 Tbsp. honey
1 Tbsp. rosewater or water
1 cup chopped pistachios

1. Place flours and salt in a food processor; pulse until blended. Add butter; pulse until butter is the size of peas. While pulsing, add ice water and lemon juice to form crumbs. Turn onto a floured surface; knead gently 8-10 times.

2. Roll dough into a 12x8-in. rectangle. Starting with a shorter side, fold dough in half. Repeat rolling and folding. Place folded dough in an airtight container and freeze for 20 minutes.

3. Roll dough into a 12x8-in. rectangle. Starting with a shorter side, fold into thirds, forming a 4x8-in. rectangle. Place folded dough with longer side facing you; repeat rolling and folding twice, always ending with a 4x8-in. rectangle. (If at any point the butter softens, chill after folding.) Cover folded dough and refrigerate overnight.

4. In a small bowl, mix sugar, cinnamon and cardamom. In another bowl, mix butter, honey and rosewater. Turn dough onto a lightly floured surface; cut in half. Roll 1 half dough into a 12x10-in. rectangle. Brush with half the butter mixture; sprinkle with half of the sugar mixture and half of the pistachios.

5. Starting with a long side, roll up the left and right sides toward the center, jelly-roll style, until rolls meet in the middle. Repeat with the remaining dough, butter mixture, sugar mixture and pistachios. Refrigerate rolls for 20 minutes or until firm enough to slice. Preheat oven to 400°.

6. Cut rolls crosswise into ¼-in. slices. Place 2 in. apart on parchment-lined baking sheets. Bake 8-10 minutes or until golden brown. Cool on pans 2 minutes. Remove to wire racks to cool.

1 PASTRY: 72 cal., 5g fat (3g sat. fat), 11mg chol., 70mg sod., 6g carb. (2g sugars, 0 fiber), 1g pro.

Peanut Butter & Cookie Knots

PREP: 1 HOUR + RISING
BAKE: 20 MIN. + COOLING
MAKES: 16 SERVINGS

These braided pastries are filled with chunks of cookies and peanut butter. They are perfect for dessert or with your morning coffee. You could use any type of chocolate cookie or chocolate candy that pairs well with peanut butter. You can also substitute hazelnut spread for the peanut butter if you'd like.
—Daniel Carberg, Roxbury, NH

2   pkg. (¼ oz. each) active dry yeast
1   cup warm buttermilk (110°-115°)
2   large eggs, room temperature
½   cup unsalted butter, softened
½   cup sugar
1   tsp. salt
4   to 4½ cups all-purpose flour

FILLING
2   cups creamy peanut butter
24   Oreo cookies, crushed
     (about 2⅔ cups)

TOPPING
1   large egg, beaten
1   cup confectioners' sugar
1   to 2 Tbsp. 2% milk
     Coarse sea salt

1. In a small bowl, dissolve yeast in warm buttermilk. In a large bowl, combine eggs, butter, sugar, salt, yeast mixture and 2 cups flour; beat on medium speed until smooth. Stir in enough remaining flour to form a soft dough (dough will be sticky).

2. Turn dough onto a floured surface; knead until smooth and elastic, 6-8 minutes. Place in a greased bowl, turning once to grease the top. Cover and let rise in a warm place until doubled, about 1¼ hours.

3. Punch down dough. Turn onto a lightly floured surface; divide into 16 portions. Roll each into 12x4-in. rectangle. Spread 1 rectangle with ¼ cup peanut butter to within ½ in. of edges; sprinkle with ⅓ cup crushed Oreos. Top with another rectangle of dough. Pinch around edges to seal.

4. Using a sharp knife, cut rectangle lengthwise in half; carefully turn each half cut side up. Loosely twist strips around each other, keeping cut surfaces facing up. Shape into a ring, pinching ends together to seal. Place on parchment-lined baking sheets. Repeat with remaining dough, peanut butter and crushed Oreos. Cover with kitchen towels; let rise in a warm place until almost doubled, about 30 minutes.

5. Preheat oven to 350°. Brush rolls with beaten egg. Bake until golden brown, 20-25 minutes. Cool on pans on wire racks for 30 minutes.

6. Combine confectioners' sugar and milk; drizzle over the cooled rolls. Sprinkle with sea salt and, if desired, additional crushed Oreos.

½ ROLL: 510 cal., 27g fat (8g sat. fat), 45mg chol., 397mg sod., 58g carb. (25g sugars, 3g fiber), 13g pro.

Cranberry Chip Monkey Bread

PREP: 15 MIN. • **BAKE:** 40 MIN.
MAKES: 16 SERVINGS

*Monkey bread is no stranger at our house.
This one with cranberries and eggnog is a
breakfast treat or knockout dessert.*
—Katherine Wollgast, Troy, MO

- ¾ **cup sugar, divided**
- 4 **tsp. ground cinnamon**
- 4 **tubes (7½ oz. each) refrigerated
  buttermilk biscuits**
- ½ **cup white baking chips**
- ½ **cup dried cranberries**
- ¼ **cup chopped walnuts or pecans**
- ¼ **cup butter, cubed**
- ½ **cup eggnog**

GLAZE
- 1 **cup confectioners' sugar**
- ½ **tsp. rum or vanilla extract**
- 2 **to 3 Tbsp. eggnog
  Optional: Additional dried
  cranberries, white baking chips
  and chopped nuts**

1. Mix ½ cup sugar and cinnamon. Cut each
biscuit into quarters; add to sugar mixture
and toss to coat. Arrange half the biscuits
in a greased 10-in. tube pan. Sprinkle with
baking chips, cranberries and walnuts. Top
with the remaining biscuits.

2. In a microwave, melt butter. Stir in the
eggnog and remaining ¼ cup sugar until
blended; pour over biscuits.

3. Bake at 350° for 40-45 minutes or until
golden brown. Cool in pan 5 minutes before
inverting onto a serving plate.

4. In a small bowl, mix confectioners' sugar,
extract and enough eggnog to reach a
drizzling consistency. Spoon over warm
bread. Sprinkle with toppings as desired.

1 SERVING: 310 cal., 13g fat (5g sat. fat),
15mg chol., 596mg sod., 47g carb. (26g
sugars, 1g fiber), 4g pro.

Butterscotch Pumpkin Puffs

PREP: 35 MIN. + CHILLING
BAKE: 35 MIN. + COOLING • **MAKES:** 5 DOZEN

Yummy things come in these little pudding-rich packages. The puffs can be made and frozen in advance, then filled before serving for a timesaving Yuletide dessert.
—Michelle Smith, Running Springs, CA

- 2 **pkg. (3.4 oz. each) instant butterscotch pudding mix**
- 1 **can (12 oz.) evaporated milk**
- ½ **tsp. ground cinnamon**
- ¼ **tsp. ground ginger**
- 1 **cup canned pumpkin**
- 1 **cup whipped topping, optional**

CREAM PUFFS

- 1½ **cups water**
- ¾ **cup butter, cubed**
- ½ **tsp. salt**
- 1½ **cups all-purpose flour**
- 6 **large eggs**
- ⅓ **cup confectioners' sugar**
- ⅓ **cup semisweet chocolate chips, melted**

1. In a bowl, combine pudding mix, milk and spices; beat on medium speed for 30 seconds. Blend in pumpkin and, if desired, whipped topping. Refrigerate for 1 hour or overnight.

2. Preheat oven to 400°. In a medium saucepan, combine water, butter and salt; bring to a boil. Reduce heat to low; add the flour all at once and stir until a smooth ball forms. Remove from heat; add the eggs, 1 at a time, beating well after each addition with an electric mixer. Continue beating until the mixture is smooth and shiny. Drop by tablespoonfuls 2 in. apart onto greased baking sheets.

3. Bake for 10 minutes. Reduce heat to 350°; bake 25 minutes longer or until golden brown. Remove from the oven; turn oven off. Cut a slit halfway through each puff; return to oven for 30 minutes with the oven door open. Cool on a wire rack. Just before serving, spoon about 1 Tbsp. filling into each puff. Dust with confectioners' sugar and drizzle with melted chocolate.

1 PUFF: 60 cal., 3g fat (2g sat. fat), 29mg chol., 80mg sod., 6g carb. (3g sugars, 0 fiber), 1g pro.

Apple Cider Cinnamon Rolls

PREP: 1 HOUR + RISING • **BAKE:** 30 MIN.
MAKES: 1 DOZEN

Feeling creative, I put an apple spin on a traditional cinnamon roll recipe. The results were yummy! A panful is perfect for a weekend morning.
—Kimberly Forni, Laconia, NH

3¼ cups all-purpose flour
¼ cup sugar
1 pkg. (¼ oz.) quick-rise yeast
½ tsp. salt
¾ cup 2% milk
¼ cup apple cider or juice
¼ cup plus ⅓ cup butter, softened, divided
1 large egg, room temperature

2 cups finely chopped peeled tart apples
1¼ cups packed brown sugar
¾ cup finely chopped walnuts
3 tsp. ground cinnamon

APPLE CIDER CREAM CHEESE FROSTING
2 cups apple cider or juice
1 cinnamon stick (3 in.)
1 pkg. (8 oz.) cream cheese, softened
¼ cup butter, softened
1 cup confectioners' sugar

1. In a large bowl, combine 2¼ cups flour, sugar, yeast and salt. In a small saucepan, heat the milk, cider and ¼ cup butter to 120°-130°. Add to dry ingredients; beat just until moistened. Add egg; beat until smooth. Stir in enough remaining flour to form a soft dough (dough will be sticky).
2. Turn onto a floured surface; knead until smooth and elastic, 6-8 minutes. Cover and let rest for 10 minutes. Roll into a 15x10-in. rectangle. Spread remaining ⅓ cup butter to within ½ in. of edges. Combine the apples, brown sugar, walnuts and cinnamon; sprinkle over butter.
3. Roll up jelly-roll style, starting with a long side; pinch seam to seal. Cut into 12 slices. Place cut side down in a greased 13x9-in. baking dish. Cover and let rise in a warm place for 30 minutes. Preheat oven to 325°.
4. Bake until golden brown, 30-35 minutes. For frosting, place cider and cinnamon stick in a small saucepan. Bring to a boil; cook until the liquid is reduced to ¼ cup, about 20 minutes. Discard the cinnamon stick; cool cider.
5. In a large bowl, beat cream cheese and butter until fluffy. Add confectioners' sugar and the reduced cider; beat until smooth. Spread over warm rolls.
1 ROLL: 540 cal., 25g fat (13g sat. fat), 73mg chol., 272mg sod., 74g carb. (44g sugars, 2g fiber), 8g pro.

German Apple Strudel

PREP: 1 HOUR + STANDING
BAKE: 45 MIN./BATCH
MAKES: 2 STRUDELS (8 PIECES EACH)

This gorgeous strudel has just what you crave—thin layers of flaky homemade crust and lots of juicy apples.
—Darlene Brenden, Salem, OR

- 3 **cups all-purpose flour**
- ½ **cup canola oil, divided**
- ¾ **cup warm water (120°)**
- 1 **large egg, room temperature, lightly beaten**

FILLING
- 1½ **cups fresh bread crumbs**
- 6 **cups chopped peeled apples (about 6 medium)**
- ½ **cup raisins**
- 1 **cup sugar**
- 1½ **tsp. ground cinnamon**
- ⅓ **cup butter, melted**
- 3 **Tbsp. sour cream**

1. Place flour in a mixer bowl; beat in ¼ cup oil (mixture will be slightly crumbly). In a small bowl, slowly whisk warm water into beaten egg; add to flour mixture, mixing well. Beat in remaining oil until smooth. Transfer to a greased bowl, turning once to grease the top. Cover and let rest in a warm place about 30 minutes.

2. Preheat oven to 350°. Spread bread crumbs into an ungreased 15x10x1-in. baking pan. Bake 10-15 minutes or until golden brown, stirring occasionally. Let cool completely.

3. Tape a 30x15-in. sheet of parchment onto a work surface; dust lightly with flour. Divide dough in half; place 1 portion on parchment and roll to a very thin 24x15-in. rectangle. (Keep the remaining dough covered.) Remove tape from parchment.

4. Sprinkle ¾ cup bread crumbs over rectangle to within 1 in. of edges. Starting 3 in. from a short side, sprinkle 3 cups apples and ¼ cup raisins over a 3-in.-wide section of dough. Mix sugar and cinnamon; sprinkle half of the mixture over the fruit. Drizzle with half of the melted butter.

5. Roll up jelly-roll style, starting at fruit-covered end and lifting with the parchment; fold in sides of dough as you roll to contain filling. Using parchment, transfer strudel to a 15x10x1-in. baking pan; trim parchment to fit pan.

6. Bake on lowest oven rack 45-55 minutes or until golden brown, brushing top with sour cream 2 times while baking. Repeat with remaining ingredients.

7. Using parchment, transfer to a wire rack to cool. Serve warm or at room temperature.

NOTE: To make fresh bread crumbs, tear bread into pieces and place in a food processor; pulse until fine crumbs form. Two to three bread slices will yield 1½ cups crumbs.

1 PIECE: 285 cal., 12g fat (3g sat. fat), 24mg chol., 61mg sod., 42g carb. (20g sugars, 2g fiber), 4g pro.

Apple Kolaches

PREP: 30 MIN. + CHILLING • **BAKE:** 10 MIN.
MAKES: 2½ DOZEN

A fellow home cook shared the recipe for this sweet, fruit-filled pastry. Even my son, who isn't a dessert fan, was disappointed when he came home to find his dad had polished off the last kolache in the batch.
—Ann Johnson, Evansville, IN

- 1 **cup butter, softened**
- 1 **pkg. (8 oz.) cream cheese, softened**
- 2 **cups all-purpose flour**
- 1½ **cups finely chopped peeled apples**
- ¼ **tsp. ground cinnamon**

ICING
- 1 **cup confectioners' sugar**
- 4½ **tsp. 2% milk**
- ½ **tsp. vanilla extract**

1. In a large bowl, beat butter and cream cheese until light and fluffy. Gradually add flour and mix well. Divide dough into 2 portions; cover and refrigerate 2 hours or until easy to handle.

2. Preheat oven to 400°. In a small bowl, combine apples and cinnamon. On a lightly floured surface, roll 1 portion of dough into a 15x9-in. rectangle; cut into fifteen 3-in. squares. Place 1 tsp. of the apple mixture in the center of each square. Overlap 2 opposite corners of dough over filling; pinch tightly to seal. Place 2 in. apart on ungreased baking sheets. Repeat with remaining dough and apple mixture.

3. Bake 10-12 minutes or until bottoms are lightly browned. Cool 1 minute before removing from pans to wire racks. Combine icing ingredients; drizzle over kolaches.

1 PASTRY: 129 cal., 9g fat (6g sat. fat), 24mg chol., 66mg sod., 11g carb. (4g sugars, 0 fiber), 2g pro.

Finger-Licking Good Mini Cream Puffs

PREP: 45 MIN. • **BAKE:** 25 MIN. + COOLING
MAKES: ABOUT 2½ DOZEN

This recipe is quick and easy to whip up and the kids will love it. These puffs are perfect to pack for a picnic or to have as a snack for family game night—I guarantee you can't eat just one!
—Jennifer Erwin, Reynoldsburg, OH

- ½ **cup water**
- ¼ **cup butter**
- ½ **cup all-purpose flour**
- ¼ **tsp. salt**
- 2 **large eggs, room temperature**

VANILLA FILLING
- 1 **pkg. (3.4 oz.) instant vanilla pudding mix**
- 1¾ **cups 2% milk**
- 1 **cup frozen whipped topping, thawed**
  Confectioners' sugar

1. Preheat oven to 400°. In a small saucepan, bring water and butter to a rolling boil over medium heat. Add flour and salt all at once; beat until blended. Cook, stirring vigorously, until a film forms at the bottom of the pan, about 4 minutes. Remove from heat; let stand 10 minutes.

2. Add eggs, 1 at a time, beating well after each addition until smooth. Continue beating until mixture is smooth and shiny. Drop dough by 1-in. balls 1½ in. apart onto parchment-lined baking sheets. Bake until puffed, very firm and golden brown, 25-30 minutes. Cool on wire racks.

3. Meanwhile, whisk pudding mix and milk for 2 minutes or until thickened; let stand for 5 minutes. Fold in whipped topping.

4. Cut puffs in half. Fill bottoms of cream puffs with vanilla filling; replace tops. Dust with confectioners' sugar; serve immediately.

1 FILLED CREAM PUFF: 52 cal., 3g fat (2g sat. fat), 18mg chol., 64mg sod., 6g carb. (4g sugars, 0 fiber), 1g pro.

Plum Streusel Kuchen

PREP: 25 MIN. • **BAKE:** 35 MIN.
MAKES: 15 SERVINGS

This recipe is actually called platz ("flat") in German, and has been in my family since before I was born. Fresh fruits of late summer make it a favorite.
—Lisa Warkentin, Winnipeg, MB

- 2 cups all-purpose flour
- ¼ cup sugar
- 2 tsp. baking powder
- ¼ tsp. salt
- 2 Tbsp. shortening
- 1 large egg, room temperature
- 1 cup heavy whipping cream
- 6 fresh plums, sliced

TOPPING
- ⅔ cup all-purpose flour
- ⅔ cup sugar
- 2 Tbsp. cold butter
- 2 Tbsp. heavy whipping cream

1. Preheat oven to 350°. In a large bowl, combine flour, sugar, baking powder and salt; cut in shortening until the mixture resembles fine crumbs. In another bowl, whisk egg and cream; add to the crumb mixture, tossing gently with a fork until mixture forms a ball.

2. Press dough into a greased 13x9-in. baking dish. Arrange plums over crust.

3. For topping, in a small bowl, combine flour and sugar; cut in butter until mixture resembles fine crumbs. Add cream, mixing gently with a fork until moist crumbs form. Sprinkle over plums.

4. Bake until a toothpick inserted in center comes out clean, 35-40 minutes. Cool on wire rack.

1 PIECE: 235 cal., 10g fat (6g sat. fat), 37mg chol., 126mg sod., 33g carb. (15g sugars, 1g fiber), 3g pro.

Kari Kelley

Plains, MT

It may take some time to make this rich, buttery treat, but it's well worth the effort! The blend of coconut, pecans and macadamia nuts is irresistible.

Double Nut Baklava

PREP: 25 MIN.
BAKE: 30 MIN. + STANDING
MAKES: ABOUT 3 DOZEN

1¼ cups sweetened shredded coconut, toasted
½ cup finely chopped macadamia nuts
½ cup finely chopped pecans
½ cup packed brown sugar
1 tsp. ground allspice
1¼ cups butter, melted
1 pkg. phyllo dough (16 oz., 14x9-in.-sheet size), thawed
1 cup sugar
½ cup water
¼ cup honey

1. In a large bowl, combine first 5 ingredients; set aside. Brush a 13x9-in. baking pan with some of the butter. Unroll the sheets of phyllo; trim to fit into pan.

2. Layer 10 sheets of phyllo in the prepared pan, brushing each with butter. (Keep the remaining dough covered with a damp towel to prevent it from drying out.) Sprinkle with a third of the nut mixture. Repeat layers twice. Top with 5 phyllo sheets, brushing each, including top sheet, with butter.

3. Using a sharp knife, cut into diamond shapes. Bake at 350° for 30-35 minutes or until golden brown. Cool completely on a wire rack.

4. In a small saucepan, bring the sugar, water and honey to a boil. Reduce heat; simmer for 5 minutes. Pour hot syrup over baklava. Let stand, covered, overnight.

1 PIECE: 174 cal., 10g fat (5g sat. fat), 17mg chol., 134mg sod., 20g carb. (12g sugars, 1g fiber), 2g pro.

Quick Cherry Turnovers

TAKES: 20 MIN. • **MAKES:** 4 SERVINGS

Refrigerated crescent rolls let you make these fruit-filled pastries in a hurry. My family loves these turnovers for breakfast, but they're so delicious, they'd be welcome any time of the day. Feel free to experiment with other pie fillings as well.
—*Elleen Oberrueter, Danbury, IA*

- 1 **tube (8 oz.) refrigerated crescent rolls**
- 1 **cup cherry pie filling**
- ½ **cup confectioners' sugar**
- 1 **to 2 Tbsp. 2% milk**

1. Preheat oven to 375°. Unroll crescent dough and separate into 4 rectangles; place on an ungreased baking sheet. Press perforations to seal. Place ¼ cup pie filling on 1 half of each rectangle. Fold the dough over filling; pinch edges to seal. Bake for 10-12 minutes or until golden.

2. Place the confectioners' sugar in a small bowl; stir in enough milk to reach a drizzling consistency. Drizzle over the turnovers. Serve warm.

1 TURNOVER: 359 cal., 12g fat (3g sat. fat), 1mg chol., 459mg sod., 56g carb. (34g sugars, 0 fiber), 4g pro.

Mini Baklava

PREP: 20 MIN. • **BAKE:** 10 MIN. + COOLING
MAKES: ABOUT 2½ DOZE

Baklava holds amazing memories for me. My best friend made it for my bridal and baby showers, and then she taught me how to make it! These delicious little miniatures give you the taste of baklava in a bite-sized package.
—*Margaret Guillory, Eunice, LA*

- ½ **cup butter**
- ¼ **cup sugar**
- 1 **tsp. ground cinnamon**
- 1 **cup finely chopped pecans**
- 1 **cup finely chopped walnuts**
- 2 **pkg. (1.9 oz. each) frozen miniature phyllo tart shells**
  Honey

1. Preheat oven to 350°. In a small saucepan over medium heat, melt butter. Stir in the sugar and cinnamon. Bring to a boil. Reduce heat; add pecans and walnuts, tossing to coat. Simmer, uncovered, until the nuts are lightly toasted, 5-10 minutes.

2. Place phyllo shells on a parchment-lined baking sheet. Spoon the nut and butter sauce mixture evenly into the shells. Bake until golden brown, 9-11 minutes. Cool completely on pan on a wire rack. Drizzle a drop of honey into each shell; let stand, covered, until serving. Serve with additional honey if desired.

1 FILLED PHYLLO CUP: 105 cal., 9g fat (2g sat. fat), 8mg chol., 33mg sod., 5g carb. (2g sugars, 1g fiber), 1g pro.

German Chocolate Ring

PREP: 30 MIN. + RISING
BAKE: 20 MIN. + COOLING
MAKES: 24 SERVINGS

This recipe is modeled after German chocolate cake, which is my favorite dessert. No wonder I enjoy making and eating this sweet-tasting bread!
—Anne Frederick, New Hartford, NY

1¼ cups sweetened shredded coconut, divided
1 cup semisweet chocolate chips, divided
¾ cup chopped pecans
3 large eggs, room temperature, divided use
4½ to 5 cups all-purpose flour
½ cup sugar
1 tsp. salt
1 pkg. (¼ oz.) active dry yeast
1 cup 2% milk
5 Tbsp. butter, divided

1. In small bowl, combine 1 cup coconut, ¾ cup chocolate chips, pecans and 1 egg; set aside. In large bowl, combine 1 cup flour, sugar, salt and yeast. In a small saucepan, heat milk and 4 Tbsp. butter to 120°-130°; add to flour mixture, beating until smooth. Add remaining 2 eggs and enough of the remaining flour to form a soft dough.

2. Turn the dough onto a lightly floured surface. Knead until smooth and elastic, 6-8 minutes. Place in greased bowl, turning once to grease top. Cover; let rise in warm place until doubled, about 1 hour.

3. Punch dough down; turn onto lightly floured surface. Roll dough into an 18x10-in. rectangle. Melt remaining 1 Tbsp. butter and brush over dough; spread with reserved chocolate mixture.

4. Roll up dough jelly-roll style, starting with a long side; pinch seam to seal. Place seam side down on greased baking sheet. Pinch ends together to form a ring.

5. With scissors, cut from outside edge two-thirds of the way toward center of ring at 1-in. intervals. Separate strips slightly; twist to allow filling to show. Cover and let rise until doubled, about 1 hour.

6. Bake at 350° for 20-25 minutes or until golden brown. Sprinkle with the remaining ¼ cup chocolate chips; let stand for 5 minutes. Spread melted chips; sprinkle with remaining ¼ cup coconut. Carefully remove from pan to a wire rack to cool.

1 PIECE: 222 cal., 10g fat (5g sat. fat), 34mg chol., 149mg sod., 30g carb. (11g sugars, 2g fiber), 4g pro.

Pear-Berry Breakfast Tarts

PREP: 45 MIN. + CHILLING • **BAKE:** 20 MIN.
MAKES: 10 SERVINGS

When my kids were small, I could never get pancakes on the table while they were all still hot. Then I got the idea for these breakfast tarts. It's a simple recipe for any busy family.
—Joan Elbourn, Gardner, MA

- ½ **cup butter, softened**
- 1 **cup sugar, divided**
- 2 **large eggs, room temperature**
- 2½ **cups all-purpose flour**
- 2 **tsp. baking powder**
- 2 **cups chopped peeled pears (about 2 large)**
- 2 **Tbsp. cornstarch**
- 2 **Tbsp. water**
- ½ **cup fresh raspberries**
- 1 **large egg white**
- 3 **to 5 Tbsp. 2% milk, divided**
- 1⅓ **cups confectioners' sugar**
  Food coloring, optional

1. Cream butter and ½ cup sugar until light and fluffy, 5-7 minutes. Add eggs, 1 at a time, beating well after each addition. In another bowl, whisk flour and baking powder; gradually beat into the creamed mixture to form a dough. Divide dough in half; shape each into a rectangle. Wrap and refrigerate 1 hour.

2. In a small saucepan over medium heat, combine pears and remaining ½ cup sugar. Cook and stir until the sugar is dissolved and the pears are softened, 6-8 minutes. In a small bowl, mix cornstarch and water until smooth; stir into the pear mixture. Return to a boil, stirring constantly; cook and stir 1-2 minutes or until thickened. Remove from heat; cool. Stir in raspberries.

3. Preheat oven to 350°. On a lightly floured surface, roll half the dough into a 15x8-in. rectangle. Cut into ten 4x3-in. rectangles. Transfer to parchment-lined baking sheets; spoon about 2 Tbsp. filling over each pastry to within ½ in. of edges. Roll remaining dough into a 15x8-in. rectangle; cut into ten 4x3-in. rectangles and place over filling. Press edges with a fork to seal. Whisk egg white and 1 Tbsp. milk; brush over pastries. Bake until golden brown and filling is bubbly, 20-25 minutes.

4. Remove from baking sheets to wire racks to cool. For icing, mix confectioners' sugar and enough of the remaining milk to reach desired consistency; tint with food coloring if desired. Spread or drizzle on pastries.

1 TART: 379 cal., 11g fat (6g sat. fat), 62mg chol., 193mg sod., 67g carb. (39g sugars, 2g fiber), 5g pro.

TEST KITCHEN TIP

For a delicious change of pace, substitute 2 cups chopped peeled apples for the pears.

AUTUMN'S BEST DESSERTS

CHEESECAKES, CUSTARDS, BREAD PUDDINGS AND MORE,

THESE LUSCIOUS SWEETS FINISH OFF A MEAL

IN IRRESISTIBLE STYLE.

GINGER PUMPKIN
CHEESECAKE, P. 279

Chai-Spiced Bread Pudding

PREP: 25 MIN. + STANDING • **BAKE:** 35 MIN.
MAKES: 9 SERVINGS

Nothing says fall to me more than the warming spices of chai. This bread pudding incorporates those flavors to make a dessert that everyone raves about.
— Jess Apfe, Berkeley, CA

- 4 large eggs, room temperature, lightly beaten
- 2 cups 2% milk
- ½ cup packed brown sugar
- 1 tsp. ground cinnamon
- 1 tsp. vanilla extract
- ¾ tsp. ground ginger
- ½ tsp. ground cardamom
- ¼ tsp. salt
- ⅛ tsp. ground cloves
- 2 Tbsp. rum, optional
- 6 slices day-old French bread (1 in. thick), cubed
- ⅓ cup slivered almonds
  Vanilla ice cream or sweetened whipped cream

1. Preheat oven to 350°. In a large bowl, whisk together first 9 ingredients and, if desired, rum. Gently stir in bread; let stand 15 minutes or until bread is softened.

2. Transfer to a greased 8-in. square baking dish. Sprinkle with almonds.

3. Bake, uncovered, until puffed, golden and a knife inserted in the center comes out clean, 35-40 minutes. Serve warm, with ice cream.

1 SERVING: 180 cal., 6g fat (2g sat. fat), 87mg chol., 218mg sod., 24g carb. (15g sugars, 1g fiber), 7g pro. **DIABETIC EXCHANGES:** 1½ starch, 1 fat.

Pumpkin Pecan Custard

PREP: 20 MIN. • **BAKE:** 35 MIN. + CHILLING
MAKES: 8 SERVINGS

My family loves pumpkin pie, but this is a delicious, creamy, healthier alternative— and we don't miss the crust at all.
—Abby Booth, Coweta, OK

- 1 can (15 oz.) pumpkin
- 1 can (12 oz.) reduced-fat evaporated milk
- ¾ cup egg substitute
- ⅓ cup packed brown sugar
- 1½ tsp. vanilla extract
- 1 tsp. ground cinnamon
- ½ tsp. ground ginger
- ¼ tsp. ground cloves
- ⅛ tsp. salt

TOPPING

- 3 Tbsp. all-purpose flour
- 3 Tbsp. brown sugar
- ½ tsp. ground cinnamon
- 2 Tbsp. cold butter
- ½ cup chopped pecans

1. Preheat oven to 325°. In a large bowl, combine the first 9 ingredients. Transfer to eight 6-oz. ramekins or custard cups. Place in a baking pan; add 1 in. boiling water to pan. Bake, uncovered, for 20 minutes.

2. Meanwhile, for topping, in a small bowl, combine flour, brown sugar and cinnamon. Cut in butter until crumbly. Stir in pecans. Sprinkle over custards. Bake 15-20 minutes longer or until a knife inserted in the center comes out clean.

3. Remove ramekins from water bath; cool for 10 minutes. Cover and refrigerate at least 4 hours.

½ CUP: 213 cal., 9g fat (3g sat. fat), 11mg chol., 160mg sod., 27g carb. (21g sugars, 3g fiber), 7g pro. **DIABETIC EXCHANGES:** 2 starch, 1½ fat.

Creamy Caramel Flan

PREP: 25 MIN. + STANDING
BAKE: 50 MIN. + CHILLING
MAKES: 10 SERVINGS

A small slice of this impressively rich, creamy treat goes a long way. What a delightful finish for a special meal or holiday celebration.
—Pat Forete, Miami, FL

¾ cup sugar
¼ cup water
1 pkg. (8 oz.) cream cheese, softened
5 large eggs
1 can (14 oz.) sweetened condensed milk
1 can (12 oz.) evaporated milk
1 tsp. vanilla extract

1. In a heavy saucepan, cook sugar and water over medium-low heat until melted and golden, about 15 minutes. Brush down crystals on the side of the pan with additional water as necessary. Quickly pour into an ungreased 2-qt. round baking or souffle dish, tilting to coat the bottom; let stand for 10 minutes.

2. Preheat oven to 350°. In a bowl, beat the cream cheese until smooth. Beat in eggs, 1 at a time, until thoroughly combined. Add remaining ingredients; mix well. Pour over caramelized sugar.

3. Place the dish in a larger baking pan. Pour boiling water into larger pan to a depth of 1 in. Bake until the center is just set (mixture will jiggle), 50-60 minutes.

4. Remove dish from a larger pan to a wire rack; cool for 1 hour. Refrigerate overnight.

5. To unmold, run a knife around edge and invert onto a large rimmed serving platter. Cut into wedges or spoon onto dessert plates; spoon sauce over each serving.

1 PIECE: 345 cal., 16g fat (9g sat. fat), 140mg chol., 189mg sod., 41g carb. (41g sugars, 0 fiber), 10g pro.

TEST KITCHEN TIP

Pay close attention when melting sugar, as it changes quickly. Be sure to find a pan for the water bath before starting to prepare the recipe.

SEE HOW IT'S DONE

Watch the flan-tastic magic happen! Just hover your camera here.

the pears are almost tender, basting occasionally with the poaching liquid, 16-20 minutes.

4. Remove pears with a slotted spoon; cool slightly. Strain and reserve 1½ cups poaching liquid; set aside.

5. Preheat oven to 400°. Unfold the puff pastry on a lightly floured surface. Cut into ½-in.-wide strips. Brush lightly with beaten egg. Starting at the bottom of a pear, wrap a pastry strip around pear, adding additional strips until the pear is completely wrapped in pastry. Repeat with the remaining pears and puff pastry.

6. Transfer to a parchment-lined 15x10x1-in. baking pan. Bake on a lower oven rack until golden brown, 25-30 minutes.

7. Meanwhile, bring the reserved poaching liquid to a boil; cook until thick and syrupy, about 10 minutes. Place pears on dessert plates and drizzle with syrup. Serve warm.

1 PEAR WITH 3 TBSP. SYRUP: 518 cal., 17g fat (4g sat. fat), 0 chol., 205mg sod., 92g carb. (49g sugars, 9g fiber), 5g pro.

Honeyed Pears in Puff Pastry

PREP: 25 MIN. • **BAKE:** 25 MIN.
MAKES: 4 SERVINGS

A honey of a salute to late-summer pear season, this cozy dessert has plenty of wow factor. Wrapped in puff pastry, it resembles a beehive.
—Heather Baird, Knoxville, TN

- 4 **small pears**
- 4 **cups water**
- 2 **cups sugar**
- 1 **cup honey**
- 1 **small lemon, halved**
- 3 **cinnamon sticks (3 in.)**
- 6 **to 8 whole cloves**
- 1 **vanilla bean**
- 1 **sheet frozen puff pastry, thawed**
- 1 **large egg, lightly beaten**

1. Core pears from bottom, leaving the stems intact. Peel pears; cut ¼ in. from the bottom of each to level if necessary.

2. In a large saucepan, combine the water, sugar, honey, lemon halves, cinnamon and cloves. Split vanilla bean and scrape the seeds; add the bean and seeds into the sugar mixture. Bring to a boil.

3. Reduce heat; place pears on their sides in saucepan and poach, uncovered, until

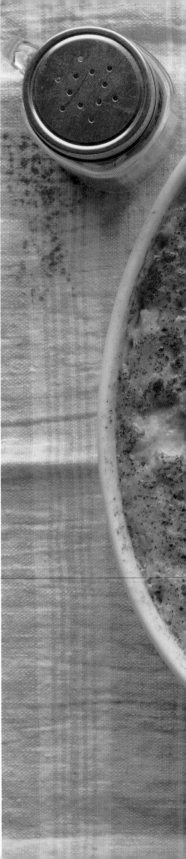

Apple Dumpling Roll-Ups

PREP: 35 MIN. • **BAKE:** 45 MIN. + STANDING
MAKES: 1 DOZEN

A family friend gave me this simple way to make apple dumplings without lots of steps. I love the sticky cinnamon topping.
—Jenny Leighty, West Salem, OH

3	cups all-purpose flour
2	tsp. baking powder
1½	tsp. salt
3	Tbsp. cold butter, cubed
1⅓	cups 2% milk
¾ to 1	cup packed brown sugar
2	tsp. ground cinnamon
4	cups chopped apples (about 4 medium)

SAUCE

1½	cups sugar
1½	cups water
2	Tbsp. all-purpose flour
1	Tbsp. butter
1	tsp. ground cinnamon

1. Preheat oven to 350°. In a large bowl, whisk the flour, baking powder and salt. Cut in butter until mixture resembles coarse crumbs. Add milk; stir just until moistened (dough will be soft and sticky).
2. Turn dough onto a floured surface. Roll into an 18x12-in. rectangle. Sprinkle brown sugar and cinnamon to within 1 in. of edges; top with apples. Roll up jelly-roll style, starting with a long side; pinch seam to seal. Using a serrated knife, cut into 12 slices. Place in a greased 13x9-in. baking pan, cut side down.
3. In a small saucepan, combine the sauce ingredients; bring to a boil, whisking to blend. Cook and stir 3-4 minutes or until thickened. Pour over top of roll-ups.
4. Bake, uncovered, until golden brown and bubbly, 45-55 minutes. Let stand 10 minutes before serving.

1 ROLL-UP: 339 cal., 5g fat (3g sat. fat), 12mg chol., 413mg sod., 71g carb. (44g sugars, 2g fiber), 4g pro.

Butternut Squash Custard

PREP: 25 MIN. • **BAKE:** 55 MIN.
MAKES: 8 SERVINGS

My husband first tried this comforting casserole more than 10 years ago when he was still my fiance. Having enjoyed it so much, he said I needed to offer it at every Thanksgiving dinner. I was happy to oblige!
—Maura Calusdian, Londonderry, NH

- 1 medium butternut squash (2 to 3 lbs.), peeled, seeded and cubed
- ½ cup all-purpose flour
- ½ cup sugar
- 2 cups 2% milk
- 3 large eggs
- 2 Tbsp. butter, melted
- ⅛ tsp. salt
- ⅛ tsp. ground cinnamon
- ⅛ tsp. ground nutmeg

1. Preheat oven to 350°. Place squash in a large saucepan and cover with water; bring to a boil. Reduce heat; cover and simmer until tender, 8-10 minutes. Drain.
2. In a large bowl, mash the squash with flour and sugar until blended; beat in the milk, eggs and butter. Pour into an ungreased 2½-qt. baking dish. Sprinkle with salt, cinnamon and nutmeg.
3. Bake until the center appears set, 55-65 minutes.

¾ CUP: 202 cal., 6g fat (3g sat. fat), 91mg chol., 118mg sod., 33g carb. (18g sugars, 3g fiber), 6g pro.

Caramel-Apple Skillet Buckle

PREP: 35 MIN. • **BAKE:** 1 HOUR + STANDING
MAKES: 12 SERVINGS

My grandma used to bake a version of this for me when I was a little girl. She would make it using fresh apples from her tree in the backyard. I've adapted her recipe because I love the combination of apples, pecans and caramel.
—Emily Hobbs, Springfield, MO

- ½ cup butter, softened
- ¾ cup sugar
- 2 large eggs, room temperature
- 1 tsp. vanilla extract
- 2 cups all-purpose flour
- 2½ tsp. baking powder
- 1¾ tsp. ground cinnamon
- ½ tsp. ground ginger
- ¼ tsp. salt
- 1½ cups buttermilk

TOPPING
- ⅔ cup packed brown sugar
- ½ cup all-purpose flour
- ¼ cup cold butter
- ¾ cup finely chopped pecans
- ½ cup old-fashioned oats
- 6 cups thinly sliced peeled Gala or other sweet apples (about 6 medium)
- 18 caramels, unwrapped
- 1 Tbsp. buttermilk
  Optional: Vanilla ice cream, whipped cream, additional chopped pecans and ground cinnamon

1. Preheat oven to 350°. In a large bowl, cream butter and sugar until light and fluffy, 5-7 minutes. Add eggs, 1 at a time, beating well after each addition. Beat in vanilla. In another bowl, whisk flour, baking powder, cinnamon, ginger and salt; add to creamed mixture alternately with buttermilk, beating well after each addition. Pour into a greased 12-in. cast-iron or other ovenproof skillet.
2. For topping, in a small bowl, mix brown sugar and flour; cut in butter until crumbly. Stir in pecans and oats; sprinkle over batter. Top with apples. Bake until the apples are golden brown, 60-70 minutes. Cool in pan on a wire rack.
3. In a microwave, melt caramels with buttermilk; stir until smooth. Drizzle over cake. Let stand until set. Serve with toppings as desired.
1 PIECE: 462 cal., 19g fat (9g sat. fat), 64mg chol., 354mg sod., 68g carb. (42g sugars, 3g fiber), 7g pro.

Salted Caramel Cappuccino Cheesecake

PREP: 30 MIN. • **BAKE:** 55 MIN. + CHILLING
MAKES: 12 SERVINGS

After spending years living in Seattle, I've become a coffee junkie! I had to relocate across the country for a time, so I created this cheesecake with the flavors of salted caramel, coffee and espresso. It lifted me up on days when I felt blue about leaving one of the world's amazing coffee destinations.
—Julie Merriman, Seattle, WA

- 1 pkg. (9 oz.) chocolate wafers
- 1 cup semisweet chocolate chips
- ½ cup packed brown sugar
- 2 Tbsp. instant espresso powder
- ⅛ tsp. ground nutmeg
- ½ cup butter, melted

FILLING

- 3 pkg. (8 oz. each) cream cheese, softened
- 1 cup packed brown sugar
- ½ cup sour cream
- ¼ cup Kahlua (coffee liqueur)
- 2 Tbsp. all-purpose flour
- 2 Tbsp. instant espresso powder
- 4 large eggs, lightly beaten

TOPPING

- ½ cup hot caramel ice cream topping
- ½ tsp. coarse sea salt

1. Preheat oven to 350°. Place a greased 9-in. springform pan on a double thickness of heavy-duty foil (about 18 in. square). Securely wrap foil around pan.
2. Place the first 5 ingredients in a food processor; cover and pulse until fine crumbs form. Gradually add the melted butter, pulsing until combined. Press mixture onto the bottom and 2 in. up side of the prepared pan.
3. In a large bowl, beat cream cheese and brown sugar until smooth. Beat in sour cream, Kahlua, flour and espresso powder. Add the eggs; beat on low speed just until blended. Pour into crust. Place springform pan in a larger baking pan; add 1 in. of hot water to larger pan.
4. Bake for 55-65 minutes or until center is just set and top appears dull. Remove springform pan from water bath; remove foil. Cool on a wire rack 10 minutes; loosen sides from pan with a knife. Cool 1 hour longer. Refrigerate overnight, covering when completely cooled.
5. Pour caramel topping over cheesecake. Refrigerate at least 15 minutes. Remove rim from pan. Sprinkle with sea salt just before serving.

1 PIECE: 618 cal., 38g fat (22g sat. fat), 160mg chol., 530mg sod., 64g carb. (42g sugars, 2g fiber), 9g pro.

TEST KITCHEN TIP

For a mirror-smooth finish on cheesecakes, be very gentle when stirring in eggs. You can also tap the filled pan gently on a firm surface a few times and pop any bubbles that rise to the top before baking.

4. Just before serving, sprinkle with almonds and remove rim of pan. Refrigerate leftovers.

1 PIECE: 329 cal., 20g fat (10g sat. fat), 100mg chol., 140mg sod., 32g carb. (26g sugars, 1g fiber), 5g pro.

Baked Pumpkin Pudding

PREP: 10 MIN. • **BAKE:** 40 MIN.
MAKES: 5 SERVINGS

Even after your favorite turkey dinner, you'll find room for this perfect pudding dessert—a treat served hot or cold. Mildly spiced, it will leave you sweetly satisfied, but not overly full.
—Gerri Saylor, Graniteville, SC

- ½ cup egg substitute
- 1 can (15 oz.) solid-pack pumpkin
- ¾ cup sugar
- 1 Tbsp. honey
- 1 tsp. ground cinnamon
- ½ tsp. ground ginger
- ¼ tsp. ground cloves
- 1½ cups fat-free evaporated milk
- 5 Tbsp. reduced-fat whipped topping

1. Preheat oven to 425°. In a large bowl, beat the egg substitute, pumpkin, sugar, honey and spices until blended. Gradually beat in milk. Pour into five 8-oz. custard cups coated with cooking spray. Place in a 13x9-in. baking pan. Pour hot water into pan to act as a water bath.
2. Bake, uncovered, for 10 minutes. Reduce heat to 350°. Bake 30-35 minutes longer or until a knife inserted in the center comes out clean.
3. Serve warm or cold. Garnish with whipped topping. Store in the refrigerator.

1 SERVING: 245 cal., 1g fat (1g sat. fat), 3mg chol., 143mg sod., 51g carb., 4g fiber), 10g pro.

Luscious Almond Cheesecake

PREP: 15 MIN. • **BAKE:** 55 MIN. + CHILLING
MAKES: 16 SERVINGS

Almonds and almond extract give this traditional sour cream-topped cheesecake a tasty twist.
—Brenda Clifford, Overland Park, KS

- 1¼ cups crushed vanilla wafers (about 40 wafers)
- ¾ cup finely chopped almonds
- ¼ cup sugar
- ⅓ cup butter, melted

FILLING
- 4 pkg. (8 oz. each) cream cheese, softened
- 1¼ cups sugar
- 4 large eggs, room temperature, lightly beaten
- 1½ tsp. almond extract
- 1 tsp. vanilla extract

TOPPING
- 2 cups sour cream
- ¼ cup sugar
- 1 tsp. vanilla extract
- ⅛ cup toasted sliced almonds

1. Preheat oven to 350°. Combine the wafer crumbs, almonds and sugar; stir in butter and mix well. Press into the bottom of a greased 10-in. springform pan; set aside.
2. In a large bowl, beat cream cheese and sugar until smooth. Add eggs; beat on low speed just until combined. Stir in extracts. Pour into crust. Place on a baking sheet.
3. Bake for 50-55 minutes or until center is almost set. Remove from the oven; let stand for 5 minutes (leave oven on). Combine the sour cream, sugar and vanilla. Spoon around edge of cheesecake; carefully spread over filling. Bake 5 minutes longer. Cool on a wire rack for 10 minutes. Carefully run a knife around edge of pan to loosen; cool 1 hour longer. Refrigerate overnight.

Toffee-Pear Crisp Bread Pudding

PREP: 20 MIN. + STANDING
BAKE: 40 MIN. + COOLING
MAKES: 12 SERVINGS

My son loves pear crisp, but one night I was making bread pudding. He asked if I could make both. I compromised by combining two desserts into this one dish. It's absolutely fantastic!
—Kurt Wait, Redwood City, CA

1¾ cups 2% milk
1 cup butterscotch-caramel ice cream topping
¼ cup butter, cubed
1 tsp. ground cinnamon
½ tsp. ground ginger
2 large eggs
4 cups cubed day-old French bread
2 cups sliced peeled fresh pears (about 2 medium)

TOPPING
½ cup all-purpose flour
½ cup packed brown sugar
⅓ cup cold butter
⅓ cup English toffee bits

1. Preheat oven to 350°. In a small saucepan, combine milk, butterscotch-caramel topping, butter, cinnamon and ginger. Cook and stir over medium-low heat until butter is melted. Remove from heat.
2. Whisk eggs in a large bowl; gradually whisk in a third of the milk mixture. Stir in remaining milk mixture. Add bread; stir to coat. Let stand 10 minutes. Gently stir in pears; transfer to a greased 11x7-in. baking dish. Bake, uncovered, 20 minutes.
3. Meanwhile, for topping, in a small bowl, combine flour and brown sugar; cut in butter until crumbly. Stir in toffee bits; sprinkle mixture over bread pudding. Bake, uncovered, 20-25 minutes longer or until puffed, golden and a knife inserted in the center comes out clean. Let stand for 10 minutes before serving. Serve warm. Refrigerate leftovers.
1 SERVING: 331 cal., 14g fat (8g sat. fat), 67mg chol., 260mg sod., 48g carb. (30g sugars, 1g fiber), 5g pro.

Baklava Cheesecake

PREP: 1¼ HOURS • **BAKE:** 50 MIN. + CHILLING
MAKES: 16 SERVINGS

With sugared cranberries and rosemary sprigs, my unique baklava cheesecake makes a grand display for office parties and other special events.
—Aryanna Gamble, New Orleans, LA

12 **sheets phyllo dough (14x9-in.)**
⅓ **cup butter, melted**
1 **cup finely chopped walnuts**
¼ **cup sugar**
½ **tsp. ground cinnamon**
¼ **tsp. ground nutmeg**
⅛ **tsp. ground allspice**
2 **pkg. (8 oz. each) cream cheese, softened**
1 **carton (8 oz.) mascarpone cheese**
⅔ **cup honey**
¼ **cup 2% milk**
3 **Tbsp. all-purpose flour**
3 **large eggs, room temperature, lightly beaten**
GARNISH
3 **Tbsp. light corn syrup**
3 **fresh rosemary sprigs**
¼ **cup sugar, divided**
½ **cup fresh or frozen cranberries, thawed and patted dry**

1. Preheat oven to 425°. Place 1 sheet of phyllo dough in a greased 9-in. springform pan, pressing phyllo onto bottom and up side of pan; brush with butter. Layer with remaining phyllo sheets, brushing each layer with butter and rotating sheets slightly to stagger the corners. (While working, keep unused phyllo covered with a damp towel to prevent it from drying out.) Place the springform pan on a 15x10x1-in. baking pan.
2. In a small bowl, mix walnuts, sugar and spices; sprinkle over bottom of phyllo. Bake for 5-7 minutes or until the edges are lightly browned (sides will puff). Cool in the springform pan on a wire rack. Reduce oven setting to 325°.
3. In a large bowl, beat cream cheese and mascarpone cheese on low speed until smooth. Beat in honey, milk and flour. Add eggs; beat on low speed just until blended. Pour into crust. Return pan to baking pan.
4. Bake 50-60 minutes or until center is almost set. Cool on a wire rack 1 hour longer. Refrigerate overnight, covering when completely cooled. Remove rim from pan.
5. For garnish, place corn syrup in a small microwave-safe bowl. Microwave, uncovered, 10 seconds or until warm. Brush lightly over both sides of rosemary sprigs. Place on waxed paper; sprinkle with 1 Tbsp. sugar.
6. If necessary, reheat remaining corn syrup until warm; gently toss cranberries in syrup. Place the remaining 3 Tbsp. sugar in a small bowl; add cranberries and toss to coat. Place on waxed paper and let stand until set, about 1 hour.
7. Just before serving, top cheesecake with sugared rosemary and cranberries.
1 PIECE: 351 cal., 26g fat (13g sat. fat), 92mg chol., 178mg sod., 26g carb. (19g sugars, 1g fiber), 6g pro.

Hot Cocoa Souffle

PREP: 20 MIN. • **BAKE:** 40 MIN.
MAKES: 6 SERVINGS

*A friend invited me to go to a church cooking
demo years ago, and one of the recipes we
prepared was this luscious souffle. It's so
decadent and delicious.*
—Joan Hallford, North Richland Hills, TX

5	**large eggs**
4	**tsp. plus ¾ cup sugar, divided**
½	**cup baking cocoa**
6	**Tbsp. all-purpose flour**
¼	**tsp. salt**
1½	**cups fat-free milk**
2	**Tbsp. butter**
1½	**tsp. vanilla extract**
	Confectioners' sugar, optional

1. Separate eggs; let stand at room temperature
for 30 minutes. Coat a 2-qt. souffle dish with
cooking spray and lightly sprinkle with 4 tsp.
sugar; set aside.

2. Preheat oven to 350°. In a small saucepan,
combine the cocoa, flour, salt and remaining
¾ cup sugar. Gradually whisk in milk. Bring to a
boil, stirring constantly. Cook and stir 1-2 minutes
longer or until thickened. Stir in butter. Transfer
to a large bowl.

3. Stir a small amount of the hot mixture into
the egg yolks; return all to the bowl, stirring
constantly. Add vanilla; cool slightly.

4. In another large bowl, with clean beaters, beat
egg whites until stiff peaks form. With a spatula,
stir a fourth of the egg whites into the chocolate
mixture until no white streaks remain. Fold in
remaining egg whites until combined.

5. Transfer to prepared dish. Bake 40-45 minutes
or until the top is puffed and the center appears
set. If desired, dust with confectioners' sugar.
Serve immediately.

1 SERVING: 272 cal., 9g fat (4g sat. fat), 188mg
chol., 209mg sod., 41g carb. (31g sugars, 2g fiber),
9g pro.

Pear Pandowdy

PREP: 20 MIN. • **BAKE:** 20 MIN.
MAKES: 2 SERVINGS

I pulled out this recipe one night when my husband was craving something sweet, and it was a big hit with both of us. It's a superb last-minute dessert that almost melts in your mouth.
—Jennifer Class, Snohomish, WA

2	medium firm pears, peeled and sliced
2	Tbsp. brown sugar
4½	tsp. butter
1½	tsp. lemon juice
⅛	tsp. ground cinnamon
⅛	tsp. ground nutmeg

TOPPING

½	cup all-purpose flour
2	Tbsp. plus ½ tsp. sugar, divided
½	tsp. baking powder
⅛	tsp. salt
¼	cup cold butter, cubed
2	Tbsp. water
	Vanilla ice cream, optional

1. Preheat oven to 375°. In a small saucepan, combine the first 6 ingredients. Cook and stir over medium heat until the pears are tender, about 5 minutes. Pour into a greased 3-cup baking dish.

2. In a small bowl, combine the flour, 2 Tbsp. sugar, the baking powder and salt; cut in butter until crumbly. Stir in water. Sprinkle over pear mixture. Sprinkle with remaining ½ cup sugar.

3. Bake, uncovered, until a toothpick inserted into topping comes out clean and topping is lightly browned, 20-25 minutes. If desired, serve warm, with ice cream.

1 SERVING: 594 cal., 32g fat (20g sat. fat), 84mg chol., 572mg sod., 76g carb. (45g sugars, 5g fiber), 4g pro.

Maple-Apple Clafoutis

PREP: 20 MIN. • **BAKE:** 40 MIN.
MAKES: 8 SERVINGS

This fruit pudding could not be easier to make! A traditional comfort food in France, it is often made with cherries. I use apples and maple syrup to give it a real midwestern flair.
—Bridget Klusman, Otsego, MI

- 4 **medium tart apples, thinly sliced**
- 2 **Tbsp. lemon juice**
- 4 **large eggs**
- 1¼ **cups 2% milk**
- ½ **cup maple syrup**
- 1 **tsp. vanilla extract**
- ½ **cup all-purpose flour**
- ½ **tsp. ground cinnamon**
  Dash salt
  Additional maple syrup, optional

1. Preheat oven to 375°. Toss apples with lemon juice; place in a greased 2-qt. baking dish. In a large bowl, whisk eggs, milk, syrup and vanilla until combined. In another bowl, combine flour, cinnamon and salt; add to egg mixture. Pour batter over apples.

2. Bake until puffed and lightly browned, 40-50 minutes. Serve warm, or cool on a wire rack. If desired, serve with additional maple syrup.

1 PIECE: 177 cal., 3g fat (1g sat. fat), 96mg chol., 75mg sod., 32g carb. (22g sugars, 2g fiber), 5g pro. **DIABETIC EXCHANGES:** 1½ starch, ½ fruit, ½ fat.

TEST KITCHEN TIP

Pulled right out of the oven, this is a showstopping masterpiece, all puffed up and golden brown. However, as it sits, it will deflate a little. So if you're looking to impress, serve it hot out of the oven. When perfectly ripe pears can be found, swap those in for the apples. Their delicate flavor shines through in this elegant dessert.

SEE HOW IT'S DONE

Watch the simple steps to making this oh-so-pretty dessert. Hover your camera here.

press onto the bottom and 1 in. up the side of a greased 10-in. springform pan. Place on a baking sheet. Bake until set, 8-10 minutes. Cool on a wire rack. Reduce oven setting to 325°.

2. Drizzle the crust with caramel topping; sprinkle with pecans. In another bowl, beat cream cheese, sugar, vanilla and flour until smooth. Beat in eggs and yolks just until combined. Stir in cream and bourbon. Pour into crust.

3. Place springform pan in larger baking pan; add 1 in. hot water to larger pan. Bake until center is almost set, 65-70 minutes. Remove springform pan from the water bath; remove foil. Cool on a wire rack for 10 minutes. Loosen side from pan with a knife, remove foil.

4. Chill for 8 hours or overnight, covering when completely cooled. Remove rim of pan. If desired, just before serving, top with whipped cream, pecans and caramel sauce. Refrigerate leftovers.

1 PIECE: 525 cal., 35g fat (18g sat. fat), 153mg chol., 378mg sod., 45g carb. (38g sugars, 1g fiber), 8g pro.

Chocolate Bourbon Pecan Cheesecake

PREP: 30 MIN. • **BAKE:** 1¼ HOURS + CHILLING
MAKES: 16 SERVINGS

This cheesecake was inspired by the Kentucky Derby, but will wow your guests and your taste buds any time. The rich flavors of chocolate, bourbon, nuts and caramel seem especially decadent in late summer and fall.
—Rashanda Cobbins, Milwaukee, WI

- 2 **cups chocolate wafer crumbs**
- 3 **Tbsp. butter, melted**
- ¾ **cup hot caramel ice cream topping**
- ¾ **cup chopped pecans, toasted**
- 5 **pkg. (8 oz. each) cream cheese, softened**
- 1¾ **cups sugar**
- 1½ **tsp. vanilla extract**
- 2 **Tbsp. all-purpose flour**
- 4 **large eggs, room temperature, lightly beaten**
- 2 **large egg yolks, room temperature, lightly beaten**
- ⅓ **cup heavy whipping cream**
- ¼ **cup bourbon**
  Optional: Whipped cream, pecans and extra caramel sauce

1. Preheat oven to 350°. Place a greased 10-in. springform pan on a double thickness of heavy duty foil. Securely wrap foil around pan. Combine cookie crumbs and butter;

Sweet Potato Crisp

PREP: 40 MIN. • **BAKE:** 35 MIN.
MAKES: 12 SERVINGS

My not-too-sweet potato crisp features a wonderful buttery crumb topping. It's a marvelous dessert that can also stand in as a welcome change from candied sweet potatoes.
—Kathy Hamsher, Moon Township, PA

- 4 **medium sweet potatoes (about 2½ lbs.), peeled and cut into 1-in. cubes**
- 1 **pkg. (8 oz.) fat-free cream cheese**
- ¼ **tsp. ground cinnamon**
- 2 **medium apples, quartered**
- 1 **cup fresh or frozen cranberries**
- ½ **cup all-purpose flour**
- ½ **cup quick-cooking oats**
- ⅓ **cup packed brown sugar**
- 3 **Tbsp. cold butter**
- ¼ **cup chopped pecans**

1. Preheat oven to 350°. Place the sweet potatoes in a large saucepan; add water to cover. Bring to a boil. Reduce heat; cook, uncovered, until tender, 10-15 minutes. Drain well.
2. In a large bowl, beat potatoes, cream cheese and cinnamon until smooth. Spread into an 11x7-in. baking dish coated with cooking spray. In a food processor, pulse apples and cranberries until chopped; spread over the potato mixture.
3. In a small bowl, mix the flour, oats and brown sugar; cut in butter until crumbly. Stir in pecans; sprinkle over top of apple and cranberry mixture. Bake, uncovered, until topping is golden brown and the apples are tender, 35-40 minutes.
1 SERVING: 206 cal., 5g fat (2g sat. fat), 10mg chol., 165mg sod., 36g carb. (19g sugars, 3g fiber), 5g pro.

Caramel Pear Pudding

PREP: 15 MIN. • **BAKE:** 45 MIN.
MAKES: 8 SERVINGS

The delicate pears and irresistible caramel topping make this old-fashioned dessert a winner whenever I serve it. It's a tempting fall sweet that puts the season's best pears to excellent use.
—Sharon Mensing, Greenfield, IA

- 1 **cup all-purpose flour**
- ⅔ **cup sugar**
- 1½ **tsp. baking powder**
- ½ **tsp. ground cinnamon**
- ¼ **tsp. salt**
  Pinch ground cloves
- ½ **cup whole milk**
- 4 **medium pears, peeled and cut into ½-in. cubes**
- ½ **cup chopped pecans**
- ¾ **cup packed brown sugar**
- ¼ **cup butter**
- ¾ **cup boiling water**
  Optional: Vanilla ice cream or whipped cream

1. Preheat oven to at 375°. In a large bowl, combine the first 6 ingredients; beat in milk until smooth. Stir in pears and pecans. Spoon into an ungreased 2-qt. baking dish.
2. In another bowl, combine the brown sugar, butter and water; pour over batter. Bake, uncovered, for 45-50 minutes. Serve warm, with ice cream or whipped cream if desired.
1 SERVING: 359 cal., 12g fat (4g sat. fat), 17mg chol., 223mg sod., 63g carb. (46g sugars, 3g fiber), 3g pro.

Pumpkin Whoopie Pies

PREP: 30 MIN. + CHILLING
BAKE: 10 MIN./BATCH + COOLING
MAKES: 2 DOZEN

My kids start begging me for these cakelike sandwich cookies as soon as autumn arrives. I haven't met a person who doesn't like these fun treats.
—Deb Stuber, Carlisle, PA

1 cup shortening
2 cups packed brown sugar
2 large eggs, room temperature
1 tsp. vanilla extract
3½ cups all-purpose flour
1½ tsp. baking powder
1½ tsp. baking soda
1 tsp. salt
1 tsp. ground cinnamon
1 tsp. ground ginger
1½ cups canned pumpkin

FILLING
¼ cup all-purpose flour
Dash salt
¾ cup 2% milk
1 cup shortening
2 cups confectioners' sugar
2 tsp. vanilla extract

1. Preheat oven to 400°. Cream shortening and brown sugar 5-7 minutes or until light and fluffy. Add eggs, 1 at a time, beating well after each addition. Beat in vanilla. In another bowl, whisk next 6 ingredients; beat into the creamed mixture alternately with pumpkin.

2. Drop batter by rounded tablespoonfuls 2 in. apart onto greased baking sheets; flatten slightly with the back of a spoon. Bake 10-11 minutes. Remove to wire racks to cool.

3. For filling, combine flour and salt in a small saucepan. Gradually whisk in milk until smooth; bring to a boil over medium-high heat. Reduce heat to medium; cook and stir until thickened, about 2 minutes. Refrigerate, covered, until completely cooled.

4. In another bowl, beat shortening, confectioners' sugar and vanilla until smooth. Add chilled milk mixture; beat until light and fluffy, about 7 minutes. Spread on the bottoms of half of the cookies; cover with remaining cookies. Store in the refrigerator.

1 SANDWICH COOKIE: 344 cal., 17g fat (4g sat. fat), 16mg chol., 284mg sod., 45g carb. (29g sugars, 1g fiber), 3g pro.

ABOUT THE GARNISH

For more about making candied citrus, hover your camera here.

2. In a large bowl, beat the cream cheese, pumpkin, sugar, cottage cheese, flour, cinnamon, vanilla, salt, nutmeg and cloves until blended. Add eggs; beat on low speed just until combined. Pour into crust.

3. Bake at 350° for 60-70 minutes or until center is almost set. Combine the sour cream, marmalade and vanilla; carefully spread over cheesecake. Bake 10 minutes longer. Cool on a wire rack for 10 minutes. Carefully run a knife around edge of pan to loosen; cool 1 hour longer.

4. Refrigerate overnight. Remove rim of pan. If desired, top with candied orange slices. Refrigerate leftovers.

1 PIECE: 342 cal., 20g fat (11g sat. fat), 77mg chol., 325mg sod., 36g carb. (24g sugars, 1g fiber), 6g pro.

TEST KITCHEN TIP

To make candied orange slices: Bring 2¼ cups sugar and 2 cups water to a boil over medium-high heat. Reduce heat to medium; add 10-12 medium orange slices. Cook until oranges are translucent, about 20 minutes. Reduce heat to low; cook until slices are tender but still intact, turning occasionally, about 10 minutes longer. Remove with slotted spoon. Cool completely on wire rack. Let stand at room temperature.

Ginger Pumpkin Cheesecake

PREP: 35 MIN. + COOLING
BAKE: 70 MIN. + CHILLING
MAKES: 16 SERVINGS

Ginger is a favorite fall flavor that I couldn't resist adding to the season's best dessert.
—Kathy Kuehn, Piedmont, SC

- 1½ cups crushed gingersnap cookies (about 32)
- 1 Tbsp. sugar
- ¼ cup butter, melted

FILLING

- 2 pkg. (8 oz. each) cream cheese, softened
- 1 can (16 oz.) pumpkin
- 1 cup sugar
- 1 cup 4% cottage cheese
- ¼ cup all-purpose flour
- 1 tsp. ground cinnamon
- 1 tsp. vanilla extract
- ½ tsp. salt
- ½ tsp. ground nutmeg
- ¼ tsp. ground cloves
- 3 large eggs, lightly beaten

TOPPING

- 1½ cups sour cream
- ⅓ cup orange marmalade
- 1 tsp. vanilla extract
  Candied orange slices, optional

1. Combine cookie crumbs, sugar and butter. Press onto the bottom and 2 in. up the side of greased 9-in. springform pan; set aside. Place pan on a baking sheet. Bake at 350° for 10 minutes. Cool on a wire rack.

Bourbon Brioche Bread Pudding

PREP: 15 MIN. + STANDING
BAKE: 35 MIN. **MAKES:** 6 SERVINGS

My husband wasn't a fan of bread pudding until I had him try a bite of mine from a local restaurant. Once he'd been won over, I replicated it at home and then experimented by adding bourbon, walnuts and a different type of bread. It's a keeper!
—Cindy Worth, Lapwai, ID

- ½ **cup bourbon, divided**
- ½ **cup raisins**
- 2½ **cups brioche bread, toasted**
- ⅓ **cup finely chopped walnuts**
- 4 **large eggs**
- 1¾ **cups heavy whipping cream**
- ⅓ **cup sugar**
- 1 **tsp. ground cinnamon**
- 1 **tsp. vanilla extract**
- ½ **tsp. ground nutmeg**
- ¼ **tsp. salt**
  Optional: Confectioners' sugar and whipped cream

1. Preheat oven to 375°. Pour ¼ cup bourbon over raisins in a small bowl; let stand 5 minutes. Place bread in a greased 8-in. square baking dish. Top with walnuts, raisins and soaking liquid.

2. In a large bowl, whisk the eggs, cream, sugar, cinnamon, vanilla, nutmeg, salt and remaining ¼ cup bourbon until blended. Pour over bread; let stand until the bread is softened, about 15 minutes.

3. Bake, uncovered, until puffed and golden and a knife inserted in the center comes out clean, 35-40 minutes. Serve warm. If desired, serve with confectioners' sugar and whipped cream.

1 SERVING: 469 cal., 34g fat (19g sat. fat), 213mg chol., 218mg sod., 30g carb. (22g sugars, 1g fiber), 9g pro.

Yogurt-Ricotta Cheesecake

PREP: 35 MIN.
BAKE: 1 HOUR 20 MIN. + CHILLING
MAKES: 16 SERVINGS

I have always loved Italian ricotta cheesecakes, but they have too much sugar for me. I made a lighter version— my family couldn't tell the difference!
—Diane Shipley, Mentor, OH

- 2 **pkg. (8 oz. each) reduced-fat cream cheese**
- 2 **cups reduced-fat ricotta cheese**
  Sugar substitute blend (made with sucralose) equivalent to 1½ cups sugar
- 2 **cups vanilla yogurt**
- ½ **cup butter, melted**
- ¼ **cup cornstarch**
- 3 **Tbsp. all-purpose flour**
- 2 **Tbsp. lemon juice**
- 1 **tsp. vanilla extract**
- 4 **large eggs, room temperature, lightly beaten**
  Halved fresh strawberries, optional

1. Beat cream cheese, ricotta and sugar blend until smooth. Beat in yogurt, butter, cornstarch, flour, lemon juice and vanilla. Add eggs; beat on low just until blended. Pour into a greased 9-in. springform pan. Place pan on a baking sheet.
2. Bake at 325° until center is almost set, 80-85 minutes. Cool on a wire rack for 10 minutes. Loosen sides from pan with a knife. Cool 1 hour. Refrigerate overnight, covering when completely cooled.
3. Remove rim from pan. If desired, serve with strawberries.
NOTE: This recipe was tested with Splenda sugar blend.
1 PIECE: 246 cal., 15g fat (9g sat. fat), 91mg chol., 231mg sod., 19g carb. (16g sugars, 0 fiber), 9g pro.

Mocha Truffle Cheesecake

PREP: 20 MIN. • **BAKE:** 50 MIN. + CHILLING
MAKES: 16 SERVINGS

I went through a phase when I couldn't get enough cheesecake or coffee, so I created this rich dessert. Its brownie-like crust and creamy mocha layer really hit the spot. It's ideal for get-togethers because it can be made in advance.
—Shannon Dormady, Great Falls, MT

1 pkg. devil's food cake mix (regular size)
6 Tbsp. butter, melted
1 large egg, room temperature
1 to 3 Tbsp. instant coffee granules

FILLING
2 pkg. (8 oz. each) cream cheese, softened
1 can (14 oz.) sweetened condensed milk
2 cups semisweet chocolate chips, melted and cooled
3 to 6 Tbsp. instant coffee granules
¼ cup hot water
3 large eggs, room temperature, lightly beaten

TOPPING
1 cup heavy whipping cream
¼ cup confectioners' sugar
½ tsp. almond extract
1 Tbsp. baking cocoa, optional

1. In a large bowl, combine cake mix, butter, egg and coffee granules until well blended. Press onto the bottom and 2 in. up the side of a greased 10-in. springform pan.
2. In another large bowl, beat cream cheese until smooth. Beat in milk and melted chips. Dissolve coffee granules in water; add to cream cheese mixture. Add eggs; beat on low speed just until combined. Pour into crust. Place pan on a baking sheet.
3. Bake at 325° until center is almost set, 50-55 minutes. Cool on a wire rack for 10 minutes. Carefully run a knife around edge of pan to loosen; cool 1 hour longer. Chill overnight.
4. Remove rim from pan. Just before serving, in a large bowl, beat cream until soft peaks form. Beat in sugar and extract until stiff peaks form. Spread over top of cheesecake. Sprinkle with cocoa if desired. Refrigerate leftovers.

1 PIECE: 484 cal., 28g fat (16g sat. fat), 109mg chol., 389mg sod., 55g carb. (41g sugars, 2g fiber), 7g pro.

5 Tbsp. cold butter, cubed
½ cup buttermilk

1. In a large bowl, combine the first 5 ingredients; transfer to a greased 12-in. cast-iron skillet or 2-qt. baking dish. Heat butter in a small saucepan over medium heat for 7 minutes or until golden brown; pour over pear mixture. Cover and bake at 350° for 20-25 minutes or until bubbly.

2. In a food processor, combine sugar and ginger; cover and process until finely chopped. Add the flour, baking powder, baking soda and salt; cover and process for 3 seconds or until blended. Add butter; process until the mixture resembles coarse crumbs. Add buttermilk and pulse just until a soft dough forms. Drop by tablespoonfuls over warm pear mixture.

3. Bake, uncovered, for 35-40 minutes or until topping is golden brown. Serve warm.

½ CUP: 332 cal., 12g fat (7g sat. fat), 31mg chol., 274mg sod., 56g carb. (33g sugars, 4g fiber), 3g pro.

Gingered Cranberry Pear Cobbler: Substitute dried cranberries for the cherries.
Gingered Raisin Pear Cobbler: Substitute golden raisins for the cherries.

Gingered Cherry Pear Cobbler

PREP: 25 MIN. • **BAKE:** 55 MIN.
MAKES: 8 SERVINGS

This is warm, sweet and filling—comfort food at its best! It's great for those crisp and cool autumn days, and it tastes best when served warm.
—Taste of Home *Test Kitchen*

4 cups chopped peeled fresh pears
½ cup dried cherries
¼ cup packed brown sugar
2 Tbsp. finely chopped crystallized ginger
1 Tbsp. all-purpose flour
3 Tbsp. butter

TOPPING
¼ cup sugar
2 Tbsp. finely chopped crystallized ginger
1 cup all-purpose flour
1½ tsp. baking powder
⅛ tsp. baking soda
¼ tsp. salt

Country Pear Puff Pancake

PREP: 20 MIN. • **BAKE:** 20 MIN.
MAKES: 4 SERVINGS

This sweet, gooey pancake is dressed up with caramelized pears and baked until golden. It's a delicious change of pace—morning or evening!
—Steffany Lohn, Brentwood, CA

- 5 Tbsp. butter, divided
- 3 medium pears, peeled and sliced
- ½ cup packed brown sugar, divided
- 1 Tbsp. lemon juice
- ½ cup all-purpose flour
- ½ cup 2% milk
- 3 large eggs, room temperature, beaten
- 2 Tbsp. maple syrup
- 1 tsp. vanilla extract
- ⅛ tsp. salt
- ½ tsp. ground cinnamon
- ¼ tsp. ground nutmeg
   Whipped cream, optional

1. Preheat oven to 450°. In a 10-in. cast-iron or other ovenproof skillet, melt 3 Tbsp. butter over medium heat. Add pears; cook and stir until tender, about 5 minutes. Stir in ¼ cup brown sugar and lemon juice.
2. In a bowl, whisk the flour, milk, eggs, syrup, vanilla and salt until smooth; pour over pears. Bake until puffy, 10-12 minutes.
3. Meanwhile, in a microwave-safe bowl, melt remaining 2 Tbsp. butter. Stir in the cinnamon, nutmeg and the remaining ¼ cup brown sugar. Spread over pancake. Bake until golden brown, 8-10 minutes. Cut into wedges and serve immediately. If desired, top with whipped cream.
1 PIECE: 468 cal., 19g fat (11g sat. fat), 181mg chol., 265mg sod., 68g carb. (48g sugars, 5g fiber), 8g pro.

Maple Dumplings

PREP: 15 MIN. • **BAKE:** 25 MIN.
MAKES: 8 SERVINGS

To give your meal a warm and cozy ending, look no further than this comforting dessert. Tender, homemade dumplings are nestled in a thick, rich maple syrup.
—Denise Boutin, Grand Isle, VT

- 2 cups all-purpose flour
- 3 tsp. baking powder
- ¼ cup shortening
- ¾ cup 2% milk
- 2 cups maple syrup
- ½ cup water
   Optional: Vanilla ice cream, maple ice cream or whipped cream

1. Preheat oven to 400°. In a large bowl, combine flour and baking powder. Cut in shortening until crumbly. Gradually add milk, tossing with a fork until dough forms a ball; set aside.
2. In a small saucepan, bring syrup and water to a boil. Carefully pour into an 11x7-in. baking dish. Drop dough by tablespoonfuls into syrup mixture.
3. Bake, uncovered, until a toothpick inserted in a dumpling comes out clean, 22-28 minutes. If desired, serve warm, with ice cream or whipped cream.
1 DUMPLING: 388 cal., 7g fat (2g sat. fat), 2mg chol., 201mg sod., 79g carb. (50g sugars, 1g fiber), 4g pro.

Pecan Date Pudding

PREP: 20 MIN. • **BAKE:** 50 MIN.
MAKES: 8 SERVINGS

This recipe was passed down from my great-grandmother to my grandmother. They lovingly served it with whipped cream on top. We never had a holiday without it.
—Patricia Rutherford, Winchester, IL

- 1 cup all-purpose flour
- 2 cups packed brown sugar, divided
- 1½ tsp. baking powder
- ¼ tsp. salt
- 2 Tbsp. butter, divided
- ¾ cup whole milk
- 1 cup chopped dates
- 1 cup chopped pecans
- 2 cups water
- Whipped cream, optional

1. Preheat oven to 350°. Combine the flour, 1 cup brown sugar, baking powder and salt. Melt 1 Tbsp. of butter; combine with milk. Stir into the flour mixture until smooth. Fold in dates and pecans. Transfer to a greased 8-in. square baking dish.

2. In a large saucepan, bring the remaining 1 cup brown sugar and the water to a boil. Cook and stir until the sugar is dissolved. Remove from heat; stir in the remaining 1 Tbsp. butter until melted. Pour over batter in baking dish.

3. Bake until a toothpick inserted near the center comes out clean, 50-60 minutes. Serve warm. If desired, top pudding with whipped cream.

1 SERVING: 452 cal., 14g fat (3g sat. fat), 10mg chol., 213mg sod., 83g carb. (67g sugars, 3g fiber), 4g pro.

Janice Elder
Charlotte, NC

Simple rice pudding gets a makeover with this upscale recipe. It has just the right thickness to soak up a hot caramel topping.

. . . .

Sticky Toffee Rice Pudding with Caramel Cream

PREP: 45 MIN.
BAKE: 35 MIN. + COOLING
MAKES: 16 SERVINGS

- 3 **cups water**
- 1 **cup uncooked medium-grain rice**
- ¼ **tsp. salt**
- 3 **cups pitted dates, chopped**
- 3 **cups 2% milk**
- 2 **tsp. vanilla extract**
- 1 **cup packed brown sugar**
- 1½ **cups heavy whipping cream, divided**
- ¼ **cup butter, cubed**
- ½ **cup sour cream**
- ¼ **cup hot caramel ice cream topping**

1. Preheat oven to 350°. In a large saucepan, bring the water, rice and salt to a boil. Reduce heat; simmer, covered, for 12-15 minutes or until rice is tender. Add dates and milk; cook and stir for 10 minutes. Remove from the heat; stir in vanilla. Set aside.

2. In a small saucepan, combine brown sugar, 1 cup cream and butter. Bring to a boil. Reduce heat; simmer for 2 minutes, stirring constantly. Stir into the rice mixture. Transfer to a greased 13x9-in. baking dish. Bake, uncovered, until bubbly, for 35-40 minutes. Cool for 15 minutes.

3. Meanwhile, in a small bowl, beat the sour cream, caramel topping and remaining ½ cup cream until slightly thickened. Serve with warm rice pudding. Refrigerate leftovers.

½ CUP RICE PUDDING WITH 1 TBSP. TOPPING: 329 cal., 14g fat (8g sat. fat), 38mg chol., 112mg sod., 50g carb. (37g sugars, 2g fiber), 4g pro.

Chocolate Cobbler

PREP: 10 MIN. • **BAKE:** 40 MIN.
MAKES: 8 SERVINGS

Talk about comfort food! This ultra moist dessert makes a decadent end to any meal. Best of all, it comes together in no time with just a few ingredients.
—Margaret McNeil, Germantown, TN

- 1 **cup self-rising flour**
- ½ **cup sugar**
- 2 **Tbsp. plus ¼ cup baking cocoa, divided**
- ½ **cup 2% milk**
- 3 **Tbsp. vegetable oil**
- 1 **cup packed brown sugar**
- 1¾ **cups hot water**
  Vanilla ice cream, optional

1. Preheat oven to 350°. In a bowl, combine the flour, sugar and 2 Tbsp. cocoa. Stir in milk and oil until smooth. Pour into a greased 8-in. square baking pan. Combine brown sugar and remaining cocoa; sprinkle over batter. Pour hot water over top (do not stir).

2. Bake at 350° until top of cake springs back when lightly touched, 40-45 minutes. Serve warm, with ice cream if desired.

NOTE: As a substitute for 1 cup of self-rising flour, place 1½ tsp. baking powder and ½ tsp. salt in a measuring cup. Add all-purpose flour to measure 1 cup.

1 SERVING: 267 cal., 6g fat (1g sat. fat), 2mg chol., 198mg sod., 53g carb. (40g sugars, 1g fiber), 3g pro.

Apple Butter Bread Pudding

PREP: 20 MIN. + STANDING
BAKE: 50 MIN.
MAKES: 12 SERVINGS

*This is one of my mother's best recipes!
Serve it as a dessert or a very special
breakfast treat.*
—Jerri Gradert, Lincoln, NE

⅓	cup raisins
1	cup apple butter
6	croissants, split

CUSTARD

8	large eggs
3	cups 2% milk
1½	cups sugar
2	tsp. vanilla extract
¼	tsp. salt

STREUSEL

½	cup all-purpose flour
½	cup packed brown sugar
¼	tsp. salt
¼	cup cold butter

1. Preheat oven to 350°. Place raisins in
a small bowl. Cover with boiling water; let
stand for 5 minutes. Drain and set aside.
2. Combine apple butter and raisins.
Spread over croissant bottoms; replace
tops. Cut each croissant into 3 pieces;
place in a greased 13x9-in. baking dish.
3. In a large bowl, combine the eggs, milk,
sugar, vanilla and salt. Pour over croissants;
let stand for 30 minutes or until the bread
is softened.
4. Combine the flour, brown sugar and salt.
Cut in butter until mixture resembles coarse
crumbs. Sprinkle over top.
5. Bake, uncovered, 50-60 minutes or until
a knife inserted in the center comes out
clean. Serve warm. Refrigerate leftovers.
1 SERVING: 433 cal., 14g fat (7g sat. fat),
175mg chol., 422mg sod., 68g carb. (51g
sugars, 1g fiber), 9g pro.

Honey Pecan Cheesecake

PREP: 20 MIN. + CHILLING
BAKE: 40 MIN. + CHILLING
MAKES: 12 SERVINGS

Birthdays and holidays are great times for cheesecake, and Thanksgiving's ideal for this particular one. In our annual church baking contest, it won first place!
—Tish Frish, Hampden, ME

1 cup crushed vanilla wafers (about 30 wafers)
¼ cup ground pecans
2 Tbsp. sugar
5 Tbsp. butter, melted

FILLING

3 pkg. (8 oz. each) cream cheese, softened
¾ cup packed dark brown sugar
3 large eggs, lightly beaten
2 Tbsp. all-purpose flour
1 Tbsp. maple flavoring
1 tsp. vanilla extract
½ cup chopped pecans

TOPPING

¼ cup honey
1 Tbsp. butter
1 Tbsp. water
½ cup chopped pecans

1. Preheat oven to 350°. In a small bowl, combine the wafer crumbs, pecans and sugar; stir in butter. Press onto the bottom of a greased 9-in. springform pan. Refrigerate.

2. In a large bowl, beat cream cheese and sugar until smooth. Add eggs; beat on low speed just until combined. Add the flour, maple flavoring and vanilla; beat until blended. Stir in pecans. Pour into crust. Place pan on a double thickness of heavy-duty foil (about 18 in. square). Securely wrap foil around pan.

3. Place in a large baking pan. Fill larger pan with hot water to a depth of 1 in. Bake for 40-45 minutes or until center is just set. Cool on a wire rack for 10 minutes. Remove foil. Carefully run a knife around edge of pan to loosen; cool for 1 hour longer. Refrigerate overnight.

4. For topping, combine the honey, butter and water in a small saucepan; cook and stir over medium heat for 2 minutes. Add nuts; cook 2 minutes longer (mixture will be thin). Spoon over cheesecake. Carefully remove rim of the pan before serving. Refrigerate leftovers.

1 PIECE: 349 cal., 23g fat (9g sat. fat), 90mg chol., 165mg sod., 32g carb. (25g sugars, 1g fiber), 5g pro.

1. Preheat oven to 375°. In a small bowl, combine the oats, flour, ¼ cup sugar, brown sugar, salt, cinnamon and nutmeg. With clean hands, work butter into the sugar mixture until well combined. Add nuts; toss to combine. Refrigerate for 15 minutes.

2. Meanwhile, in a large bowl, combine the plums, tapioca, lemon juice and remaining 2 Tbsp. sugar. Transfer to a greased 9-in. pie plate. Let stand for 15 minutes. Sprinkle topping over plum mixture.

3. Bake until the topping is golden brown and the plums are tender, 40-45 minutes. Serve warm.

1 SERVING: 233 cal., 8g fat (3g sat. fat), 11mg chol., 107mg sod., 40g carb. (27g sugars, 3g fiber), 3g pro.

TEST KITCHEN TIP

Plums come in a variety of colors, including green, yellow, purple, red and black. You can use any variety of plum to make this crisp, but you may want to adjust the amount of sugar if the plums you choose are particularly sweet or tart.

Plum Crisp with Crunchy Oat Topping

PREP: 25 MIN. + STANDING • **BAKE:** 40 MIN.
MAKES: 8 SERVINGS

Made with fresh plums and a crunchy oat topping, this crisp is a lighter alternative to classic fruit pie. It goes over well with the women in my church group.
—Deidre Kobel, Boulder, CO

- ¾ cup old-fashioned oats
- ⅓ cup all-purpose flour
- ¼ cup plus 2 Tbsp. sugar, divided
- ¼ cup packed brown sugar
- ¼ tsp. salt
- ¼ tsp. ground cinnamon
- ¼ tsp. ground nutmeg
- 3 Tbsp. butter, softened
- ¼ cup chopped walnuts
- 5 cups sliced fresh plums (about 2 lbs.)
- 1 Tbsp. quick-cooking tapioca
- 2 tsp. lemon juice

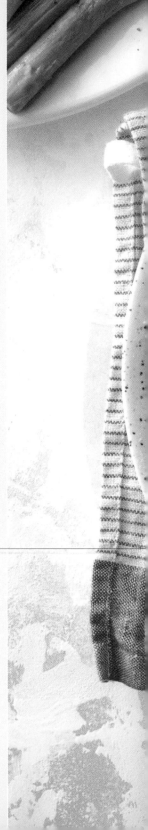

BONUS: POTPIES & OTHER COZY DINNERS

WHEN IT COMES TO BAKING, SOMETIMES SAVORY
IS JUST AS WELCOME AS SWEET. THESE HEARTY,
DELECTABLE DISHES ARE PERFECT FOR A FALL DINNER.

SALMON QUICHE, P. 298

Bacon Quiche Tarts

PREP: 15 MIN. • **BAKE:** 20 MIN.
MAKES: 8 SERVINGS

Here's a fun way to make single-serving quiches that people of all ages are sure to enjoy. Flavored with bacon, cheese and veggies, these little bites are just the thing as an appetizer or served up with a pot of chili.
—Kendra Schertz, Nappanee, IN

- 6 oz. cream cheese, softened
- 5 tsp. 2% milk
- 2 large eggs
- ½ cup shredded Colby cheese
- 2 Tbsp. chopped green pepper
- 1 Tbsp. finely chopped onion
- 1 tube (8 oz.) refrigerated crescent rolls
- 5 bacon strips, cooked and crumbled
  Thinly sliced green onions, optional

1. Preheat oven to 375°. In a small bowl, beat cream cheese and milk until smooth. Add eggs, cheese, green pepper and onion.
2. Separate crescent dough into 8 triangles; press onto the bottom and up the sides of 8 greased muffin cups. Sprinkle half the bacon into the cups. Pour egg mixture over bacon; top with the remaining bacon.
3. Bake, uncovered, for 18-22 minutes or until a knife inserted in the center comes out clean. Serve warm. If desired, top with chopped green onion.
FREEZE OPTION: Freeze cooled baked tarts in a freezer container. To use, reheat tarts on a baking sheet in a preheated 375° oven until heated through.
1 TART: 258 cal., 19g fat (9g sat. fat), 87mg chol., 409mg sod., 12g carb. (3g sugars, 0 fiber), 8g pro.

Chicken Biscuit Potpie

PREP: 10 MIN. • **BAKE:** 25 MIN.
MAKES: 4 SERVINGS

This hearty meal in one takes just 10 minutes to assemble before you pop it into the oven.
—Dorothy Smith, El Dorado, AR

- 1⅔ cups frozen mixed vegetables, thawed
- 1½ cups cubed cooked chicken
- 1 can (10¾ oz.) condensed cream of chicken soup, undiluted
- ¼ tsp. dried thyme
- 1 cup biscuit/baking mix
- ½ cup 2% milk
- 1 large egg

1. Preheat oven to 400°. In a large bowl, combine the vegetables, chicken, soup and thyme. Pour into an ungreased deep-dish 9-in. pie plate. Combine the biscuit mix, milk and egg; spoon over chicken mixture.
2. Bake until topping is golden brown and a toothpick inserted in the center comes out clean, 25-30 minutes.
1 SERVING: 376 cal., 14g fat (4g sat. fat), 103mg chol., 966mg sod., 38g carb. (5g sugars, 5g fiber), 23g pro.

TEST KITCHEN TIP

If you prefer fresh vegetables to frozen, precook them to almost done before adding them; it will help everything cook evenly. Feel free to use whatever vegetables you like, or add mushrooms.

Cranberry Bacon Galette

PREP: 25 MIN. • **BAKE:** 20 MIN. + COOLING
MAKES: 9 SERVINGS

Sweet, smoky, tangy, fresh: The flavors in this distinctive appetizer are sure to perk up taste buds for dinner. I sprinkle the warm squares with basil, and everyone loves a dollop or two of the mascarpone cheese topping.
—Merry Graham, Newhall, CA

- 1 carton (8 oz.) mascarpone cheese
- 1 Tbsp. orange marmalade
- 1 Tbsp. jellied cranberry sauce
- 2 Tbsp. sugar
- 1 cup chopped red onion
- 1 cup dried cranberries
- ¾ cup chopped fresh mushrooms
- 1 Tbsp. olive oil
- ½ tsp. lemon-pepper seasoning
- ¼ tsp. salt
- ¼ tsp. smoked paprika
- 3 Tbsp. cranberry-tangerine juice
- 1 sheet frozen puff pastry, thawed
- 5 cooked bacon strips, crumbled
- ¼ cup minced fresh basil

1. Preheat oven to 400°. For topping, in a small bowl, combine the cheese, marmalade and cranberry sauce. Refrigerate until serving.

2. In a large skillet, cook sugar over medium-high heat 1-2 minutes or until it just begins to melt. Add onion; cook and stir 2 minutes longer.

3. Stir in cranberries, mushrooms, oil, lemon pepper, salt and paprika; cook and stir 2 minutes. Reduce heat. Stir in juice; cook and stir until mushrooms are tender, about 4 minutes.

4. Roll out puff pastry and shape the galette crust (shown at right).

5. Spread cranberry mixture to edges; sprinkle with bacon. Bake 18-22 minutes or until pastry is golden brown. Cool 10 minutes. Sprinkle with basil. Serve warm with topping.

1 PIECE: 355 cal., 23g fat (9g sat. fat), 38mg chol., 299mg sod., 34g carb. (15g sugars, 3g fiber), 6g pro.

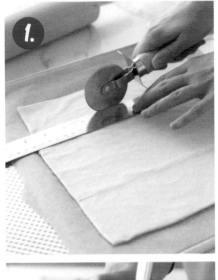

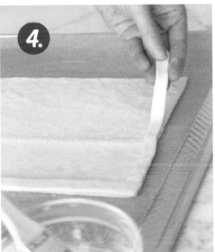

HOW-TO

MAKE THE GALETTE CRUST

1. On a parchment-lined baking sheet, unfold puff pasty and form a 10-in. square, using a rolling pin if necessary. With a ruler, cut a 10x2-in. rectangle with a long sharp knife or pastry wheel.

2. From the 10x2-in. strip, cut two 10x½-in. strips and two 7x½-in. strips. Remove and discard trimmings.

3. Prick the remaining 10x8-in. pastry base all over with a fork.

4. Brush water ½ in. around the edges of the pastry base. Place the 10x½-in. and 7x½-in. strips along the edges to form the sides. Press lightly.

Salmon Quiche

PREP: 15 MIN. • **BAKE:** 1 HOUR
MAKES: 8 SERVINGS

This recipe came to me from my mother—it's the kind you request after just one bite! The quiche is hearty enough to satisfy the biggest appetite; serve it alongside a salad or with a side of fresh vegetables.
—Deanna Baldwin, Bermuda Dunes, CA

- 1 **sheet refrigerated pie crust**
- 1 **medium onion, chopped**
- 1 **Tbsp. butter**
- 2 **cups shredded Swiss cheese**
- 1 **can (14¾ oz.) salmon, drained, flaked and cartilage removed**
- 5 **large eggs**
- 2 **cups half-and-half cream**
- ¼ **tsp. salt**
  Minced fresh parsley, optional

1. Preheat oven to 450°. Line unpricked pie crust with a double thickness of heavy-duty foil. Bake for 8 minutes. Remove foil; bake 5 minutes longer. Cool on a wire rack. Reset oven temperature to 350°.

2. In a small skillet, saute onion in butter until tender. Sprinkle cheese in the crust; top with salmon and onion.

3. In a small bowl, whisk the eggs, cream and salt; pour over salmon mixture. Bake at 350° for 45-50 minutes or until a knife inserted in center comes out clean. Sprinkle with parsley if desired. Let stand 5 minutes before cutting.

1 PIECE: 448 cal., 29g fat (15g sat. fat), 219mg chol., 610mg sod., 18g carb. (5g sugars, 0 fiber), 26g pro.

Broccoli Beef Braids

TAKES: 30 MIN.
MAKES: 2 LOAVES (4 SERVINGS EACH)

Each slice of this fast-to-fix golden bread is like a hot sandwich packed with beef, broccoli and mozzarella.
—Penny Lapp, North Royalton, OH

- 1 **lb. ground beef**
- ½ **cup chopped onion**
- 3 **cups frozen chopped broccoli**
- 1 **cup shredded part-skim mozzarella cheese**
- ½ **cup sour cream**
- ¼ **tsp. salt**
- ¼ **tsp. pepper**
- 2 **tubes (8 oz. each) refrigerated crescent rolls**

1. Preheat oven to 350°. In a large skillet, cook beef and onion over medium heat for 6-8 minutes or until beef is no longer pink, breaking beef into crumbles; drain. Stir in broccoli, cheese, sour cream, salt and pepper; heat through.
2. Unroll 1 tube of crescent dough onto a greased baking sheet; form into a 12x8-in. rectangle, pressing perforations to seal. Spoon half the beef mixture lengthwise down center of rectangle.
3. On each long side, cut 1-in.-wide strips at an angle, about 3 in. into the center. Fold 1 strip from each side over filling and pinch ends together; repeat.
4. Repeat with the remaining ingredients to make second braid. Bake for 15-20 minutes or until golden brown.
1 PIECE: 396 cal., 23g fat (6g sat. fat), 48mg chol., 644mg sod., 29g carb. (8g sugars, 2g fiber), 20g pro.

Beef Stew Skillet Pie

PREP: 1½ HOURS • **BAKE:** 30 MIN. + STANDING
MAKES: 6 SERVINGS

*Puff pastry makes a pretty topping for
this homey skillet potpie.*
—Josh Rink, Milwaukee, WI

6 **Tbsp. all-purpose flour, divided**
1½ **tsp. salt**
½ **tsp. pepper**

1 **lb. boneless beef round steak,
cut into 1-in. pieces**
2 **Tbsp. canola oil**
1 **large onion, chopped**
2 **garlic cloves, minced**
¼ **cup dry red wine**
2 **cups beef broth, divided**
1 **Tbsp. tomato paste**
½ **tsp. Italian seasoning**
½ **tsp. dried basil**
1 **bay leaf**

2 **medium potatoes, cubed**
3 **large carrots, peeled and sliced**
1 **sheet frozen puff pastry, thawed**
½ **cup frozen peas**
2 **Tbsp. minced fresh parsley**
1 **large egg, beaten**

1. Preheat the oven to 425°. In a large
resealable container, combine 3 Tbsp.
flour, salt and pepper. Add beef in batches;
shake to coat. Invert a 10-in. cast-iron or
other ovenproof skillet onto a piece of
parchment; trace circle around pan ¼ in.
larger than rim. Cut out circle and set aside.

2. In the same skillet, saute beef in oil until
browned. Add onion and garlic; cook and
stir until onion is tender. Add wine, stirring
to loosen browned bits.

3. Combine 1½ cups broth, tomato paste,
Italian seasoning and basil; stir into skillet.
Add bay leaf. Bring to a boil. Reduce heat;
simmer, covered, until meat is tender,
about 45 minutes. Add potatoes and
carrots; cook until vegetables are tender,
20-25 minutes longer.

4. Meanwhile, roll out puff pastry to fit
skillet, using parchment circle as a guide;
cut venting slits in pastry. Keep chilled until
ready to use.

5. Combine the remaining 3 Tbsp. flour
and ½ cup broth until smooth; gradually stir
into skillet. Bring to a boil; cook and stir until
thickened and bubbly, about 2 minutes.
Discard bay leaf. Stir in peas and parsley.

6. Brush beaten egg around edge of skillet
to help pastry adhere; carefully place pastry
over filling. Using a fork, press the pastry
firmly onto rim of pan; brush with egg.
Bake pie until the pastry is dark golden
brown, 30-35 minutes. Let stand for
10 minutes before serving.

1 SERVING: 473 cal., 19g fat (4g sat. fat),
73mg chol., 1088mg sod., 49g carb. (4g
sugars, 6g fiber), 25g pro.

Chicken Potpie Galette with Cheddar-Thyme Crust

PREP: 45 MIN. + CHILLING
BAKE: 30 MIN. + COOLING
MAKES: 8 SERVINGS

This gorgeous galette takes traditional chicken potpie and gives it a fun open-faced spin. The rich filling and flaky cheddar-flecked crust make it taste comforting and satisfying.
—Elisabeth Larsen, Pleasant Grove, UT

- 1¼ cups all-purpose flour
- ½ cup shredded sharp cheddar cheese
- 2 Tbsp. minced fresh thyme
- ¼ tsp. salt
- ½ cup cold butter, cubed
- ¼ cup ice water

FILLING
- 3 Tbsp. butter
- 2 large carrots, sliced
- 1 celery rib, diced
- 1 small onion, diced
- 8 oz. sliced fresh mushrooms
- 3 cups julienned Swiss chard
- 3 garlic cloves, minced
- 1 cup chicken broth
- 3 Tbsp. all-purpose flour
- ½ tsp. salt
- ¼ tsp. pepper
- 2 cups shredded cooked chicken
- ½ tsp. minced fresh oregano
- 2 Tbsp. minced fresh parsley

1. Combine flour, cheese, thyme and salt; cut in butter until crumbly. Gradually add ice water, tossing with a fork until dough holds together when pressed. Shape into a disk; refrigerate 1 hour.
2. For filling, melt butter in a large saucepan over medium-high heat. Add carrots, celery and onion; cook and stir until slightly softened, 5-7 minutes. Add mushrooms; cook 3 minutes longer. Add Swiss chard and garlic; cook until the chard is wilted, 2-3 minutes.
3. Whisk together broth, flour, salt and pepper; slowly pour over the vegetables, stirring constantly. Cook until thickened, 2-3 minutes. Stir in chicken and oregano.
4. Preheat oven to 400°. On a floured sheet of parchment, roll dough into a 12-in. circle. Transfer to a baking sheet. Spoon filling over crust to within 2 in. of edge. Fold crust edge over filling, pleating as you go, leaving the center uncovered. Bake on a lower oven rack until crust is golden brown and filling is bubbly, 30-35 minutes. Cool 15 minutes before slicing. Sprinkle with parsley.
1 PIECE: 342 cal., 21g fat (12g sat. fat), 81mg chol., 594mg sod., 22g carb. (2g sugars, 2g fiber), 16g pro.

SEE HOW IT'S DONE
Watch how this gorgeous galette comes together! Just hover your camera here.

TEST KITCHEN TIP
Fill the galette with any meat/cheese/veggie combo you like. It would be just as amazing, for example, with sausage, golden beets and kale. The filling may start to bubble up a bit toward the end of the bake time, so be sure to use parchment paper or a silicone mat.

Herbed Leek Tarts

PREP: 25 MIN. • **BAKE:** 20 MIN. + COOLING
MAKES: 2 TARTS (8 SERVINGS EACH)

This savory tart is a favorite among our family and friends! It's delicious and different—and surprisingly easy to make.
—Jean Ecos, Hartland, WI

- 3 **cups thinly sliced leeks**
  (about 4 medium)
- ½ **cup chopped sweet red pepper**
- 4 **garlic cloves, minced**
- 2 **Tbsp. olive oil**
- 1½ **cups shredded Swiss cheese**
- 2 **Tbsp. Dijon mustard**
- 1 **tsp. herbes de Provence**
- 2 **sheets refrigerated pie crust**
- 1 **tsp. 2% milk**
- 2 **Tbsp. chopped almonds**
  or walnuts, optional

1. Preheat oven to 375°. In a large skillet, saute leeks, red pepper and garlic in oil until tender. Remove from the heat; cool for 5 minutes. Stir in the cheese, mustard and herbs; set aside.
2. On a lightly floured surface, roll each sheet of crust into a 12-in. circle. Transfer to parchment-lined baking sheets. Spoon leek mixture over crusts to within 2 in. of edges. Fold edges of crust over filling, leaving center uncovered. Brush folded crust with milk; sprinkle with nuts if desired.
3. Bake for 20-25 minutes or until the crust is golden and filling is bubbly. Using parchment, slide tarts onto wire racks. Cool for 10 minutes before cutting. Serve warm. Refrigerate leftovers.
NOTE: Look for herbes de Provence in the spice aisle.
1 PIECE: 194 cal., 12g fat (5g sat. fat), 14mg chol., 177mg sod., 17g carb. (2g sugars, 1g fiber), 5g pro.

Brie & Caramelized Onion Flatbread

PREP: 45 MIN. • **BAKE:** 20 MIN. + STANDING
MAKES: 1 FLATBREAD (12 PIECES)

If you're prepping for a party, saute the onions and garlic for this flatbread a day ahead so it's easy to put together on the day of the event. Prepared pizza dough makes it a snap.
—Trisha Kruse, Eagle, ID

- 2 **Tbsp. butter**
- 3 **large sweet onions, halved and**
  thinly sliced (about 6 cups)
- 2 **garlic cloves, minced**
- 1 **Tbsp. brown sugar**
- 1 **Tbsp. balsamic vinegar**
- ½ **tsp. salt**
- ¼ **tsp. pepper**
- 1 **loaf (1 lb.) frozen pizza dough,**
  thawed
- 8 **oz. Brie cheese, cut into ½-in. pieces**

1. Grease a 15x10x1-in. baking pan; set aside. In a large skillet, heat butter over medium heat. Add onions; cook and stir until softened, 4-6 minutes. Reduce heat to medium-low; cook 25-30 minutes or until deep golden brown, stirring occasionally. Add garlic; cook and stir 1 minute longer.
2. Preheat oven to 425°. Add brown sugar, vinegar, salt and pepper to onion mixture. Cook and stir 5 minutes longer. Press dough into a 12x10-in. rectangle on prepared pan. Top with onion mixture and cheese. Bake 20-25 minutes or until golden brown. Let stand 10 minutes before cutting.
1 PIECE: 206 cal., 9g fat (5g sat. fat), 24mg chol., 333mg sod., 25g carb. (6g sugars, 1g fiber), 8g pro.

Mini Sausage Pies

PREP: 35 MIN. • **BAKE:** 30 MIN.
MAKES: 1 DOZEN

The simple ingredients and family-friendly flavor of these little sausage cups make them a go-to dinner favorite. The fact that every person gets his or her own pie (or two!) makes them even better.
—Kerry Dingwall, Wilmington, NC

- 1 **pkg. (17.3 oz.) frozen puff pastry, thawed**
- 1 **lb. bulk sage pork sausage**
- 6 **green onions, chopped**
- ½ **cup chopped dried apricots**
- ¼ **tsp. pepper**
- ⅛ **tsp. ground nutmeg**
- 1 **large egg, lightly beaten**

1. Preheat oven to 375°. On a lightly floured surface, unfold pastry sheets; roll each into a 16x12-in. rectangle. Using a floured cutter, cut twelve 4-in. circles from 1 sheet; press onto bottoms and up sides of 12 ungreased muffin cups. Using a floured cutter, cut twelve 3½-in. circles from remaining sheet.

2. Mix sausage, green onions, apricots and spices lightly but thoroughly. Place ¼ cup mixture in each pastry cup. Brush edges of smaller pastry circles with egg; place over pies, pressing edges to seal. Brush with egg. Cut slits in top.

3. Bake until crust is golden brown and a thermometer inserted in filling reads 160°, 30-35 minutes. Cool 5 minutes before removing from pan to a wire rack.

FREEZE OPTION: Cool baked pies and freeze in freezer containers. To use, partially thaw pies in refrigerator overnight. Reheat on a baking sheet in a preheated 350° oven until heated through, 14-17 minutes.

2 MINI PIES: 551 cal., 36g fat (10g sat. fat), 82mg chol., 784mg sod., 42g carb. (5g sugars, 5g fiber), 16g pro.

TEST KITCHEN TIP

The slits on the top of the pies are for venting. You can change up the look of these cuties by altering the shape of the vents. We love the rustic look of x's, but small teardrops and fork tine marks look charming as well.

SEE HOW IT'S DONE
Watch how we make these cute mini pies by hovering your camera over the code.

onion, relish and bacon. Transfer to the prepared crust.

2. In a large bowl, whisk the eggs, cream, milk, mustard, pepper sauce, salt and pepper. Pour over the beef mixture. Sprinkle with cheeses.

3. Bake until a knife inserted in center comes out clean, 50-60 minutes. If necessary, cover the edges with foil during the last 15 minutes to prevent overbrowning. Let stand for 10 minutes before cutting. Garnish with optional ingredients as desired.

1 PIECE: 502 cal., 35g fat (19g sat. fat), 236mg chol., 954mg sod., 24g carb. (8g sugars, 1g fiber), 23g pro.

TEST KITCHEN TIP

Using lean ground beef instead of beef that's 80% lean saves 45 calories per 4-oz. serving of beef. Lean ground beef is also 29% lower in saturated fat.

Roadside Diner Cheeseburger Quiche

PREP: 20 MIN. • **BAKE:** 50 MIN. + STANDING
MAKES: 8 SERVINGS

Here's an unforgettable quiche that tastes just like its burger counterpart. Easy and appealing, it's perfect for guests and fun for the whole family.
—Barbara J. Miller, Oakdale, MN

1   sheet refrigerated pie crust
¾   lb. ground beef
2   plum tomatoes, seeded and chopped
1   medium onion, chopped
½   cup dill pickle relish
½   cup crumbled cooked bacon
5   large eggs
1   cup heavy whipping cream
½   cup 2% milk
2   tsp. prepared mustard
1   tsp. hot pepper sauce
½   tsp. salt
¼   tsp. pepper
1½ cups shredded cheddar cheese
½   cup shredded Parmesan cheese
    Optional: Mayonnaise, additional pickle relish, crumbled cooked bacon, chopped onion and chopped tomato

1. Preheat oven to 375°. Unroll crust into a 9-in. deep-dish pie plate; flute edges and set aside. In a large skillet, cook beef over medium heat until no longer pink, breaking it into crumbles; drain. Stir in the tomatoes,

Basil Tomato Tart

PREP: 20 MIN. • **BAKE:** 20 MIN.
MAKES: 8 SERVINGS

*I received this recipe from a good friend of mine.
It's a great way to use up fresh tomatoes from
the garden, and it tastes a lot like pizza.*
—Connie Stumpf, North Myrtle Beach, SC

 Dough for a single-crust pie (9 in.)
1½ **cups shredded part-skim mozzarella
 cheese, divided**
 5 **to 6 fresh plum tomatoes**
 1 **cup loosely packed fresh basil leaves**
 4 **garlic cloves**
 ½ **cup mayonnaise**
 ¼ **cup grated Parmesan cheese**
 ⅛ **tsp. pepper**

1. Roll dough to fit a 9-in. tart pan or pie plate;
place in pan. Do not prick. Line crust with a
double thickness of heavy-duty foil.
2. Bake at 450° for 5 minutes. Remove foil; bake
8 minutes more. Remove from the oven. Reduce
heat to 375°. Sprinkle ½ cup mozzarella over the
hot crust.
3. Cut each tomato into 8 wedges; remove seeds.
Arrange over cheese.
4. In a food processor, process the basil and garlic
until coarsely chopped; sprinkle over tomatoes.
5. Combine mayonnaise, Parmesan, pepper and
the remaining mozzarella; spoon over basil. Bake,
uncovered, until the cheese is browned and
bubbly, 20-25 minutes.
1 PIECE: 345 cal., 27g fat (12g sat. fat), 47mg
chol., 413mg sod., 19g carb. (2g sugars, 1g fiber),
8g pro.

Turkey Lattice Pie

PREP: 20 MIN. • **BAKE:** 25 MIN.
MAKES: 12 SERVINGS

With its pretty lattice crust, this cheesy baked dish is as appealing as it is tasty. It's easy to make, too, since it uses ready-to-go crescent roll dough.
—Lorraine Naig, Emmetsburg, IA

- 3 tubes (8 oz. each) refrigerated crescent rolls
- 4 cups cubed cooked turkey
- 1½ cups shredded cheddar or Swiss cheese
- 3 cups frozen chopped broccoli, thawed and drained
- 1 can (10¾ oz.) condensed cream of chicken soup, undiluted
- 1⅓ cups 2% milk
- 2 Tbsp. Dijon mustard
- 1 Tbsp. dried minced onion
- ½ tsp. salt
  Dash pepper
- 1 large egg, lightly beaten

1. Unroll 2 tubes of crescent roll dough; separate into rectangles. Place rectangles in an ungreased 15x10x1-in. baking pan; press onto the bottom and ¼ in. up sides of the pan to form a crust, sealing seams and perforations. Bake at 375° for 5-7 minutes or until light golden brown.
2. Combine turkey, cheese, broccoli, soup, milk, mustard, onion, salt and pepper. Spoon over crust.
3. Unroll the remaining dough; divide into 2 rectangles. Seal perforations. Cut each rectangle lengthwise into 1-in. strips. Using strips, make a lattice design on top of the turkey mixture. Brush with egg. Bake for 17-22 minutes longer or until top crust is golden brown and filling is bubbly.
1 PIECE: 396 cal., 20g fat (4g sat. fat), 81mg chol., 934mg sod., 30g carb. (8g sugars, 2g fiber), 24g pro.

Pork & Cabbage Pockets

PREP: 25 MIN. + RISING • **BAKE:** 25 MIN.
MAKES: 8 SERVINGS

I like to welcome my family home on fall days to the aroma of these hearty pork pie pockets. I sometimes double the recipe so I can have leftovers for busy-day dinners.
—Jan Smith, Kalispell, MT

1 pkg. (¼ oz.) active dry yeast
1 cup warm water (110° to 115°)
¼ cup shortening
¼ cup sugar
1 large egg
1 tsp. salt, divided
3 to 3¾ cups all-purpose flour
1 lb. bulk pork sausage
3 cups shredded cabbage

1 medium onion, chopped
¼ cup water
1½ tsp. dried oregano
1½ tsp. ground cumin
¼ tsp. pepper
1 Tbsp. butter, melted

1. In a large bowl, dissolve yeast in water. Add shortening, sugar, egg, ½ tsp. salt and 2 cups flour; beat until smooth. Add enough remaining flour to form a soft dough. Turn onto a floured surface; knead until smooth and elastic, 6-8 minutes. Place in a greased bowl, turning once to grease top. Cover and let rise in a warm place until doubled, about 1 hour.

2. Meanwhile, in a skillet, cook sausage until no longer pink; drain. Add cabbage, onion, water, oregano, cumin, pepper and remaining ½ tsp. salt. Cook, uncovered, until vegetables are tender and no liquid remains, about 15 minutes. Cool to room temperature.

3. Punch dough down. Roll into a 24x12-in. rectangle; cut into eight 6-in. squares. Spoon ⅓ cup filling into the center of each square. Bring corners to the center and pinch to seal; pinch seams together. Place on greased baking sheets. Cover and let rise for 30 minutes.

4. Brush with melted butter. Bake at 375° until golden brown, 25-30 minutes.

1 POCKET: 405 cal., 19g fat (6g sat. fat), 51mg chol., 558mg sod., 47g carb. (10g sugars, 3g fiber), 11g pro.

TEST KITCHEN TIP

If you're on a tight schedule, you can use frozen bread dough from the market for this recipe instead. It will still need to go through its second rise, but you'll save time on mixing and the initial rise.

Mile-High Chicken Potpie

PREP: 40 MIN. + CHILLING
BAKE: 50 MIN. + STANDING
MAKES: 6 SERVINGS

Classic chicken potpie gets extra homey when it's loaded with a creamy filling and baked tall in a springform pan. This deep-dish marvel is perfect for Sunday dinners.
—Shannon Norris, Cudahy, WI

- 1 large egg, separated
- 4 to 6 Tbsp. cold water, divided
- 2 cups all-purpose flour
- ¼ tsp. salt
- ⅔ cup cold butter, cubed

FILLING

- 3 Tbsp. butter
- 2 medium potatoes, peeled and cut into ½-in. cubes
- 4 medium carrots, thinly sliced
- 2 celery ribs, finely chopped
- ¼ cup finely chopped onion
- 3 Tbsp. all-purpose flour
- 2 Tbsp. chicken bouillon granules
- 1½ tsp. dried tarragon
- ½ tsp. coarsely ground pepper
- 1½ cups half-and-half cream
- 2½ cups cubed cooked chicken
- 1½ cups fresh peas or frozen peas
- ½ to 1 tsp. celery seed

1. In a small bowl, beat egg yolk with 2 Tbsp. water. In a large bowl, combine flour and salt; cut in butter until crumbly. Gradually add yolk mixture, tossing with a fork; add additional water 1 Tbsp. at a time, as needed, until dough forms a ball. Divide dough into 2 portions, 1 with three-quarters of the dough and 1 with the remainder. Shape each into a disk; cover and refrigerate 1 hour or overnight.

2. For filling, in a Dutch oven, melt butter. Saute potatoes, carrots, celery and onion until crisp-tender, 5-7 minutes. Stir in flour, bouillon, tarragon and pepper. Gradually stir in cream. Bring to a boil; cook and stir until thickened, about 2 minutes. Stir in the chicken and peas; set aside to cool completely.

3. On a lightly floured surface, roll out the larger portion of dough to fit bottom and all the way up the inside of an 8-in. springform pan. Place crust in pan; add cooled filling. Roll remaining dough to fit over the top. Place over filling. Trim, seal and flute edge. Cut slits in top. Chill for at least 1 hour.

4. Lightly beat egg white with 1 tsp. water. Brush over top crust; sprinkle with celery seed. Place pie on a rimmed baking tray.

5. Bake at 400° until the crust is golden brown and filling is bubbly, 50-55 minutes. Cool on a wire rack for at least 30 minutes before serving.

1 PIECE: 700 cal., 38g fat (22g sat. fat), 183mg chol., 1282mg sod., 58g carb. (8g sugars, 6g fiber), 29g pro.

Buffalo Chicken Crescent Rolls

PREP: 20 MIN. • **BAKE:** 15 MIN.
MAKES: 16 ROLLS

My husband loves Buffalo wings, but they are so messy! These chicken rolls are mess-free—and they're much tastier than regular Buffalo wings, if you ask me.
—Tiffinie Cichon, Gulfport, MS

- 1 **cup shredded cooked chicken**
- 4 **oz. cream cheese, cubed**
- ½ **cup shredded cheddar cheese**
- 2 **Tbsp. prepared ranch salad dressing**
- 2 **Tbsp. Buffalo wing sauce**
- 2 **tubes (8 oz. each) refrigerated crescent rolls**
- ⅓ **cup crumbled blue cheese**

1. Preheat the oven to 375°. In a small saucepan, combine chicken, cream cheese, cheddar cheese, ranch dressing and wing sauce. Cook and stir over low heat until cheeses are melted, about 5 minutes. Remove from the heat.
2. Unroll tubes of crescent dough; separate into 16 triangles. Place 1 Tbsp. chicken mixture in the center of each triangle; sprinkle with 1 tsp. blue cheese. Bring corners of dough over filling and twist; pinch seams to seal (filling will not be completely enclosed). Place on ungreased baking sheets.
3. Bake until golden brown, 15-20 minutes. Serve warm.
1 ROLL: 175 cal., 11g fat (3g sat. fat), 21mg chol., 372mg sod., 13g carb. (3g sugars, 0 fiber), 6g pro.

Fontina Asparagus Tart

PREP: 15 MIN. • **BAKE:** 20 MIN.
MAKES: 16 SERVINGS

This lemony tart is loaded with fontina cheese and fresh asparagus. It's a snap to make but looks really impressive. Be advised: Your guests will be vying for the last tasty slice.
—Heidi Meek, Grand Rapids, MI

- 1 **lb. fresh asparagus, trimmed**
- 1 **sheet frozen puff pastry, thawed**
- 2 **cups shredded fontina cheese**
- 1 **tsp. grated lemon zest**
- 2 **Tbsp. lemon juice**
- 1 **Tbsp. olive oil**
- ¼ **tsp. salt**
- ¼ **tsp. pepper**

1. Preheat oven to 400°. In a large skillet, bring 1 in. of water to a boil; add the asparagus. Cook, covered, until crisp-tender, 3-5 minutes. Drain and pat dry.
2. On a lightly floured surface, roll pastry sheet into a 16x12-in. rectangle. Transfer to a parchment-lined large baking sheet. Bake until golden brown, about 10 minutes.
3. Sprinkle 1½ cups cheese over pastry to within ½ in. of edges. Place asparagus over top; sprinkle with remaining ½ cup cheese. Mix the remaining ingredients; drizzle over top. Bake until the cheese is melted, 10-15 minutes. Serve warm.
1 PIECE: 142 cal., 9g fat (4g sat. fat), 16mg chol., 202mg sod., 10g carb. (1g sugars, 1g fiber), 5g pro.

Jamaican Beef Patties

PREP: 35 MIN. • **BAKE:** 25 MIN.
MAKES: 8 SERVINGS

Born in Jamaica, my mother brought this recipe with her when she moved to the States. The savory flavor and spices are just right, and the crust is flaky and delicious.
—Natasha Watson, Douglasville, GA

- 1 **lb. ground beef**
- 1 **medium onion, chopped**
- 1 **tsp. curry powder**
- 1 **tsp. dried thyme**
- 1 **tsp. pepper**
- ¾ **tsp. salt**

CRUST

- 2 **cups all-purpose flour**
- 1½ **tsp. curry powder**
- **Dash salt**
- ½ **cup cold butter**
- ⅓ **cup ice water**
- 1 **large egg, lightly beaten**

1. Preheat oven to 350°. In a large skillet, cook beef and onion over medium heat until beef is no longer pink and onion is tender, 6-8 minutes, breaking up beef into crumbles; drain. Stir in curry powder, thyme, pepper and salt; set aside.
2. For crust, whisk together flour, curry powder and salt. Cut in butter until mixture resembles coarse crumbs. Add water; stir just until moistened. Divide dough into 8 portions. On a lightly floured surface, roll each portion into a 6-in. circle. Place about ¼ cup filling on half of each circle. Fold crust over filling. Press edges with a fork to seal.
3. Transfer to parchment-lined baking sheets; brush with beaten egg. Bake until light brown, 22-25 minutes. Remove to wire racks. Serve warm.
1 PATTY: 336 cal., 19g fat (10g sat. fat), 89mg chol., 373mg sod., 26g carb. (1g sugars, 2g fiber), 14g pro.

Judy Batson
Tampa, FL

This elegant, rustic recipe goes together in minutes and is so simple. It's perfect for entertaining!

. . . .

Beef & Blue Cheese Tart

PREP: 20 MIN. • **BAKE:** 15 MIN.
MAKES: 6 SERVINGS

- ½ **lb. lean ground beef (90% lean)**
- 1¾ **cups sliced fresh mushrooms**
- ½ **medium red onion, thinly sliced**
- ¼ **tsp. salt**
- ¼ **tsp. pepper**
- 1 **tube (13.8 oz.) refrigerated pizza crust**
- ½ **cup reduced-fat sour cream**
- 2 **tsp. Italian seasoning**
- ½ **tsp. garlic powder**
- ¾ **cup crumbled blue cheese**

1. Preheat oven to 425°. In a large skillet, cook the beef, mushrooms and onion over medium heat, crumbling beef, until beef is no longer pink, 5-7 minutes; drain. Stir in salt and pepper; set aside.

2. On a lightly floured surface, roll crust into a 15x12-in. rectangle. Transfer the crust to a parchment-lined baking sheet.

3. In a small bowl, combine the sour cream, Italian seasoning and garlic powder; spread over crust to within 2 in. of edges. Spoon the beef mixture over top. Fold up edges of crust over filling, leaving center uncovered.

4. Bake 15-18 minutes or until the crust is golden. Using the parchment, slide tart onto a wire rack. Sprinkle with blue cheese; let stand for 5 minutes before slicing.

1 PIECE: 328 cal., 12g fat (5g sat. fat), 43mg chol., 803mg sod., 35g carb. (6g sugars, 1g fiber), 19g pro.
DIABETIC EXCHANGES: 2 starch, 2 lean meat, 2 fat.

INDEX

FALL FLAVORS